# THE EMERGENCE OF ARAB NATIONALISM

A bibliography

# The Emergence
# of
# ARAB
# NATIONALISM

from the Nineteenth Century to 1921

compiled and annotated by
FRANK CLEMENTS

\*

**SR** *Scholarly Resources Inc.*
1508 Pennsylvania Avenue · Wilmington, Delaware 19806

1976
SCHOLARLY RESOURCES INC.
1508 Pennsylvania Avenue, Wilmington, Delaware 19806

International Standard Book Number 0 8420 2096 9
Library of Congress Catalog Card Number 76 5160

Printed in Great Britain

# CONTENTS

## ACKNOWLEDGEMENTS

I owe a great debt to my supervisor, Dr. Derek Hopwood of the Middle East Centre, St. Antony's College, Oxford, whose guidance, judgement and friendship has been of inestimable value throughout the preparation of this thesis.

My thanks are also due to Madame Sama el Mohassini of the Zahiriah National Library in Damascus for her assistance in interpreting the spirit of the early Syrian Nationalist Movement.

*Foreword by*
# DR. DEREK HOPWOOD
*Middle Eastern Bibliographer,*
*St. Antony's College, Oxford*

The rise of Arab nationalism has been a phenomenon influenced by many factors. The entry into the Middle East of European men and concepts, the decline of the Ottoman Empire, the First World War, the growth of Zionism – all these and others combined to shape and vivify Arab consciousness. These largely external factors came face to face with the long existing Arab pride in an historical and Islamic heritage stretching back over many centuries. The Arab renaissance took place in the knowledge that the West, once the recipient of the benefits of Arab science and culture, had moved ahead and was clearly superior in material and military terms. Thus the Arabs regarded the West ambivalently, with envy but also with a confidence in their own past achievements. The fact that by the end of the First World War most of the Arab world was under some form of European colonisation tended to deepen the ambivalence and to emphasise the elements of alienation and separateness.

Many volumes have been devoted to all aspects of this subject and doubtless many more are in store. Some subjects seem inexhaustible – Lawrence, Sykes-Picot, the Balfour Declaration. There are scholars writing with reasonable impartiality, those who wish only to propagate one side of a question, and the downright eccentrics who find the Middle East exotic, slightly dangerous and, hopefully, commercially profitable. To keep abreast of this flood of literature is difficult and while most academics have their own views on its value it is rare to find someone who has the energy and the patience to read and assess it all.

Frank Clements has done so and has produced more than a bibliography. His summaries of each book or article together with the connecting narrative provide a comprehensive overall view of an important period. The production of bibliographies is a uniquely altruistic task – work that few are ready to undertake but many are prepared to criticise. Mr. Clements has undertaken it and has put all librarians and students of the Middle East in his debt. It will not prevent authors from retreading well-trodden ground, but they will now at least have no excuse for not being aware of what has already been written.

# INTRODUCTION

The aim of this bibliography is to list and evaluate material of significance related to the Arab Nationalist Movement from its beginnings in the nineteenth century to the granting of the mandates and the Cairo Conference of 1921.

The starting date for this work is indeterminate because authorities differ as to whether the movement began with changes in the middle of the nineteenth century or with the landing of Napoleon in Egypt. The end of the project is also indeterminate as the implementation of the mandates and the decisions of the Cairo Conference varied according to the country.

The bibliography includes books, periodical articles and pamphlets and gives the author, title and bibliographical details. Only works in English or in translation are included and books which are purely travel works or guides have also been excluded. Each entry is annotated wherever necessary though in some cases the item is only annotated once with added entries in other sections and in the case of items of a general nature or limited interest only an entry is made.

Essential works have been indicated by an asterisk and this may be consistent throughout the work or only limited to one particular section.

Restriction of area has also been followed and this work does not cover Egypt and southern Arabia. The nationalist movements in these areas, during the period under consideration, can be considered separately from the countries covered by this bibliography though this is not true of modern day developments.

The work is divided into three main sections, the first dealing with the Arab provinces under the Ottoman administration and ending with the Arab Revolt and the war in the Middle East. The second section deals with the Cairo Conference. The work concludes with a consideration of the Fertile Crescent under the Mandate system and a small collection of general bibliographies related to the area. It has not been considered necessary to list general national and trade bibliographies such as the *British Museum Catalogue*, the *Cumulative Book Index* or *Whitaker's Cumulative Book List*. Each section is further subdivided according to the natural subdivisions of the subject as detailed in the Contents List.

The index is a straight through sequence of authors and titles with the point of reference being to page numbers. As some titles tend to be lengthy these have been shortened wherever possible.

The inclusion of titles in the bibliography is very much a subjective conclusion as are the comments regarding importance or otherwise. However, the general comments in the annotations represent the views of the author of the original work.

# Section 1

# The Struggle between the Arabs and Turks

This section deals with the period from about the middle of the nineteenth century when influences were at work upon the Arabs leading to the beginning of the Arab Nationalist Movement and the Arab Revolt.

## (a) The Ottoman Empire – aspects of administration and diplomacy.

This section deals with aspects of Ottoman administration in the Arab provinces prior to the beginnings of the Arab nationalist movement and considers these in relation to changes in the Ottoman Empire as a whole.

The general administration of the Arab provinces is dealt with most significantly by Gibb and Bowen in *Islamic Society in the West* and Zeine's *Arab-Turkish relations and the emergence of Arab Nationalism*, and in specific areas through works such as Longrigg's *Four Centuries of Modern Iraq* and Peake's *A History of Jordan and its Tribes*.

Specific administrative problems can be examined through a study of works such as Churchill's study of Turkish rule in the Lebanon entitled *The Druzes and Maronites under Turkish rule from 1840–1860* and Scheltma's translation of *The Lebanon in turmoil Syria and the powers in 1860* which consider the conditions and events leading up to the massacres of the Christian minorities. In fact the problem of the minorities is of great significance as each province had its minority community and a general study of the situation is provided by Albert Hourani's *Minorities in the Arab World* whilst in Palestine, an area of great concern, a useful study is that of Mandel's entitled 'Turks, Arabs and Jewish Immigration into Palestine, 1822–1914' which appears in *Middle Eastern Affairs No. 4*.

The Ottoman rule through the system of vilayets and millets must also be seen in relation to the process of reform which was being undertaken by the Ottoman Empire as a whole. Significant entries include Davison's 'Reform in the Ottoman Empire 1856–

1876'; Hourani's 'Beginnings of modernisation in the Middle East' and Polk and Chambers' 'Beginnings of modernisation in the Middle East'. Also of significance are Zeine's work cited above and particularly the bibliography of Midhat Pasha by his son Ali Midhat as the reforms of Midhat Pasha were extremely important in the vilayets of Syria.

This period in the history of the Arab provinces was significantly affected by Turkey's diplomatic dealings with the other powers through the capitulatory concessions and the problems of the Christian minorities. In addition to Gibb and Bowen's work Sousa deals with this aspect in *The Capitulatory Regime of Turkey. Its history, origin and nature*. Direct Great Power involvement can be seen in the 1860 *Convention for pacifying Syria (and Lebanon)* and the 1861 *Regulation for the Administration of Lebanon* both of which were a response to the massacres of the Christian minorities in 1860.

## (b) The beginnings of the Arab Nationalist Movement.

The tentative movements within the Ottoman Empire and the gradual changes in the administrative pattern led to the beginnings of the nationalist movement which can be considered in two parts. At first the movement was an attempt to obtain reforms of the Ottoman Empire with the hopes of obtaining autonomy for the Arab provinces whilst still remaining part of the Islamic Empire. These hopes were raised and dashed by the Young Turks which led to the policy of the movement developing into one which sought independence from the Empire. This was partly as a result of the Turkification policy of the Committee of Union and Progress and the eventual opening of negotiations between Britain and the Sherif of Mecca following the outbreak of the war and subsequent repressive measures by the Turkish authorities in the Arab provinces.

This section is well represented by literary output both in books and periodicals which is a reflection on the significance of this subject which was to greatly influence events in the Middle East during the twentieth century. Although aspects of the movement can be divided into two phases as outlined above many of the works cover both phases and any split would be purely artificial. The most significant contribution in the English language is George Antonius' *The Arab Awakening*, which, despite its faults, remains a standard work on the subject and covers both phases of the development of the movement. Although this work will only be mentioned here it can be assumed that it is relevant throughout this section.

2

The movement in its stage of seeking reform and autonomy within the framework of the Ottoman Empire was also linked with the effects of Western influences and education in the area and this is reflected by Abu Lughod's *Arab rediscovery of Europe*; Hourani's *Arabic thought in the Liberal Age 1789–1939*, and Sharabi's *Arab intellectuals and the West*. The autonomy aspect is covered in depth by Saab in his *Arab Federalists of the Ottoman Empire* and also by Zeine in *Arab-Turkish relations and the emergence of Arab nationalism*. The gradual change of emphasis from Ottomanism to Arabism is dealt with in several articles by Professor Dawn, also collected in book form, articles by Rasheeduddin Khan and Haim's *Arab nationalism: an anthology*. The change as typified by one particular figure is well covered by Cleveland's *The making of an Arab Nationalist: Ottomanism and Arabism in the life and thought of Sati 'al-Husri* with the collective voice being represented by the 1905 *Programme of the League of the Arab Fatherland*.

The nationalist movement as an independence movement gained ground with the Turkification policy of the Committee of Union and Progress and the supression of the Arab societies thus fomenting the unrest which existed in the Arab provinces. In these developments the Arab officers in the Turkish army played an extremely important role and this aspect is dealt with by Be'eri's *Army officers in Arab politics and society*. The whole development is also covered in works already cited by Dawn, Khan, Saab and Zeine to which one should add certain articles in Kedourie's *The Chatham House version and other Middle Eastern Studies*. Negotiations between the Arabs and Britain are also dealt with in Kedourie's work and although the main negotiations are part of the next section the early exchange of letters between Hussein and Britain are of relevance here. Collective Arab thought, amongst those involved in the movement, can be found in the *Resolutions of the Arab–Syrian Congress at Paris 1913* and the *Arab Nationalist Manifesto* which was issued from Cairo at the beginning of World War I. All of these items need to be contrasted with the 'Sykes–Picot Agreement' of 1916 which was an agreement between Britain and France and seemingly at variance with the promises made through the McMahon–Hussein correspondence.

## (c) The Arab Revolt and the War in the Middle East.

The Arab Revolt which began in 1916 was only part of the theatre of war in the Middle East and controversy has continued as to the significance of the Arab contribution with opinion often being dependent upon the writer's support or otherwise for the Arab cause. It is, however, accepted that the Arab contribution, although only a small part of the campaign, did succeed in tying down a large number of Turkish troops in the Hedjaz and was a useful flanking force for Allenby's advance through Palestine to Damascus.

Because of this the war needs to be studied both from the general as well as from the specific in order to set the Arab role into context. There are several general works on the war in the Middle East with one of the most useful being the two-volume history compiled by MacMunn, Falls and Beck entitled *History of the Great War, Military Operations Egypt and Palestine*. Also of significance are Bray's highly critical *Shifting Sands*, Falls' *Armageddon 1918*; Wavell's *The Palestine Campaign* and the biography of Allenby by Gardner entitled *Allenby*.

Concerning the Arab part of the campaign as a specific topic Lawrence's *Seven Pillars of Wisdom* and its abridgement *Revolt in the Desert* are essential works. Controversy has raged as to whether Lawrence's account is an accurate record or one designed to show Lawrence and the Arabs in the best possible light. However, despite its failings the *Seven Pillars of Wisdom* is the major work on the revolt though the abridgement is easier to read as it concentrates on the military campaign and omits the soul search- ing of the parent work. As the leading figure in the Arab revolt both in the public eye and through his literary output the majority of Lawrence's work is of relevance and are too many to cite individually though his *Evolution of a Revolt* edited by Weintraub and *Secret Despatches from Arabia* should be read.

The subject is also covered by Kirkbride's account under the title *An Awakening: The Arab campaign 1917–18* and an article by Dawn entitled 'Ideological influences in the Arab Revolt'. Regarding the war and its political side an essential study is Busch's *Britain, India and the Arabs 1914–1921* which investigates the Arab cause in relation to the political divisions between the British Foreign Office as represented by the Arab Bureau and the India Office with its interests in Mesopotamia. This theme is also contained in Troeller's *Ibn Saud and Sherif Hussein: A comparison in importance in the early years of the First World War* which examines the effect of divided British policies upon the two major figures in the Arab world at that time. The political problems during the revolt were also apparent in connection with Palestine with conflicting aims and motives and of particular value are two studies by Friedman entitled *The McMahon Hussein Corres-*

*pondence and the Question of Palestine* and *The Question of Palestine 1914–18: British-Jewish-Arab relations.*

The question of the Arab Revolt and the war in the Middle East can be examined through general and specific works cited and through many other works on the Allied operations in the Middle East not mentioned which will give a good account of the military part of the war. However, it is the political background and events during the period which were to have far-reaching consequences in the peace settlement and its aftermath though these were complicated by the successful Arab participation in the war.

## (a) OTTOMAN ADMINISTRATION AND ASPECTS OF DIPLOMACY

## GENERAL WORKS

ALLEN, RICHARD
**Imperialism and nationalism in the Fertile Crescent:** Sources and prospects of the Arab–Israeli conflict.
*London: O.U.P. 1974.*
*x, 686 pp., maps, bibl., index, 20½ cms.*
*(Chapters Six and Seven, pp. 106–159.)*

In the section which follows the consideration of the Arab Empires the author deals with the question of the Arab provinces within the Ottoman Empire, considering especially the position of the minority peoples. The millet system '. . . which gave a large measure of autonomy to the non-Muslim religious communities (despite its advantages for the Turks and their subjects in the early years), developed into another divisive and controversial factor'. Attempts were also made to reform the Turkish administration resulting in the introduction of the Tanzimat which broke the Ulamas' monopoly of law and introduced a judicial system based on that of France.

*ANTONIUS, GEORGE
**The Arab Awakening:** The story of the Arab nationalist movement.
*London: Hamish Hamilton. 1938.*
*xii, 13–471 pp., maps, app., index, 22 cms.*

For many years this was the standard work in English on the Arab nationalist movement and it is still an extremely valuable contribution to the subject. The work begins by discussing the background which deals with a definition of the Arab people and the geographical area forming the Arab world, though the study is confined to the Arabian peninsula and the Fertile Crescent.

The second chapter deals with what Antonius calls the 'False Start', that of the movements begun by Mohammed Ali in Egypt, Ibrahim Pasha in Syria and the Wahhabi movement which was defeated by Mohammed Ali, whose ambitions were in turn defeated by the British and the lack of an Arab national consciousness. This leads to a study of the revival of the Arab culture through the growth of missionary activity in Syria which led to increased educational prospects and the rise of an Arab press.

6

The disturbances and massacres of the mid-nineteenth century in Syria are also examined and are seen to have established the sectarian differences within the Ottoman Empire.

CAMBRIDGE HISTORY OF ISLAM
**Vol. 1. The Central Islamic Lands,** edited by P. M. Holt, Ann K. S. Lambton and Bernard Lewis.
*London: C.U.P. 1970.*
*xviii, 815 pp., bibl., index, 23½ cms.*

Inevitably with a work of this nature much of the content is outside the scope of this study though three of the articles in this authoritative work are of direct interest.

> Holt, P. M. *The Later Ottoman Empire in Egypt and the Fertile Crescent*, pp. 374–393.
> Zeine, Z. N. *The Central Islamic Lands in Recent Times: The Arab Lands*, pp. 566–594.
> Rustow, O. A. *The Central Islamic Lands in Recent Times:* The political impact of the West, pp. 673–697.

Annotations to these contributions will be found under the author entry in the relevant section.

COKE, RICHARD
**The Arab's place in the sun.**
*London: Butterworth. 1929.*
*318 pp., illus., maps, index, 22 cms.*

The first part of this study deals with the early history of the area from the time of the Arab Empire to the position of the Arab Provinces within the Ottoman Empire. This section is an attempt to substantiate the historical claim of the Arab peoples to nationhood in the twentieth century.

FISHER, SYDNEY NETTLETON
**The Middle East:** A history.
*London: Routledge & Kegan Paul. 2nd ed. 1971.*
*xxx, 749 pp., maps, bibl., index, 22 cms.*

A general work providing a very useful survey of the Middle East during the period of this study though the earlier and later sections are irrelevant by virtue of date.

The section of relevance is as follows and each section has its own bibliography.
Part II: The Ottoman Empire
    Chapter 19. *The Decline and Retreat of the Ottoman Empire.*

*LANDEN, ROBERT G., ED.
**The Emergence of the Modern Middle East:** Selected readings.
*London: Van Nostrand Reinhold. 1970.*
*xiii, 366 pp., 22½ cms.*

A selection of primary source material to illustrate the growth of modernisation in the Middle East from the late eighteenth century to date. It is aimed at the student of Middle Eastern history and politics and attempts to provide a comprehensive 'sampler' of the numerous varieties of source material including, for example, historical essays, newspaper editorials, state papers and memoirs.

The work is arranged in a rough chronological order with each section built around a particular theme with each section having an introductory essay:

1. The Intrusion of the modern world in the Middle East.
2. Defensive modernisation: The Military–Administrative Phase.
3. Defensive modernisation: The Intellectual Phase.
4. Imposed modernisation: Imperialism as a vehicle for change.
5. World War I and Political reorientation.
6. Assertions of national identity.
7. Creating a new Economic and Social Order.

As with all works of this nature not all of the items are of relevance to a specialised study such as this. Where a contribution is of significance an annotated entry will be found under the author or title in the relevant section.

LENCZOWSKI, GEORGE
**The Middle East in World Affairs.**
*New York: Cornell University Press. 2nd ed. 1956.*
*xix, 576 pp., maps, bibl., index, 24 cms.*

Part One of this work is entitled the 'First World War and the Peace' with the first chapter dealing with the historical background of the Ottoman Empire prior to the outbreak of war. In this section the author deals with the rise of Mohammed Ali in Egypt and Ibrahim Pasha in Syria which sowed the seeds of Christian and Syrian Arab nationalism. It also deals with the effects of European diplomacy on the Ottoman Empire and the attempts at reform prior to the Young Turks coup d'état of 1908.

LENCZOWSKI, GEORGE, ED.
**The Political Awakening in the Middle East.**
*New Jersey: Prentice-Hall. 1970.*
*ix, 180 pp., map, bibl., 21 cms.*

The aim of this collection of readings is to trace both historically and topically the political transition of the Middle East. The work examines the traditional structure of the Ottoman Empire as a basis through primary and secondary sources.

The work is divided into topics with section one being of relevance to this area:

1. Administrative and military reform.
   Two readings of interest in this section are those dealing with the first reforms in the Ottoman Empire and an appraisal of Mohammed Ali.

## OTTOMAN ADMINISTRATION

ABU-JABER, KAMEL S.
**The Millet system in the nineteenth-century Ottoman Empire.**
*Muslim World. Vol. 57, 1967, pp. 212–223.*

Although not restricted to the Arab provinces this article is of relevance as the millet system operated throughout the Ottoman Empire '. . . as a political organisation which granted to the non-Muslims the right to organise into communities possessing certain delegated powers under their own ecclesiastical heads. In time such communities or millets developed their own peculiar characteristics and traditions, in this way becoming identified with the various nationalities'. The principle of this system is examined and its place within the Ottoman Empire as is the administration and jurisdiction of the millets.

The latter part of the article deals with the impact of the West on the millets and the reasons leading to the discontent of the millets during the latter part of the nineteenth century with the weakness of the Ottoman state encouraging the aspirations of some of the minority groups towards independence. Also discussed are the attempts made to reform the system which failed because of the opposition of the Muslims and the Christians each because of their own fears and because of a lack of dedicated administrators who were needed to effect reforms, in a traditional society. 'The reforms were sabotaged by corrupt officials, and by the important ulema who, while paying lip service, undermined any effective means to seriously applying them.'

'But the millet system did not work well. What began as a unilateral concession by a benevolent ruler was turned into a rigid system by his successors. Nor were the non-Muslims any better. They clung tenaciously to their comparatively privileged position, especially their ecclesiastical leadership which struggled against the reform. The foreign powers used the millets to their own ends and to gain advantage from the Porte.'

BOWERING, JOHN
**Report on the Commercial statistics of Syria.**
*Great Britain: House of Lords, Sessional Papers 1840.*
*Vol. xxxv, pp. 9–10.*
*In: Landen, Robert G., ed.*
*The Emergence of the Modern Middle East: Selected readings, pp. 56–58.*

A report on the attempts of Ibrahim Pasha to revitalise the Syrian economy which was designed to pay for Mohammed Ali's modernisation programme. The inhabitants of each town were obliged to utilise the agricultural land suitable for development and Ibrahim Pasha and his army officers invested large sums in the development. It failed, however, due to adverse weather conditions and the lack of an agricultural population and livestock but it was another move in the transition of the Middle East.

*CHURCHILL, COLONEL CHARLES HENRY
**The Druzes and the Maronites under the Turkish rule from 1840–1860.**
*London: Quaritch. 1862.*
*viii, 300 pp., index, 22 cms.*

This work deals with the Turkish rule in the Lebanon and in particular the relationship between the Druzes and Maronites leading to the massacres of the Christian minority by the Druzes in 1860. This was done with the apparent approval of the Turkish authorities and was ended only as a result of pressure from France and Britain.

The author lived in the Lebanon during this period and this is a first-hand account of the situation leading up to the massacres and the arrival of the French troops to protect the Christians. It also deals with the trial of the Druze prisoners after the massacres which Churchill maintains was merely a mockery as the accused were never punished.

It should be remembered, however, that this work although invaluable as a contemporary account has been superseded by later research.

COX, PERCY
**Iraq.**
*United Empire. March 1929, pp. 132–144.*

The early part of the article deals with the early history of Iraq eventually leading up to the conquest of the area by the Ottoman though it was not until after the Crimean War that closer control was exercised over the province by the Ottoman Government. This resulted in some improvement in general conditions especially under the control of Midhat Pasha during his governorship of Baghdad from 1869–1872 as he laboured in the cause of progress and reform. However, improvements only lasted as long as his period in Baghdad and conditions soon relapsed into a state of stagnation.

Progress was once again apparent following the rise to power of the Committee of Union and Progress which encouraged education and made some attempts to get to grips with the problem of agriculture. These developments were halted by the Italian and Balkan wars which weakened the authority of the central government and the Arab provinces became restless. 'In Iraq, nearly every summer at the time of harvest or revenue collection, rebellious outbreaks occurred at one place or another, travel became unsafe and river piracies frequent.'

\*DAVISON, RODERIC H.
**Reform in the Ottoman Empire 1856–1876.**
*Princeton: Princeton University Press. 1963.*
*xiv, 479 pp., glossary, app., bibl., index, 24 cms.*

This work is particularly valuable for the section dealing with the provincial government and the vilayet system of 1864 and 1867. It considers the problems of administering the provinces of the Ottoman Empire and the reform of the system that the vilayet law of 1864 was designed to bring about. It considers the vilayet administration with its various subdivisions and the first attempts to instill some form of elected representation into the administrative system.

It is stressed, however, that although the vilayet system was not perfect it could be made to work by capable and honest officials. It was still open to abuse because of the system of appointment of the valis and officials with the posts often being purchased by bribery and the policy of changing valis at frequent intervals. The work also deals with the internal dissension within the Ottoman Empire and the growth of the Young Turk movement.

DAVISON, RODERIC H.
**Turkish attitudes concerning Christian Muslim equality in the nineteenth century.**
*American Historial Review. Vol. LIX, No. 4, July 1954, pp. 845–864.*

A consideration of the millet system in the Ottoman Empire which, whilst giving partial autonomy to the communities, at the same time preserved and emphasised the religious differences within the Empire. The ecclesiastical hierarchy which controlled the millet supervised the religious, educational and charitable affairs of the community whilst also controlling personal affairs such as marriage and divorce and collecting some taxes. This system of government served the Ottoman Empire for four hundred years as a mosaic pattern within which the two communities lived side by side under the same ruler but under different laws and control by different officials.

During the latter part of the nineteenth century attempts were made to reform the system notably by administrators such as Midhat Pasha who attempted to realise some measure of Ottoman equality involving the equality of Muslims and Christians but the Turkish mind was not ready to accept absolute equality. 'While Arab nationalism developed, like the Christian nationalisms, as a reaction to Ottoman Turkish control, the Turks themselves found the source for a nationalism of their own in the Osmanlilik of the Tanzimat . . .'

FOREIGN OFFICE: HISTORICAL SECTION. HANDBOOK 96b.
**The Pan-Islamic Movement.**
*London: Foreign Office. 1919.*
*24 pp., 21½ cms.*

A brief account of the Pan-Islamic movement outlining the historical roots of the movement and its development under the Young Turks into a policy of Turkification throughout the Ottoman Empire. It is also seen as a factor in preventing the break up of the Ottoman Empire during the latter part of the nineteenth century as the leaders of Syria and Mesopotamia refrained from taking any action for fear of destroying the Empire of Islam. This was, however, destroyed by the attitude of the Committee of Union and Progress who pursued a policy of Turkification which the Arabs felt was a danger to Islam and the Arabic language.

*GIBB, H. A. R. and BOWEN, HAROLD
**Islamic Society and the West.** Vol. I, Islamic society in the Eighteenth Century, Parts 1 and 2.

*London: O.U.P. (for Royal Institute of International Affairs). Part 1, 1950; Part 2, 1957. Vol. 1: Part 1, xi, 386 pp., notes, opp., index, 22 cms. Vol. 1: Part 2, vi, 285 pp., bibl., index, 22 cms.*

Part one of this two-part work begins by examining the basic structure of the Ottoman Empire and the part played in its running by the Sacred Law. This is followed by an examination of the tradition in the Empire and in particular the significance of the Caliphate and the Sultan to which the governing class attached great importance as did the mass of the Muslim population. The next major consideration is the study of the ruling institution which includes the army, the Imperial Household, the navy and the Central Administration.

Also in this section is a segment on the government of the provinces in which the aspect is considered in depth with a chapter being devoted to the Arab provinces. The aim of the administration in the Arab provinces was to preserve them in the condition in which they were taken over and to ensure the authority of the Sultan. In the light of the structure and nature of the Ottoman Empire the system is seen as 'eminently practical, and neither harsh nor unjust', recognising 'the traditional and recognised division of mankind into a variety of social orders' and drawing up regulations to ensure 'that none should interfere with or infringe the functions or rights of others'. The situation in the Arab provinces was complicated by the usual rivalry between the Central Administration and the local troops supplemented by the lawlessness of the Bedouin tribes and in Iraq by the Kurdish minority.

The question of the peasantry, land tenure and agriculture also has a special section on the Arab provinces which had the village as the unit of agriculture but with rights and usages varying from province to province and even district to district. Agriculture was depressed by the financial intendants whose administration in part was responsible for the depopulation of the country though this was surpassed for effect by the ravaging of the cultivated areas by the Bedouin with Palestine, which was poorly protected, being described as 'one of the most devastated regions of Syria'. The volume concludes with a study of the city, industry and commerce with the contrast between city and country being seen as a contrast of civilizations with little or no tie save that of economics. In terms of commerce the real power rested with the non Muslim subjects who were able to trade with Europe and by doing so enjoyed the protection of the European Consols and some freedom from the restrictions of the bribery and corruption of the local administration.

Part two of this volume concludes the consideration of the institutions of Islamic society in the Ottoman Empire. The opening section deals with the system of taxation and finance. 'The system was thus, in essentials, one of exploitation of the provinces for the benefit of the Imperial Court, Treasury, and army, offset in part by the obligations of external defence and maintenance of the Islamic religion.'

The study continues by examining the religious institutions in the Empire and in particular the role these played in the legal and social structure with the authorities having greater powers of interference and control. Education in the provinces was based on much the same system as in the rest of the Empire though the language of instruction was Arabic and no real general education was given. In Syria education was less centralised with schools in Aleppo and Damascus and in the more important provincial towns with the opportunity being given to those with ability to enrol in the Turkish cadres. In Iraq the position was less satisfactory though Baghdad had good schools as did Basra and Mosul. The conditions and standards of the schools fluctuated as they were sustained by endowments and the success of the establishment depended upon its income.

The volume concluded by reviewing the constitution and status of the minority communities in the Empire and the political and social effects that these had on the future of the Empire in terms of divisions of population.

GILBERT, MARTIN
**The Arab–Israeli Conflict:** Its history in maps.
*London : Weidenfeld & Nicolson. 1974.*
*101 pp., maps, 25 cms.*

An extremely valuable collection of maps illustrating the Arab–Israeli conflict though only parts one and two are of relevance by virtue of date.

Part one is entitled 'Prelude to Conflict' and the following maps are of interest:

4. The Jews of Palestine 636 to 1880.
5. Jewish Settlement in Palestine 1880–1914.
6. Arab–Jewish Conflict under Turkish Rule 1882–1914.

HITTI, PHILIP K.
**A short history of Lebanon.**

14

*London: Macmillan. 1965.*
*xi, 249 pp., maps, index, 20 cms.*

This work is based on the author's *The Lebanon in History* and is an account from the earliest settlements of the Canaanites up to 1964, though for the purposes of this study the work begins at page 184 with the chapter entitled 'Between Medievalism and Modernism'. This deals with the rule of Bashir who began the evolution of Lebanon from its medieval character into the modern world with a less autocratic form of government though his rule was eventually ended in 1840 due to his involvement with Mohammed Ali, in the revolt against the Sultan which was put down by the Great Powers.

Hitti then continues to deal with the civil disturbances in 1860 and the massacres which resulted in action being taken by the Great Powers to protect the Christian minority eventually leading to Lebanon being granted autonomy in 1867.

HOURANI, ALBERT, ED.
**Middle Eastern Affairs Number Four.**
*London: O.U.P. 1965.*
*165 pp., 22 cms.*

(St. Antony Papers Number 17.)
Contents of Relevance:

Mandel, Neville. 'Turks, Arabs and Jewish Immigration into Palestine, 1882–1914', pp. 77–108.
Khadduri, Majid. ' "Aziz" Ali Misri and the Arab Nationalist Movement', pp. 140–163.

Annotations for these two essays will be found under the author concerned.

HOURANI, ALBERT H.
**Minorities in the Arab World.**
*London: O.U.P. 1947 (for Royal Institute of International Affairs).*

This is a study of minorities in the Arab World which are defined as being those communities who are Arabic speaking but not Sunni Moslem by faith in the countries of Egypt, Palestine, Transjordan, Lebanon, Syria and Iraq.

The early part of the work deals with the origin and development of minorities and in part considers their position within the Ottoman Empire which recognised and perpetuated these differences. This is considered in the light of the Millet System which allowed autonomous millets each coterminous with the

15

Empire and recognised by the government. This section also deals with the social position of the Christians and Jews which was at times precarious being dependent upon the ruler at any particular time.

HOURANI, ALBERT
**The Ottoman background of the Modern Middle East.**
*London: Longmans. 1970.*
*iv, 48 pp., illus., 21½ cms.*
*(Carrears Arab Lecture 1969.)*

The work is in Arabic and English with the English version occupying twenty-four pages. The lecture was an attempt to redress the balance regarding the value, or otherwise, of the Ottoman Empire in the Middle East and an answer to the charge that the rule of the Ottomans prevented the development of Arab and Muslim civilisation. Hourani maintains that this is a fairly common view which is nationalistic in nature and one which does not stand close examination and Hourani illustrates this by examining the establishment of the Ottoman Empire and the legacy it left to the Middle East.

The second part of the lecture deals with the Ottoman Empire in the latter part of the nineteenth century when it was going through a period of reform in an attempt to re-establish its authority but these reforms in themselves proved to be factors which led to the eventual breakdown of the Empire. The major change as seen by Hourani was the intellectual one brought about by new schools especially in Lebanon and Syria, the increase in contact with the Western world and the greater availability of books and newspapers all of which contributed to the idea that society should be organised on a nationalist basis '. . . of a sentiment of national loyalty and unity in which members of different religions and social communities should join in a nationalism explicitly secular but having, like everything in the Middle East, a concealed religious element.'

Hourani concludes by summarising the effects of the Ottoman society in the Middle East especially with regard to the position of the leaders of the Arab provinces who had put their families through Turkish schools, had often served in the administration and the army and indeed many of them had served in the Arab Revolt with grave misgivings about the breach in the Muslim Empire. Initially the post World War I Arab leaders brought to the movement '. . . a certain style of political action and a memory of Ottoman unity'.

IRELAND, PHILIP WILLARD
**Iraq:** A study in political development.
*London: Cape. 1937.*
*510 pp., illus., maps, app., bibl., index.*

See Section 3a for annotation to this work.

IZZEDDIN, NEJLA
**The Arab World:** Past, present and future.
*Chicago: Henry Regnery Co. 1953.*
*xvi, 412 pp., illus., index, 24 cms.*

This work is an attempt to present an appreciation of the Arab
spirit and an understanding of the issues affecting Arab life
beginning with a consideration of the composition of the Arab
world and what constitutes an Arab. The early sections consider
the cultural heritage of Islam, the rise of the Arab Empire, the
Arab world in the Middle Ages and the eclipse of Arab society
following the Mongol invasions of the mid-thirteenth century.

The work goes on to deal with the rise of the Ottoman Empire
in the Arab world leading to the impact of Mohammed Ali on the
Ottoman Empire in Egypt and that of Ibrahim Pasha in Syria. It
also considers the rise of the Wahhabi movement and the religious
concept of the movement.

KEDOURIE, ELIE
**England and the Middle East:** The destruction of the Ottoman
Empire 1914–1921.
*London: Bowes and Bowes. 1956.*
*xiii, c–236 pp., app., bibl., index, 21½ cms.*

The first chapter of this book considers the bases of English
policy in the Middle East from 1830–1914 and though it does not
consider the Ottoman provincial administration or the Arab
question it is of relevance as this formed the basis for all future
policy in the area.

The remainder of the chapters deal with specific aspects of the
question as follows and these are considered in the relevant
sections:

| | |
|---|---|
| The Making of the Sykes–Picot agreement | – Section 1b |
| Sir Mark Sykes | – Section 1c |
| Colonel Lawrence | – Section 1c |
| The Unmaking of the Sykes–Picot agreement | – Section 2a |
| Syria, 1918–1920 | – Section 3b |
| Mesopotamia, 1918–1921 | – Section 3a |

KORTEPETER, C. M.
**Another look at the Tanzimat.**
*Connecticut : The Muslim World. Vol. LIV, 964, pp. 49–55.*

(A review article of 'The Genesis of Young Ottoman Thought' by Serif Mardin, Princeton University Press, 1962.)

The article is critical of Dr. Mardin's book on some aspects of its organisation and over some omissions but considers that it is 'a real contribution to the study of Islamic political history and theory'.

The book is an examination of the Young Turk movement from a Turkish viewpoint with the aim of describing the process by which Western political concepts were introduced into Turkey. The approach is by means of a consideration of three problems; that of the state of political ideas in the Empire at the time of the reforms, the influences to which these ideals were subjected, and the changes that took place as a result of these pressures. The work is well indexed and has a useful bibliography.

LONGRIGG, STEPHEN HEMSLEY
**Four Centuries of Modern Iraq.**
*London : O.U.P. 1925.*
*xii, 378 pp., illus., bibl., map, index.*

A history of Iraq from the Ottoman conquest to the turn of the twentieth century which although general in nature and less detailed than his other works does provide an excellent introduction to the Iraq of the mandate. Only the latter part of the work falls within the period of this study dealing with the period from the arrival of Midhat Pasha as Vali to the beginning of the twentieth century.

*LONGRIGG, STEPHEN HEMSLEY
**Iraq 1900–1950:** A political, social and economic history.
*London : O.U.P. 1953.*
*x, 436 pp., app., bibl., map, index, 22 cms.*

An extremely detailed history of Iraq covering a period of great importance in the fortunes of the country beginning with the last few years of Turkish rule.

The work begins by considering the situation in Iraq in 1900 with a survey of the country and its people, its position in relation to its neighbours and the two main sectors in Iraq, those of the urban dweller and the rural dweller. This opening survey also considers the resources of the country and its communications problems both of which were characterised by the all pervading poverty of the country and its government. This section also deals with the last years of Turkish rule and especially the relations between the Turkish rulers and the Arab nationalists prior to the outbreak of war.

LONGRIGG, STEPHEN HEMSLEY
**Syria and Lebanon under French Mandate.**
*London : O.U.P. 1958.*
*xii, 404 pp., maps, bibl., index, 21½ cms.*

See entry under Section 3b for annotation to this work.

MANDEL, NEVILLE
**Attempts at an Arab-Zionist Entente: 1913–1914.**
*Middle Eastern Studies. Vol. 1, No. 3, April 1965, pp. 238–267.*

This article examines the attempt at an Arab-Jewish entente prior to the outbreak of war against a background of increased Jewish immigration into Palestine and increasing Arab nationalism. At the same time as this attempt was being made the Zionists were also in contact with the Ottoman government regarding the restrictions placed on immigration into Syria. However, although the Ottoman government was keen to demonstrate its sympathy for the Jews the Grand Vezir said that the Jews 'must before all else make an entente with the Arabs; we shall do the rest'.

The Arabs, however, received responses from the Ottoman government in the summer of 1913 which led to their dropping the negotiations with the Zionists. Interests were reawakened in April 1914 following the failure of the Ottoman government to fulfil its promises and the agreement amongst all Arab nationalists that the time had come to achieve independence and to achieve this aim Jewish support seemed attractive. An entente was never worked out and it was doubtful if it would have succeeded or lasted as popular feeling in Palestine was too hostile to the Zionists to have allowed it to stand.

MANDEL, NEVILLE
**Turks, Arabs and Jewish Immigration into Palestine 1882–1914.**
*In : Hourani, Albert, ed.*
*Middle Eastern Affairs Number Four (pp. 77–108).*

This essay examines the whole question of Jewish immigration into Palestine from the end of the nineteenth century when increased numbers began to arrive from Eastern Europe. It examines the view that the Arabs were not opposed to Jewish settlement until the Balfour declaration and seeks to prove that opposition did exist in the 1880s. The Ottoman administration in Istanbul granted permission for Jewish settlement from the East but not in Palestine partly because of the delicate question of the status quo in the Holy Places, though this restriction was often breached. This increased settlement caused unrest because of the Jewish purchase of land and their method of controlled agriculture which conflicted with the traditional common usage of natural pastureland.

The rise to power of the Young Turks brought about a new spirit in the Arab lands and gave rise to the Arab nationalist movement based, initially, on a hope for autonomy within the Empire. This new spirit also manifested itself in ill feeling against the Jews both on a level between the felleheen and the settlers at local settlements and at government level in Istanbul. The Zionist movement was also viewed with suspicion by the Turkish government regarding it as a separatist movement within the Empire. The relaxation of the restrictions against the Jews by the C.U.P. also led to unrest between the Arabs and Jews as the former suspected the Turks of selling out Arab interests in Palestine. Eventually this led to Arab politicians campaigning on a basis of anti-Zionism, murders of Jewish settlers and general unrest. All of this was prior to the Balfour declaration and the problems of the peace settlement and mandate after the war.

*Ma'oz, Moshe
**Ottoman reform in Syria and Palestine 1840–1861:** The impact of the Tanzimat on politics and society.
*London: O.U.P. 1968.*
*xi, 265 pp., illus., maps, bibl., index, 22½ cms.*

This work deals in detail with the Tanzimat period of reform in the Ottoman Empire which was a crucial stage in the attempts to reform and modernise the decaying Empire. The study begins in 1840 when the Syrian provinces were retaken from the Egyptians and the reforms were first introduced and it concludes in 1861 following the Christian massacres in Syria. This period saw attempts at modernisation though these were only small beginnings and were not far reaching enough to improve the administration for the benefit of Arabs and Turks alike.

The study is divided into five main areas:

1. Introduction: the background to the Tanzimat in Syria and Palestine.

2. Aspects of government and administration.
3. Ottoman rule in Syria and Palestine 1840–1861.
4. Social and economic welfare.
5. The state of the Christians and Jews and the Moslem's attitude towards them.

The work has an extensive bibliography giving published and unpublished sources in Turkish, Arabic, Hebrew and European languages.

MILLER, WILLIAM
**The Ottoman Empire and its Successors 1801–1927 with an appendix, 1927–1936.**
*London: C.U.P. 1936.*
*xv, 644 pp., bibl., maps, index, 18½ cms.*

A general history of the Ottoman Empire and its eclipse with the main work ending at 1927 and the updating in the form of a brief appendix. The work considers the situation in the Arab provinces though not in great detail but in the context of the Ottoman Empire as a whole. The work has an extensive bibliography with works in all languages.

*MOOSA, Dr. MATTI I.
**The Land policy of Midhat Pasha in Iraq, 1869–1872.**
*Islamic Quarterly. Vol. 12, 1968, pp. 146–159.*

Midhat Pasha fought for a constitutional democratic system of government based on equality and freedom and although he had remarkable administrative ability his ideas were too revolutionary to be accepted by the Sublime Porte, especially under the despotic regime of Abdul Hamid II.

This paper discusses one aspect of Midhat Pasha's work in Iraq, that of reform of the land tenure system, though it is stressed that this cannot be separated from the remainder of his reform schemes, nor can his success, or failure, in Iraq be judged solely on his land tenure policy. The question of land tenure was a perpetual problem because of the tribal system which was organised according to traditional customs and the attempts of the Ottoman Government to solve this by legal means.

Essentially Midhat Pasha's policy was to sell large and small tracts of state-owned land to holders who had held title deeds, to villagers who cultivated an area and to sub-tribal chiefs for their tribal areas. It was hoped that this policy would benefit the country in several ways as it would give the land holders security of tenure, it would eliminate inter-tribal rivalry and it would make the semi-nomadic tribesmen settle and become respectable citizens. Although the land policy was not a complete success it was not a complete failure. 'In an age of internal corruption, maladministration, and social and economic chaos in the decaying Ottoman Empire in the nineteenth century, the land tenure policy of Midhat Pasha in Iraq, together with his other reform policies, can be considered successful. Its success was limited by the fears of the local sheiks regarding their authority, by the big landlords who feared the loss of their estates and the greed of the officials in Istanbul who saw the provinces only as a source of revenue.'

PEAKE, F. G.
**A History of Jordan and Its Tribes.**
*Florida: University of Miami Press. 1958.*
*x, 253 pp., notes, maps, 27½ cms.*

The greater part of the work is outside of the scope of this study as it is a history of the various tribes in the Jordan area. Although the Jordan area was nominally under Ottoman rule the measure of control varied from area to area though by the second half of the nineteenth century considerable progress had been made towards restoring order and in restraining the tribes. In common with Turkish policy throughout the Empire no attempt was made to prevent feuding between the tribes.

Revolts against Turkish rule were not completely eliminated, however, as revolts took place in 1905 and 1910 which were put down with severity and the leaders of the rebellion put to death. The area was never completely under Turkish rule but such was the nature of the area and the feuding between the tribes that it did not present any united threat to the Ottoman Empire.

POLK, WILLIAM R. and CHAMBERS, RICHARD L., EDS.
**Beginnings of modernization in the Middle East: The** Nineteenth Century.
*London: University of Chicago Press. 1968.*
*x, 427 pp., notes, index, 23½ cms.*

A publication of the Centre for Middle Eastern Studies which presents a collection of essays on the subject of modernisation in the Middle East though not all of the essays are of relevance to this study. The work is divided into six sections each devoted to an aspect of the process of modernisation.

The work opens with a collection of three essays dealing with the movement towards the reform of the Ottoman Empire and the section is entitled 'Notables and Bureaucrats'. It deals with the aims and achievements of the Ottoman Reformers of the nineteenth century, the eventual constitutional reforms and the final modernisation of the Ottoman Empire. Although concerned essentially with the Ottoman Empire as a whole all aspects are of relevance when considering the Ottoman rule in the Middle East.

The second section deals with the process of 'Ideological Change' though only two essays are of relevance as the third deals with Iran. The first essay deals with the introduction of the principle of representation in the government of the Empire and in the Arab world particularly the 'elections' to the councils of the subdivisions of the vilayets. The second essay deals with the impact of nationalism in Turkish society which although not of direct relevance is of interest because it gave rise to the Young Turk movement and the beginnings of the policy of Turkification.

In section three dealing with 'Social Movements' only one contribution is of relevance dealing with the 1860 religious troubles in Damascus which resulted in the massacre of members of the Christian minority. The final section of this collection is concerned with problems in modernisation with two of the four essays being of particular relevance. The first deals with the effects of modernisation on Syrian politics and society from the time of Sultan Mahmud (1808–1839) until the 1850s. The second deals with the period from 1870 when the Ottoman government was increasing its efforts to modernise the vilayet system whilst still preserving political domination and exploitation of the provinces.

SALIBI, KAMAL S.
**The Lebanese identity.**
*Journal Contemporary History. Vol. 6, No. 1, 1971, pp. 76–86.*

Although of interest to a consideration of the Ottoman administration in the Lebanon this article is mainly a consideration of the growth of Arab nationalism. A full annotation to this article will be found in the section dealing with the beginnings of the Arab nationalist movement.

*SCHELTEMA, J. F., TRS.
**The Lebanon in turmoil Syria and the powers in 1860.**
*Book of the marvels of the time concerning the massacres in the Arab country by Iskander Ibn Yarg'ub Abkarius.*
*New Haven: Yale University Press. 1920.*
*(Yale Oriental Series Researches: Vol. vii.) 203 pp., 24½ cms.*

This work is an account of the Christian massacres in Damascus in 1860 written by a Christian possibly of Armenian birth and a resident in Syria for a number of years. The translator considers that the account is of great subsidiary importance to the history of Lebanon and Syria because of the accuracy of the account and what it implies. In the examination of these events it is also evident that the massacres of 1860 were in part due to the actions of the Christians themselves and from interference from the Great Powers.

\*SHAMIR, SHIMON
**Midhat Pasha and the anti-Turkish agitation in Syria.**
*Middle Eastern Studies. Vol. 10, No. 2, May 1974, pp. 115–141.*

Midhat Pasha was appointed Vali to Syria in November 1878 having been dismissed as Grand Vezir and banished from Istanbul in 1876. He began to work energetically in his new position urging the Sultan to extend his powers so that the provincial government could be an instrument for reform. His ideas were met with opposition, however, and although he submitted his resignation twice in two years, on both occasions it was rejected. After the second rejection political agitation in Syria increased and anti-Ottoman placards began to appear calling on Syrian Arabs to take over the management of their own affairs.

This situation has been examined by scholars using consular reports and memoirs of contemporary Syrians, though no one had examined in depth the Yildiz Palace section of the Ottoman archives. This article is an attempt to utilise documents from the Yildiz and to re-examine the driving forces behind the Syrian agitation and the role played by Midhat himself.

In the journals are reports of state functionaries and informers sent to spy on Midhat Pasha and these seem to indicate that he was securing support from amongst population and from associates whom he had given posts of authority in addition to support from some of the consuls-general in Syria. 'The presence of Midhat Pasha in Syria – considering the fact that it has a sensitive and important position vis-à-vis the foreigners and one in which the authority of the government is not limited – is not free from danger, and the wisdom of the Sublime Porte is very well aware of that.'

It was evident that Midhat Pasha aimed at being something more than Vali of Syria seeking to obtain a measure of autonomy for himself and the province. The only question asked in Istanbul was whether there was an organisation amongst the Syrian Arabs in which Midhat was implicated or whether the agitation was the result of external influences from either Britain or France. It seems that Midhat opposed by the Sublime Porte sought to utilise the support of Britain to enable him to carry out his reforms and to organise the provincial government on his own lines.

The suggestion is also made that the author of the anonymous placards was none other than Midhat Pasha and though this case is not proved it is evident that 'the Syrians of his time regarded Midhat as the prime mover of the affair'. This conclusion also indicated that the Syrians regarded this as an Ottoman intrigue 'and any interpretation in terms of a genuine struggle for Arab-Syrian autonomy was simply beyond their horizon'. In conclusion the author considers that the period was not one of patriotic fervour expressed in secret societies but one shaped by the politics of the Ottoman élite acting on this society. 'These two facts were moulded by Abdulhamid into a forceful Ottoman-Islamic policy, and it was this line that dominated the Syrian scene in the subsequent decades.'

STEVENS, RICHARD P., ED.
**Zionism and Palestine before the Mandate.**
*Beirut: Institute for Palestine Studies. 1972.*
*xiii, 153 pp., index, 21 cms.*

Although not strictly relevant to the development of the Arab nationalist movement this work is included because of the importance of the Palestine problem and also because of the representation given to the Arab viewpoint. Of particular importance as a survey of the problem is the introductory essay by the Editor which occupies the first forty-eight pages of the work and which presents a balanced approach to the problem.

TIBAWI, A. L.
**A modern history of Syria including Lebanon and Palestine.**
*London: Macmillan. 1969.*
*441 pp., plates, maps, notes, bibl., index, 23 cms.*

A comprehensive history of Syria, Lebanon and Palestine from the end of the eighteenth century to 1921 and subsequently the state of Syria to 1967. The first part of the work deals with the period of Ottoman rule.

In the first part of the work the author deals with the invasion of Egypt by Napoleon which is seen as a false dawn in the evolution of present day Arab nationalism. The work then deals with the British occupation in Egypt and the situation in the remaining part of the Ottoman Empire and in particular the civil war in Syria in 1860. The section concludes with a consideration of the rise of Arab nationalism.

*ZEINE, ZEINE N.
**Arab-Turkish relations and the emergence of Arab Nationalism.**
*Lebanon : Khayat's. 2nd ed. 1966.*
*156 pp., bibl., index, 21 cms.*

An important work which discusses the relationship between the Arabs and Turks in the nineteenth century and the beginning of the twentieth century and their bearing on the genesis of Arab nationalism. In this study the Arabs are essentially those who lived in the Syrian and Beirut Vilayets of the Ottoman Empire because it was here that opposition to Turkish rule began.

1. The Ottomans and the Ottoman Conquest of the Near East.

This section discusses the origin of the Ottomans and the establishment of their Empire in the Near East. The most important point made is that the Turks did not defeat the Arabs in conquering the Arab lands as their military activities were directed against the Mamluks. It also seems evident that the Arab lands were not directly administered from Constantinople as they were, in the beginning, granted a certain deference because of their sacred language and a common religion. Indeed almost complete local independence was left to Lebanon.

The point is also made that the religious bond was the cardinal element in Arab–Turkish relations for nearly four hundred years and was the reason for the acceptance by the Arabs of nationally alien rule. The popular misconception that the Turk was responsible for Arab backwardness is countered by the author using a quotation from Gibb and Bowen's *Islamic Society and the West* in which they wrote that Syria '. . . had probably benefited materially more than any other Asiatic province from incorporation in the Ottoman Empire, as a result of the commercial connections thus formed'.

2. Ottoman Government in Arab Lands.

This chapter deals with the form of administration in the Arab Lands which was based on the Vilayet and Sandjak system which were adaptations of Midhat Pasha's system and based on the laws of the vilayet of 1864 and 1871. This section also discusses the legal machinery of the Ottoman Empire which was gradually remodelled on Western ideas with a new penal code being introduced in 1840 based on that of the French. The administrative units were further reorganised in the Arab provinces following the 1860 massacres in Mount Lebanon and Damascus and in 1867 Jerusalem was created a Sandjak in its own right in recognition of its growing importance.

# ASPECTS OF DIPLOMACY.

**Convention on measures for pacifying Syria (and Lebanon): Austria, France, Great Britain, Prussia, Russia and the Ottoman Empire. 5 September 1860.**
Great Britain, *Parliamentary Papers*, 1861, vol. 68, pp. 5-6.
In: Hurewitz, J. C.
*Diplomacy in the Near and Middle East*, pp. 163-164.

This followed the massacre of the Christian minorities by the Druzes in the Lebanon and by the Muslims in Damascus which was in part supported by the Turkish authorities. The British and French governments vied with each other to intervene with Britain suspecting the French of territorial designs and the convention aimed at providing a formula for intervention without territorial aspirations.

The main body of the convention was;

1. A body of European troops to be sent to Syria to re-establish peace.
2. The French to provide half of the required number of troops with any increase being provided from other countries after negotiation with the Sublime Porte.
3. The C. in C. of the expeditionary force to negotiate with the Turkish officials as to means of fulfilling the convention.
4. Britain, Austria, Prussia and Russia to provide naval forces to ensure its success.
5. The stay of the expeditionary force to be limited to six months.
6. The Sublime Porte to furnish supplies and provisions for the expeditionary force.

FARMAN, T. F.
**French claims on Syria.**
*Contemporary Review. September 1915, pp. 343-353.*

This article considers the historical aspects of the French interest in Syria which evolved from her traditional role as protector of the Christians in Lebanon. It continues by dealing with German attempts to usurp France's position mainly through the construction of the Baghdad railway and the reasons for the continuing French influence.
'Regulation for the Administration of Lebanon.' 9 June 1861.
(French text in Great Britain, *Parliamentary Papers*, 1861, vol. 68, pp. 683-686.)

In: Hurewitz, J. C.
*Diplomacy in the Near and Middle East*, pp. 165–168.
A commission of the five great powers was created to investigate the 1860 massacres and to recommend changes in the administration. The regulations consisted of seventeen articles dealing in detail with the administration but the essential component was the provision for a non-Lebanese, Ottoman Christian Governor nominated by the Porte after consulting with the European powers. This regulation transferred the Lebanon into the best administered province in the Ottoman Empire lasting until October 1914 when it was terminated by the Sublime Porte.

SAUSA, NASIM
**The Capitulatory Regime of Turkey:** Its history, origin and nature.
*Baltimore: Johns Hopkins Press. 1933.*
*xxiii, 378 pp., bibl., index, 21 cms.*

This work deals with the conditions of foreigners in the Ottoman Empire as regulated by a series of treaties between the Ottoman Empire and the Christian States of Europe and America. It has interest because of the background it throws on the administration of the Empire and the position of minorities within the Empire.

SHARROCK, WILLIAM I.
**The origin of the French Mandate in Syria and Lebanon: The Railroad Question, 1901–14.**
*International Journal of Middle East Studies. Vol. 1, No. 2, April 1970, pp. 133–153.*

This article seeks to illustrate that the French mandate in Syria and the Lebanon was not the direct result of the Sykes-Picot agreement but of an internationally recognised claim before war was declared. Initially such a claim was based on France's claim to be the protecting power for the Christian minorities in the area. This developed into an influence based on commerce and finance which led to France having a large stake in the finances of the Ottoman Empire.

   This financial involvement was reflected in the financial interests that she had in the Baghdad railway as although France withdrew on an official basis because of wrangling with Germany, private sources still provided a third of the capital. Of equal importance was France's involvement in the Syrian network of railways which was an attempt to expand and solidify her influence in the area. This situation was further strengthened by concessions made by the Turks in return for a further loan which was raised in 1914. 'As a result of the Franco–Turk accord of 9 April 1914, an economic sphere of influence was delineated for France in Syria. This fact was recognised by both Germany and Turkey.'

## BIOGRAPHICAL WORKS

*ABDULLAH I, KING OF TRANSJORDAN
**Memoirs of King Abdullah of Transjordan,** edited by Philip P. Graves.
*London: Cape. 1950.*
*278 pp., illus., refs., app., index, 20½ cms.*

The early part of these memoirs deal with the relationship between the Sherifian family and the Ottoman Government which begins with the political exile of Hussein in Constantinople until his appointment as Emir in 1908 following the deposing of Sherif Ali by the Sublime Porte.

However, following the abdication of Abdul Hamid and the rule of the Young Turks relations began to deteriorate with disagreements between the Vali and Hussein over who was vested with the authority of the Sultan in the Hedjaz and accusations of unrest among the tribes against the authority of the Sultan. Further trouble was caused by the proposed railway to Mecca and the enforcing of the law for 'The Administration of Provinces'. The prospects of impending war were not well received by Hussein as he felt that it was not possible to defend the area and he wrote to the Sultan that 'I therefore entreat your Majesty in the name of God not to enter the war on the side of Germany, as this would be either ignorance or high treason.'

*MIDHAT, ALI HAYDOR
**The Life of Midhat Pasha.**
*London: Murray. 1903.*
*xii, 292 pp., 23 cms.*

This biography of Midhat Pasha by his son was written in an attempt to clear his father's name following his trial and assassination. The interest in this work lies in the sections dealing with Midhat Pasha's reforms in the vilayets in the Middle East especially in Baghdad and Syria where he continued the reforms that he had begun in the Danube Province. It also deals with Midhat's relationship with the Sultan which was one of conflict over the proposed reforms in Syria and the problem of the Christian minorities.

# (b) THE BEGINNING OF THE ARAB NATIONALIST MOVEMENT

## GENERAL WORKS

General works on the Middle East with relevance to the beginnings of the Arab nationalist movement.

AHMAD, FEROZ
**The Young Turks:** The Committee of Union and Progress in Turkish Politics 1908–1914.
*London: O.U.P. 1969.*
*xiii, 205 pp., bibl., index, 20 cms.*

References to the Arabs and the Arab provinces are scattered throughout the early part of this book but the main section falls in the final two chapters dealing with 'The Consolidation of Power' and 'The Politics of Union and Progress'.

This work is important because the C.U.P. was in being at the critical period in the growth of the Arab nationalist movement. 'Even after the introduction of decentralized administration in the provinces, agitation of local autonomy continued in Syria and Iraq . . .' The Turks countered the nationalist movements in the Arab provinces by giving a more definite form to their own nationalism thus alienating the Arab intellectuals in the Ottoman parliament and the politically conscious Arab officers in the Ottoman Empire.

ALLEN, RICHARD
**Imperialism and nationalism in the Fertile Crescent:** Sources and prospects of the Arab–Israeli conflict.
*London: O.U.P. 1974.*
*x, 686 pp., maps, bibl., index, 20½ cms.*
*(Chapter 7, pp. 133–159.)*

The Arab nationalist movement began in the latter part of the nineteenth century though it really came into its own following the rise to power of the Young Turks in 1908 which resulted in a shift from Ottomanism to Arabism. 'Inevitably the Arab revival meant conflict with the Turkish patriotism of the Young Turk triumvirate. . . . For their part most Arab Muslims, before the rise of nationalism, had normally felt loyal to the Sultan-Caliph because of their common faith. Yet the two peoples were basically out of tune.'

This section deals with the development of the movement from the early influences of Mohammed Ali, the Western influence through the educational activities of the missionaries in Syria and the rise of an educated middle class and an Arab press. At first the movement aimed at securing autonomy within the Ottoman Empire but the intransigence of the Young Turks with their policy of Turkification caused the now Muslim nationalist movement to become a separatist movement.

AL-MARAYATI, ABID A., *et al.*
**The Middle East:** Its Governments and Politics.
*California : Duxbury Press. 1972.*
*xiv, 516 pp., maps, glossary, bibl., index, 24 cms.*

This work is divided into three sections, the first dealing with various aspects of the area in general terms, the second considers the area by country and the final section considers the international implications and the problems of Palestinian nationalism. Each contribution is by a specialist in the field and the result is an expression of personal viewpoint which may be at variance with other contributors. The approach is interdisciplinary as the politics of the area cannot be considered in isolation from its history, culture, social structure or economic conditions.

Part 1 of this work consists of the interdisciplinary chapters and these are intended to lead the reader into the region and to provide a basis for the country by country study in Part 2. The chapters in the second part provide a brief introduction to the history, economics and social structure of each country followed by an analysis of its political structure and foreign policies though in the latter case the emphasis is on the post World War II period. The last part deals with the external international pressures on the Middle East and the vexed question of Palestinian nationalism.

Some sections of the work are outside of the scope of this study as they deal with Iran, Israel, Egypt, Saudi Arabia and the Gulf States. Each section has its own select bibliography and notes with a final glossary defining terms used in the text.

ARMAJANI, YAHYA
**Middle East Past and Present.**
*New Jersey : Prentice-Hall. 1970.*
*xii, 432 pp., maps, illus., bibl., index, 23½ cms.*

Aimed at students and the general reader with no knowledge of the history and culture of the Middle East this work is divided into four parts dealing with the advent of Islam, the Ottoman

Empire, Western Imperialism and the Middle East, and the modern history of the Middle East. The work also has an introductory section dealing with the land and its people, religious groups, diversity and unity, nationalism and Islam.

In the introductory section on nationalism the author considers the five main ingredients of nationalism in the Middle East which although in itself divisive has common characteristics regardless of country. The first ingredient is pride in the past based on the great empires of the past and on the cultural heritage of the past. This is linked by the author with the second ingredient which is one of a feeling of inferiority when compared with the past and when compared with the technology of the Western world. Secularism is the third ingredient with the struggle being between those who favour a return to puritanism in Islam and those who favour complete modernisation. The fourth ingredient is that of suspicion of the policies of countries outside the area who are considered to be opposed to the 'Arab Awakening' and the fifth that of confusion caused by the problem of knowing what of the ancient culture to retain or discard.

The work then continues to deal with the history of the area from the decay of the Ottoman Empire through the Arab Revolt and the mandates down to the Arab–Israeli war of 1967, and much of the considerations are outside of the scope of this study. The bibliography is selective and arranged according to the four sections of the book.

CARMICHAEL, JOEL
**The Shaping of the Arabs:** A study in ethnic identity.
*London: Allen & Unwin. 1969.*
*iv, 407 pp., bibl., index, 22 cms.*

This book attempts to outline the growth of an ethnic community over 1,300 years concluding with a discussion of the present-day problems of Arab unity. It begins by a consideration of what is an 'Arab' concluding that the best criteria is that of language with the exception of communities where some other criteria is more important.

Main Contents:

1. Arab origins; Muhammed and the Koran.
2. The Outpouring from the desert; Bedouin conquests.
3. A New State; The Arab Kingdom and the Muslim empire.
4. The Flowering of a Civilization: The Islamic World Empire.
5. A Medieval Confrontation – Islam and Christendom.

6. The Empire crumbles; The Turkish come in; The Long stagnation.
7. Stirrings of nationalism; The Reshaping of Arab identity.
8. Modern times.
   Epilogue: The Arabs in the Modern World; Arab Unification.

In the beginning the true Arab was a member of the Bedouin tribes and other groups would not think of themselves as Arabs but as Muslims. It is only in the last generations that has changed the pattern as 'the potent effects of mythologising – and more particularly the polarising of propaganda emotions, and agitations around the conflicts with the Turks and later on with the Jewish Zionists – have finally begun, but only just begun, to make the phrase "Arab Nationalist Movement" an understandable category of politics.'
Carmichael in the Epilogue considers the position as it is in the present-day Arab World and its prospects for the future. 'The Arabic-speaking world, on the verge, perhaps, of ethnic, crystallisation, and in any case already functioning as a political complex, has appeared on the world stage at a singularly entangled conjuncture. It is a question whether its resources, mental and material will enable it to keep pace with the improvisations of life . . .'

COKE, RICHARD
**The Arab's place in the sun.**
London: Butterworth. 1929.
318 pp., illus., maps, index, 22 cms.

The second part of this work deals with the place of the Arab in the modern world beginning with the national re-awakening based on Wahhabi movement and the brief rule of Ibrahim Pasha in Syria. The author traces the movement from this development through the secret societies and the unrest in certain areas at the time of the outbreak of World War I. This section also deals with the negotiations between Britain and Sherif Hussein which led to the declaration of the Arab Revolt.

ELLIS, HARRY B.
**Heritage of the Desert:** The Arabs and the Middle East.
New York: The Roland Press Co. 1956.
vii, 311 pp., illus., maps, bibl., index, 21 cms.

A light treatment of the Arabs and the Middle East in world

affairs based on the author's experiences as Middle East corres-
pondent for *The Christian Science Monitor*. The book deals with
the early history of the Arab and Ottoman Empires, the mandates
and their administration and the problems of Westernisation and
Communism. The real value of the work lies, however, not so
much in its consideration of the political aspects of the area but in
its evaluation of the Arab peoples.

*FISHER, SYDNEY NETTLETON
**The Middle East:** A History.
*London: Routledge & Kegan Paul. 2nd ed. 1971.*
*xxx, 749 pp., maps, bibl., index, 22 cms.*

See Section 1a for main annotation.

Chapters of relevance to this section are as follows:

Part III: European Imperialism in the Modern Middle East.
    Chapter 20   The era of the French Revolution and Napoleon.
    Chapter 21   Mahmud II – Nationalism and Reform.
    Chapter 22   Muhammed Ali and the development of modern
                 Egypt.
    Chapter 23   European ambitions and diplomacy in the Middle
                 East.
    Chapter 24   From Tanzimat to the Constitution.
    Chapter 25   Abdul Hamid II and Despotism.
    Chapter 26   The Young Turks.
    Chapter 27   Arab Nationalism.

GIBB, H. A. R.
**The Arabs.**
*London: O.U.P. 1940.*
*32 pp., maps, 17½ cms.*
*(Oxford Pamphlets on World Affairs No. 40.)*

A consideration of the Arab world in general terms dealing with
its background and history. The pamphlet also considers the
impact of the West on the area and the re-awakening of Arab
self-consciousness and Arab nationalism. 'Gone is the lethargy,
the political apathy, the calm acceptance of good and evil as the
Will of God. From end to end the Arab world is in travail.'

GIBB, H. A. R.
**Social change in the Near East.**
*In: Ireland, Philip W., ed.*
*The Near East Problems and Prospects.*
*Chicago: University of Chicago Press. 1942.*

Gibb begins by considering the Arab peoples in terms of history and geography and then considers the break up of the Ottoman Empire in the face of Western influences with the Arabs considering that the existence of the Turkish vilayets provided for a successful combination of areas into an Arab nation. Certain factors, however, legislated against the uniting of the various areas into an Arab state namely, the feudal system, the minorities in race and religion and the differing social systems. None of these problems had been solved by the administration of the Ottomans and indeed many had been accentuated in the pursuit of a policy of divide and rule.

IRELAND, PHILIP W., ED.
**The Near East:** Problems and prospects.
*Chicago : University of Chicago Press. 1942.*
*xiv, 266 pp., app., map, index, 19½ cms.*

A collection of essays based on a series of lectures delivered at the Harris Institute in 1942 with the object of providing an interpretation of the Near East in terms of its internal problems, international relationships and post-war prospects.

The essay of relevance to this study is by H. A. R. Gibb and is concerned with the social changes in the Near East. The annotation to this article will be found under the author's name.

JECKH, ERNEST, ED.
**Background of the Middle East.**
*New York: Cornell University Press. 1952.*
*viii, 236 pp., maps, bibl., index 23 cms.*

This work consists of a collection of contributions designed to provide the reader with information necessary for an understanding of the Middle East. Although the work is of general interest the following sections are of particular relevance to this study.

Thomas, Lewis V. 'European imperialism in the Middle East', pp. 118–127.
Kohn, Hans. 'Nationalism', pp. 145–156. This contribution is of particular value providing a useful summary of the development of Arab nationalism together with an assessment of its failings and problems.
Each section is followed by a short bibliographical listing.

KARPAT, KEMAL H.
**Political and social thought in the contemporary Middle East.**
*London : Pall Mall Press. 1968.*
*xiii, 397 pp., notes, index, 23½ cms.*

This work is aimed at providing the student of the East with access to the writings of Arabs, Turkish and Iranian intellectuals to give an insight into the political and social thought of contemporary Middle East writers.

Only part of this collection is of relevance as the latter part deals with the modern nationalist movement and the impact of communism. The first part of the study deals with the background to Arab nationalism considering its historical roots, its relationship to the Koran, its ideology and its characteristics. Section four deals with the regional and local forms of nationalism and is concerned with the growth of the nationalist movements in Syria and Lebanon. The tenth section is also of interest as it deals with Arab unity and ideology beginning with the concept of a greater Syria and the Pan-Arabism plan of King Abdullah of Transjordan. It also deals with the concept of Arab unity and Federalism and the ideological problems affecting the Arab world and its desire for unity.

Each contribution is introduced by a short paragraph giving biographical and bibliographical details of the writer with a synopsis of the writer's viewpoint.

*LAQUEUR, WALTER
**The Middle East in transition:** Studies in contemporary history.
*London : Routledge & Kegan Paul. 1958.*
*xix, 513 pp., index, 21½ cms.*

A collection of essays dealing with various aspects of the Middle East considering social and political changes and the influences of communism and the Soviet Union on the Middle East. The contributions are by distinguished writers on the Middle East and all aspects of social, political and economic change are considered. Although not all of the essays are of relevance to this work the following are worthy of study:

Tutsch, Hans E. 'Arab unity and Arab dissensions', pp. 33–51.
Himadeh, Sa'id B. 'Social awakening and economic development in the Middle East', pp. 52–60.
Kedourie, Elie. 'Pan-Arabism and British policy', pp. 100–111.
Rejwar, Nissim. 'Arab nationalism', pp. 145–165.

Haim, Sylvia G. 'Islam and the theory of Arab nationalism',
pp. 280–307.

KHADDURI, MAJID
**Political trends in the Arab World:** The Role of ideas and
ideals in politics.
*London: Johns Hopkins Press. 1970.*
*xi, 298 pp., refs., notes, index.*

This work is a study of the mainstreams of contemporary Arab
thought dealing with some of the major problems with which the
Arabs have been involved. It does not deal with North Africa
except where this matches the mainstream of Arab political ideas,
and is concerned only with political trends and not with
personalities and the question of leadership in the Arab World.

The introduction deals with the question of Islam in the Arab
World and its role in a changing Arab society as it became
exposed to the ideas of the West and the decay of the Ottoman
Empire. This leads to a consideration of the rise of nationalism, an
idea which Khadduri considers second only to Islam in its
domination of the Arab mind. In addition the idea of nationalism
has had an impact in areas of Arab society which until its advent
had been the sole province of Islam. The chapter also deals with
the genesis of nationalism beginning with the Christian Arabs in
Lebanon and Syria and the gradual involvement of the Muslim
Arabs leading to the leadership of the movement changing hands.

In its initial stages Arab nationalism was a cultural movement
rather than a political one with the Arab language, rich in
literature, providing the source of national pride and identity.
Indeed Lawrence, in his *Seven Pillars of Wisdom*, wrote that the
Arabs '. . . had lost their geographical sense, their racial and
political memories, but they clung the more tightly to their
language, and erected it almost into a fatherland of its own'.
Khadduri concludes that these ingredients might have eventually
been moulded into a motive social force were it not for the events
of World War I and the imposition of the mandates.

The remainder of the book deals with a later period than this
study covering the period between the two wars and the rise of
Arab socialism and contemporary forms of nationalism.

LENCZOWSKI, GEORGE
**The Middle East in world affairs.**
*New York: Cornell University Press. 2nd ed. 1956.*
*xix, 576 pp., maps, bibl., index, 24 cms.*
*(Chapter One.)*

In this section dealing with the historical background to World War I the question of the Young Turks rise to power is considered though not the effect on the Arab provinces. This section also deals with the problem of the loyalty of the Arabs prior to the declaration of the Arab Revolt in the light of the Turkification policy of the C.U.P. and in contrast with the secret societies formed by the politically conscious Arab army officers including Emir Faisal.

LENCZOWSKI, GEORGE, ED.
**The Political awakening in the Middle East.**
*New Jersey: Prentice-Hall. 1970.*
*ix, 180 pp., map, bibl., 21 cms.*

This collection of readings uses the Ottoman Empire as a basis and proceeds to examine the departures from this traditional structure through primary and secondary sources. The following topics are of relevance to this section.
2. Reform within Islam: Fundamentalism and Modernism.
    Interest in this section centres on the Wahhabi movement and its role in Arab nationalism.
3. Early Constitutionalism and Nationalism. Readings of relevance in this section are as follows:
    'The Young Turks', G. L. Lewis.
    'The Committee of Union and Progress', H. Luke.
    'The Birth of Arab Nationalism', G. Antonius.
    'Arab Turkish relations', Z. N. Zeine.
    'The struggle for Arab self-determination', Z. N. Zeine.

*LENGYEL, EMIL
**World Without End:** The Middle East.
*New York: John Day Co. 1953.*
*viii, 374 pp., maps, bibl., index, 22 cms.*

An interesting work which considers the whole concept of the Middle East with the most detailed consideration being given to the nineteenth century. It is a work which looks at the region in a compassionate way considering its history, its exploitation, its position as a battlefront for the great powers, its strengths and its weaknesses.

The work begins with a consideration of the social and economic aspects of the area, concluding that it is the poorhouse of the world and that the fact that oil has meant improving conditions brings with it the threat of revolution. The work continues with an examination of the history of the area from earliest times through the early Arab Empire and the Ottoman Empire to the era of independence following the Second World War. It deals with the Arab Revolt and the problems of the mandates and the struggle of the Arabs for independence. It also deals with the problem of Palestine which above all else has shown the inherent weakness of the concept of Arab unity. Each country is dealt with briefly in relation to the great powers and their new-found independence and the struggle to establish themselves as nations.

Also considered is the make-up of the Middle East as a political and ethnic area in an attempt to answer the question as to what constitutes an Arab. This section also deals with the impact of Islam on the Arab World, its appeal to the people and the dissension which it also brings and the nationalism which it encourages, e.g. the Wahhabi movement. The work concludes with a study of the revival of Turkey, the position of oil in the Middle East, the strategic problems and the problems created for America by Britain relinquishing its role as the Great Power in the area. The writer concludes that this role is vital as the assistance given by America will determine the future of the area as 'Only then will the Middle East cease to be a power vacuum, inviting aggression. The Middle East is a world without end and may therefore become the site of new beginning.'

MANSFIELD, PETER
**Arab political movements.**
*In: Mansfield, Peter, ed.*
*The Middle East: A political and economic survey, pp. 66–90.*

This thematic study begins by considering the awakening of the Arab peoples which began following the invasion of Egypt by Napoleon though this was an isolated incident and the real beginning came with the influence of Mohammed Ali in Egypt and Ibrahim Pasha in Syria. The essay continues by discussing the impact of Western education in Syria with the intellectual revival providing the essential background for a political renaissance. This leads to a discussion of the Arab secret societies and the gradual change of leadership of the movement from the Christian to the Muslim Arabs together with a change in policy from Ottomanism to Arabism.

*MANSFIELD, PETER, ED.
**The Middle East:** A political and economic survey.
*London: O.U.P. 4th ed. 1973.*
*xi, 591 pp., map, app., index, 22½ cms.*

An extremely useful work though a large part is irrelevant by virtue of geography or date. The work has an introductory section which defines the area, summarises its history and politics and the social and economic aspects of the area in addition to a consideration of the various sects and faiths. In this section are also a series of thematic studies only two of which are relevant and these are considered separately.

Monroe, E. 'The origins of the Palestine problem'. Section 1c.
Mansfield, P. 'Arab political movements'. Section 1c.

The remainder of the work deals with the region country by country with each entry following the same pattern of content though some coverage is irrelevant by virtue of date.

(*a*) The land and the people.
(*b*) History and politics.
(*c*) Government, constitution and administration.
(*d*) Social and economic survey.

The following chapters are of relevance:
Chapter V. Iraq, pp. 311–339.
Chapter VII. The Hashemite Kingdom of Jordan, pp. 375–398.
Chapter VIII. Lebanon, pp. 399–418.
Chapter X. Syria, pp. 452–483.

NUTTING, ANTHONY
**The Arabs:** A Narrative history from Mohammed to the present.
*London: Hollis and Carter. 1964.*
*vi, 424 pp., maps, bibl., index, 22 cms.*

A general history of the Arab peoples from the beginnings of the Arab Empire of which only the latter part is of interest to this study. In view of the coverage of the work it is impossible for each section to go into detail but this is a very readable account providing a useful introduction to the history of the Arab peoples.

POLK, WILLIAM R. AND CHAMBERS, RICHARD L., EDS.
**Beginnings of modernization in the Middle East:** The Nineteenth Century.
*London: University of Chicago Press. 1968.*
*x, 427 pp., notes, index, 23½ cms.*

Section four of this work deals with the importance of 'Foreign Intervention'. The aspect of the intervention mainly considered is the impact of the Western economy as the unrest in the latter part of the nineteenth century was partly due to the conflict between the culture and pre-industrial revolution economy of the east and the sophisticated mechanised European economy.

\*SACHAR, HOWARD M.
**The Emergence of the Middle East 1914–1924.**
*London : Allen Lane, The Penguin Press. 1969.*
*xiii, 518 pp., xxix, maps, notes, bibl., index, 24 cms.*
*(Chapter V, pp. 116–151.)*

This work deals with the emergence of the Middle East resulting from World War I which gave rise to a concerted nationalist movement and the disintegration of the Ottoman Empire.

The section on the Arab Revolt considers the negotiations between McMahon and Hussein and the extent to which nationalist feeling was evident concluding that only in areas where Turkish repression was not likely did any tangible Arab involvement emerge. Also considered is the involvement of Lawrence and the Sherifian army in the Middle East war though Lawrence's idea of Arab independence was different from that of Hussein as he wrote 'Their idea of nationality is the independence of tribes and parishes and their idea of national union is episodic, combined resistance to an intruder. Constructive policies, an organised state, and an extensive empire are not only beyond their capacity, but anathema to their instincts . . .'

SHARABI, HISHAM
**Governments and Politics of the Middle East in the Twentieth Century.**
*London: Van Nostrand. 1962.*
*xiii, 296 pp., illus., maps, notes, index, 23½ cms.*

The work aims at providing a summary and guide to the structure and functioning of the government of the Middle East through three main lines of development, governmental structures, political organisation and behaviour, regional and international relations. In two sections the Middle East is dealt with as a single unit, Part One being the Political Framework and Part Seven the question of Democracy versus Autocracy with other aspects being considered on a regional basis and as such some of these sections are irrelevant to this study.

Apart from sections one and seven section four is also of relevance to this study as it deals with the first bid for independence through a consideration of the Ottoman rule, the nationalist movement and the Arab Revolt, and the post-war settlement. The section then continues to deal with the countries in turn through the three main lines indicated.

The notes are extensive and the author draws particular

attention to the documentary evidence to which most of the footnotes refer.

*STEWART, DESMOND
**The Middle East:** Temple of Janus.
*London: Hamish Hamilton. 1972.*
*viii, 414 pp., bibl., index, 24 cms.*

The greater part of this work is of relevance to this study though one must exclude the last part of the book by virtue of date and some of the earlier material by virtue of geography.

The first section of relevance is that entitled 'God's Hook-Nosed Shadow' which deals with the reign of Sultan Abdul Hamid and in particular the work of Midhat Pasha in reforming the Ottoman administration in Mesopotamia. However, as Hamid's reign progressed the Empire continued its decline with no leadership to repair the system as the Sultan had become a recluse on all but religious occasions leaving the affairs of the Empire in the hands of Albanians and Arabs who were unlikely to conspire against him. In 1908, however, the Young Turk movement started a revolt in anticipation of being banned by the Sultan and forced the restoration of Midhat Pasha's constitution.

The prospects for peace in the Empire seemed to be good and in the Arab provinces the Hedjaz railway was inaugurated and Hussein became Emir of Mecca. In the new Ottoman Empire Abdullah was elected to represent Mecca and he became the parliament's vice-chairman whilst Faisal was elected to represent Jeddah. Events in Europe precipitated a crisis and the Committee of Unions and Progress assumed power with Mehemet V installed as the new Sultan. However, events in Europe and growing discontent at home caused the Young Turks to order the disbanding of groups such as the Ottoman Arab Fraternity followed by the establishment of a dictatorship which pursued a policy of Turkification. These moves led to some Ottoman officials regarding the Arabs as inferiors thus creating friction which led to rifts in national unity. From this point onwards the Arabs instead of pursuing a policy of autonomy within the Empire began to move towards a policy of independence for the Arab provinces.

# ARAB NATIONALISM – GENERAL WORKS

ABD AL KADIR HUSAINI SAIJID
(HUSAINI, DR. S. A. Q.)
**Constitution of the Arab Empire.**

*Karachi: Muhammed Ashraf. 1958.*
*x, 152 pp., index, 21½ cms.*

Although not strictly relevant to this study the inclusion of this work is justified because of the detailed account it gives of the Arab form of government. The work begins by discussing the nature of the Arab constitution, the historical derivation of its various parts and the way in which the constitution developed over the years. The work then deals with various offices under the constitution, the Arab judiciary and finally the form of local government. Although related directly to the time of the Arab Empire much of it lasted through the Ottoman Empire because of its dependence upon and inter-relation with Islam.

AL-MIYAHID, SHARIF
**Arab Nationalism:** A historical analysis.
*Pakistan Horizon (Karachi). 1963, pp. 37–46.*

A discussion of the rise of Arab nationalism which had its foundation in the last decades of the nineteenth century as a purely intellectual movement based on the study of the Arabic language, history and literature and the revival of an Arabic culture. Gradually a political movement developed and it gained momentum as a result of the Young Turk revolution which made the intelligentsia more conscious of Arabism though at this stage the motivation was decentralisation and not separation from the Ottoman Empire.

*ANTONIUS, GEORGE
**The Arab Awakening:** The story of the Arab nationalist movement.
*London: Hamish Hamilton. 1938.*
*xii, 13–471 pp., maps, app., index, 22 cms.*
*(Chapters Three to Six.)*

The next significant part of this work deals with the various secret societies and clubs which were formed to combat the Turkish Empire and to seek a measure of autonomy for the Arab provinces. This is one of the fullest accounts of Arab political activities in Syria to be found in English. It was from these beginnings that the growth of the Arab nationalist movement can be traced as these societies became the vehicle for the expression of Arabism in place of the original demands for reform within the existing framework. The Committee of Union and Progress attempted to suppress these movements and one of the leaders 'Aziz 'Ali was arrested and secretly sentenced to death though this was commuted to fifteen years hard labour. 'His trial had shaken the Arab world more profoundly, perhaps, than any single act of Turkish tyranny, and greatly hardened the Arab will to freedom, for it had moved the masses as well as the thinkers.'

The negotiations between Britain and Hussein form a substantial part of this work and indeed the question of Palestine becomes a major theme as Antonius argues the case that it was included in the area promised to the Arabs. The argument is based on two premises, firstly that the British never excluded Palestine from the pledged territories and that no Arab leader ever assumed the area to be excluded nor would they have agreed to its exclusion.

\*Arab Nationalist Manifesto disseminated from Cairo at the beginning of the First World War
*In: Anderson, M. S.*
*The Great Powers and the Near East: 1774–1923, pp. 153–155.*

This manifesto is an appeal to the ancestral traditions of the Arabs coupled with a denouncement of economic imperialism. It stresses the linguistic character of Arab nationalism with the ability to rise above traditional religious antagonisms. The appeal is emotive and the language, at times, violent. 'You have become humiliated slaves in the hands of the usurping tyrant: the foreigner unjustly dispossesses you of the fruit of your work and labour and leaves you to suffer the pangs of hunger.' . . . 'Till when will you go on acquiesing in this utter humiliation, when your honour is made free of, your wives raped, your children orphaned . . .'

Appeal is also made to the Christian and Jewish Arabs to join in the struggle as 'The Muslim Arabs are your brethren in patriotism, and if you find among them some who are seized with an ugly fanaticism, so likewise are such to be found among you'. The manifesto concludes by declaring the intention to achieve complete independence, and the formation of a decentralised Arab state which will revive ancient glories and rule the country on autonomous lines, according to the needs of each province.

Aziz, M. A.
**The Origins of Arab Nationalism.**
*Pakistan Horizon. Vol. 9, March 1956, pp. 29–37.*

In this article the author sees the impetus to the Arab awakening as the invasion of Napoleon in 1798 followed by the rule of Mohammed Ali in Egypt and his son Ibrahim Pasha in Syria. The second half of the nineteenth century saw the centre of the nationalist movement move to Syria and Lebanon with the influence of the West and the advances in education.

Motivation for freedom from the Ottoman Empire followed the advent of the Young Turks in 1908 as prior to their policy of Turkification the Arab wish was for greater autonomy within the framework of the Ottoman Empire.

The remainder of the article sketches over the period of the Arab Revolt, the peace settlement, the mandate system and concludes by examining the situation through and following World War II, seeing the Arab League as a new chapter in the Arab nationalist movement.

★Be'eri, Eliezer
**Army Officers in Arab Politics and Society.**
*London : Pall Mall Press. 1970.*
*xii, 514 pp., app., bibl., index, 23½ cms.*

A large proportion of this work is outside of the scope of this study dealing, as it does, with the period following independence in the various Arab states. Certain sections of this study are, however, extremely important dealing with the role of the Arab officers in the Arab awakening and the historical and social origins of the Arab officer class.

The section considering the role of the officers in the Arab awakening deals with the effects of the Young Turk movement the thoughts of which were well received in military circles and the subsequent disenchantment with Ottomanism which resulted in the formation of secret societies such as al-'Ahd. The actions of the Young Turks and the post-war activities of Ataturk provided examples which the Arab officers were quick to draw upon when the Arab provinces gained independence.

The section dealing with historical and social origins of the Officer class treats the subject by dealing firstly with Turkey and Egypt and although of interest they are not as important as the sections on Syria, Iraq and Jordan. The author considers the position of the officer class from these areas during their service in the Turkish army, their involvement in the Arab Revolt and the post-war situation. All of the figures dominant in the Arab Revolt and post-war politics were former members of the Ottoman army some of whom had joined the secret societies and joined in the Arab Revolt whilst others had remained loyal to the Sultan until the end of the war. The author then goes on to discuss the increasing role of the military in Arab politics which he sees as '. . . a continuation of the political heritage of Islamic civilization and of the underground tradition of Arab nationalism'.

BEN-GURION, DAVID
**My talks with Arab Leaders.**
*London: Wiley. 1974.*
*x, 343 pp., frontis., app., 24½ cms.*

Only the early part of this work is of relevance by nature of period and some is not relevant because it is a treatment of the Zionist cause. However, it does deal with the situation prior to World War I especially the relationship between the Arabs and the Jewish settlers with the periodic unrest often resulting in bloodshed. One point of interest is made whilst Ben-Gurion was in prison as a result of Djemal Pasha's moves against the Jews which followed his suppression of the Arab nationalists. Ben-Gurion met in the same prison an Arab student whom he had known in Constantinople and on telling him that he was being banished from the country the Arab replied 'As your friend, I am sorry to hear it; as an Arab I am glad'.

In this early section the author also deals with the Weizmann–Faisal agreement which was reached in 1919 but which had no practical value as it did not bind a single Arab. This meant that although the Arab presence could not be ignored the only things that the Jews could rely on was the Balfour Declaration and the possibility of Britain being given the mandate for Palestine.

BURU, TAWFIK
**The Arabic Nationality in the Nineteenth Century.**
*Damascus: Ministry of Culture. 1955.*
*218 pp., 16 cms.*

The Arab national consciousness is considered from the middle of the nineteenth century dealing with the various factors that affected its development. These factors include the fundamental changes in the structure of society through the advances in education which gave rise to an educated middle class and the revival of an Arabic press and literature.

CHURCH, LESLIE F.
**Problems of the Arab Countries** (Editorial).
*London Quarterly Review. Vol. 121, July 1946, pp. 193–198.*

In tracing the development of the nationalist movement this article concentrates on the part played by the Christians through the work of the missionaries and their schools. This resulted in a desire for the revival of Arab literature and culture which was fostered by the missionary schools and their printing presses. At a later date, however, they found it more convenient to use books in European languages and as a result the leadership of the nationalist movement passed into Muslim hands as the Muslim schools continued to use Arabic for teaching.

*DAWN, C. ERNEST
**The Rise and Progress of Middle Eastern Nationalism.**
*Social Education. Vol. XXV, No. 1, January 1961, pp. 20–24.*

In this article Professor Dawn discusses the rise of nationalism in the Middle East with its two main facets being opposition to foreign interest in the area which assumed a dominance over the second facet that of building a nation.

Initially the nationalism motivated by opposition to foreign interests did not exist among the Arabs because there was no Western influence in the Middle East and even when the area was conquered by the Ottomans there was the unity of the one religion. This situation changed from about the middle of the nineteenth century with the rise of a nationalist movement among the Christian Arabs in the Lebanon and Syria which eventually spread to the Muslim Arabs who assumed its leadership. The movement was given further impetus by the policies of the Young Turks which alienated Arab political thought and turned it from Ottomanism to Arabism.

Professor Dawn also discusses the part played by Islam in the evolution of Arab nationalism and this influence was apparent amongst both the conservatives and modernists, the former being unwilling to admit that the West was superior and the latter accepting the fact but resenting it. This interplay between Arabism and Islam was very evident in the beginnings of the movement and Arab politicians still find it difficult to separate the two even today.

FARAH, CAESAR E.
**The Dilemma of Arab Nationalism.**
*Die Welt des Islam. 1963, 8, pp. 140–164.*

In dealing with the beginning of the nationalist movement the article considers the pattern of evolution based upon the views of the articulate minority mainly from the Christian community of Lebanon, whose ideas on nationalism were different from those of the Iraqis and Syrians. In all cases though the awakening national sentiment was intellectual in nature 'an inflamed pride in the rediscovered literary and imperial exploits of the Arab nation in the distant past'.

Initially the national consciousness was reflected only in a demand for autonomy within the Ottoman Empire by the granting of a 'large measure of political and literary rights from their Ottoman overlords within the existing framework of government'.

*FARIS, NABIH AMIN AND HUSAYNE, MOHAMMED
**The Crescent in Crisis:** An interpretive study of the modern Arab world.
*Lawrence: University of Kansas Press. 1955.*
*191 pp., notes, index, 21½ cms.*

An extremely valuable work which deals with the problems of the Arab world as a national unit considering both the unifying factors and those factors that have legislated against national unity. The work begins with a section introducing the Arab world and considering the geographical and political divisions.
Unifying Factors:

(a) Basic unifying factors
   i   Language – considered the most important effective unifying factor.
   ii  One History – a unifying factor because the Arabs live their history.
   iii One Religion – Islam had and still has influence in bringing the Arabs close together and strengthening.
   iv  One mentality – similarity of mentality and temperament in general.
(b) New unifying factors
   i   Schools.
   ii  The press, radio and cinema.
   iii Political parties.
   iv  Modern means of communication.
   v   Modern economics developments.

Divisive Factors
(a) Dynastic rivalries
   This section deals with the actions of the Arab rulers in dividing the Arab world and in particular the rivalries between the Sherifian family and Ibn Saud both in relation to each other and in their dealings with the Great Powers.
(b) The Foreign Powers
   Deals with the effects of the Foreign Powers on the Arab world and the responsibility which they must bear for 'destroying the unity of the Arab world by liberation and unity within it, retarding its economic development, and obstructing its educational and cultural progress . . .' It does not consider any of the

benefits gained from this association but this is a deliberate policy on the writers' part as the work is concerned only with the disunifying of the foreign powers.

(c) Religious sectarianism

Argues that sectarianism dissipates national effort, drains its vitality and diverts its attention from fundamental issues. 'It cuts up every Arab society into fragmentary social islands, self-contained, hating one another and hostile to one another.'

(d) National minorities

The problems of national minorities became a relevant consideration towards the end of the nineteenth century when Arab nationalism began to make itself felt. It is considered that these national minorities were used by the Great Powers to drive a further wedge between the Arab peoples.

(e) Diversity of political aims

The spread of nationalism and the idea of national identity hampered by provincialism amongst Arabs which had its basis long before nationalism became a force in the Arab world. These diverse aims amongst the various areas of the Arab world 'have caused the dissipation of much energy in resisting their inroads, refuting their arguments and deflecting their attacks' when these energies could have been directed against colonialism and backwardness. At the same time these provincial movements have been of service to the cause of Arab nationalism as 'They have stirred Arab nationalists from their apathy, warned them of the necessity for clarifying their aims and unifying their forces, and have impressed upon them the importance of co-ordinated and positive action among the rank and file of the Arab public'.

The work also considers the problems of disparity in political development, economic and social disparity and cultural disparity. The notes to the work are extremely detailed and contain both Arabic and English references.

FATEMI, NASROLLAH S.
**The Roots of Arab Nationalism.**
*Orbis (Philadelphia). 1959, pp. 437–456.*

The roots of Arab nationalism are in two main eras, the Islamic which ended in the nineteenth century and the modern which began with Napoleon's invasion in Egypt. The concern of this study relates to the modern era which is considered from section IV onwards beginning with Napoleon's invasion of Egypt and the subsequent rule of Mohammed Ali and Ibrahim Pasha in Syria.

GABRIELLI, FRANCESO
**The Arab Revival.**
*London: Thames & Hudson. 1961.*
*178 pp., maps, index, 21 cms.*

This work deals with the Arab awakening from the middle of the nineteenth century after an introduction which covers the Arab Empire prior to the Ottoman conquest. In this period the revival was mainly cultural with a revival of literature and in particular Arab journalism which was a significant development in the revival. The work deals with the Arab aspirations prior to 1914 and especially with developments following the coming to power in 1908 of the Young Turks.

The Arab part in the World War is considered together with the problem of the promises made to the Arabs as a result of their participation in relation to the Sykes–Picot agreement. The author maintains that these secret agreements and the mandate system contributed '. . . to the series of political crisis that beset the whole Arab world during those twenty years, and to the new phase of Arab extremist nationalism, that marks the period closest to us'.

GLIDDEN, HAROLD W.
**Arab Unity: Ideal and reality.**
*In: Kritzeck, James and Winder, R. Bayly, eds.*
*The World of Islam.*
*London: Macmillan. 1960.*
*pp. 249–254.*

This article seeks to challenge the concept that were it not for the policies of Britain and France Arab unity would be a reality. Indeed Khadduri attributes the basic problem of the Middle East to these policies which 'created either internal insecurity and confusion, or contention among rival powers which has often invited foreign intervention'. However, Glidden contends that whilst British and French actions adversely affected Arab unity it did not destroy it, as a unified Arab political state ceased to exist in A.D. 756 with the establishment of the Umayyad amirate in Spain. In A.D. 773 the 'Abbasid caliphal authority in Spain was abolished thus marking the end of this unity, a fact often concealed by modern promoters of Arab unity.

The present day concept of Arab unity dates from about 1880 when demands for independence began to be heard but this was only in the context of Syria and Lebanon. Indeed later events did little to present a united Arab front as the nationalism of Hussein did not include the whole of the Arab world where support was only given to the Turks especially by the Rashids of Ha'il. This lack of unity also was apparent with regard to the Caliphate which although endorsed by the McMahon–Hussein correspondence was done without consultation with other Arab leaders who would have voiced their opposition.

\*HAIM, SYLVIA G.
**Arab Nationalism:** An anthology.
*London: University of California Press. 1962.*
*x, 255 pp., notes, bibl., 22 cms.*

This work aims at giving a complete picture of the literature of the subject and each item was chosen either for its historical importance or because it best represents some noteworthy current opinion.

The introduction deals with the birth of Arab nationalism placing it in the twentieth century contrary to the work of George Antonius' *The Arab Awakening* which places it in the eighteenth century. The introduction then goes on to discuss the thinking of Arab leaders with regard to Islam, national unity, the effects of the First World War and the present day trends in Arab political parties.

The contents are a collection of writings on Arab nationalism beginning with Rashid Rida on Islam and national unity and ending with writings on the Arab Ba'th Party. The bibliography is in two sections, the first concerned with Western publications and the other Arabic.

HANNA, SAMI A. AND GARDNER, GEORGE H.
**Al-Shu Ubiyyah up-dated.** A study of the twentieth-century revival of an eighth-century concept.
*Middle East Journal. Vol. 20, Summer 1966, pp. 335–351.*

The first section of relevance is that dealing with the period from 1839–1918 which is considered to be an extension of the classical shu'ubiyyah movement and in a publication by Anis Sayigh four major characteristics are discerned following four centuries of Ottoman rule:

1. The Arabs never enjoyed independence or freedom and those Arabs who achieved high positions did so by suppressing their Arabness.
2. The Arabs were second-class citizens.
3. The Arab language deteriorated and was ignored.
4. The Turks were able to castrate the Arab mind.

These views are further strengthened by the writings of Mustafa al-Shihabi in 1961, Al-Fikayki in 1961 and the Umm al-qura of 'Abd al Rahman al-Kawahibi in 1899 in which he severely criticised the Ottoman government's policy. 'It is one of the necessities that each people must obtain from the people of Turkey some sort of administrative independence which agrees with their habits and national character.'

The second section entitled 'Shu' ubiyyah Gharbiyyah' covering the period 1798-1939 deals with the impact of the West and the concern shown by conservative Arab leaders about the undermining effects of Westernisation upon the traditional Arab way of life.

HOGARTH, DAVID GEORGE
**Arabs and Turks.**
*Cairo: The Arab Bulletin. No. 48, 21 April 1917.*

An assessment of the problem of the Arab peoples in relation to the Allied policy of removing Turkish control from all areas in which the Arab speaking races were more numerous. Hogarth examines the demise of the Arab Empire and its replacement by the Ottoman Empire into which the Arabs were assimilated.

The new attitude towards Turkey saw the support of the Allies being given to the Arabs but Hogarth had doubts as to the strength of the cause being supported. The control of Islam had been too long in the hands of Turkey for it to become part of the spiritual-political force of the Arabs. 'The ruling house of Mecca owes, in all men's sight, its elevation and present wealth to an Albanian Pasha of Egypt, and its present head will have to rely on very much more than his pedigree if he is to be the agent of a new Arab unity.'

HOLT, P. M.
**The Later Ottoman Empire in Egypt and the Fertile Crescent.**
*In: The Cambridge History of Islam. Vol. 1. The Central Islamic Lands, pp. 374-393.*

This chapter deals with the Ottoman Empire from the seventeenth to the twentieth centuries in Egypt, which is not included in this study, and the Fertile Crescent. As such this chapter deals with the decline of the Ottoman Empire and the increasing impact of the West with the author considering that the latter part of the eighteenth century shows developments which anticipate some of the major themes in the history of the area for the following one hundred years.

The first of these themes is seen as the impact on the region of European military power which begins with the Russo-Turkish war of 1768–1774, was reinforced by Bonaparte's occupation of Egypt and the intervention of Britain and France in the area. The second development was the revival of interest in Syria from Egypt which began in 1770 but which really manifested itself with the rule of Mohammed Ali in the following century. Lastly came the attempts by the Ottoman government to break the power of local despots, aimed at restoring the power of the Sultan, but in fact setting the pattern for future unrest in the area. The chapter ends by discussing the end of Ottoman rule in the Fertile Crescent dealing with the Young Turk movement, the rise of the Arab nationalist movement and the impact of World War I.

HOURANI, ALBERT H.
**Minorities in the Arab World.**
*London: O.U.P. (for Royal Institute of International Affairs). 1947.*
*viii, 140 pp., maps, index, 22 cms.*

The nineteenth century saw the intervention of the European Powers in the affairs of the Ottoman Empire mainly on the pretext of the relationship between the Porte and its Christian subjects. The latter part of the century saw the growth of a national consciousness which sought to establish the Ottoman community on the basis of constitutional government, individual liberty and the equality of all nations and sects in the Empire. Although a large number of the Christian Arabs regarded the nationalist movement with fear 'as no more than a scarcely-disguised religious movement' support was forthcoming from those who had an increasing consciousness of the Arab heritage and the ideas of Western democracy.

Also considered is the distinctive nationalist movement of the Christian Arabs in the Lebanon who wanted an independent state under French protection and with increased frontiers. Similar movements were evident elsewhere in the Empire especially among the Kurds although the progress of this movement was slow.

HOWARD, HARRY N.
**Nationalism in the Middle East.**
*Orbis (Philadelphia), 1967, 10, pp. 1200–1213.*
Only the early part of this article is of relevance as it deals with the early developments of the Arab nationalist movement from

the period prior to the Young Turks and the events leading up to World War I. In the main this is a restatement and reappraisal of thoughts of Hans Kohn.

KATIBAH, H. I.
**The New Spirit in Arab Lands.**
*New York: Published by the author. 1940.*
*320 pp., bibl., index, 23 cms.*

In his preface to the work the author states that it was written as a result of the need for a study of the nationalist movement from the inside '. . . based on the living experience of one who has accompanied the Arab nationalist movement as an active participant and disinterested observer . . .'

The work begins with the problem of a definition of the Arab peoples and concludes that the Arabs are those who speak the Arabic language and share the traditions and associations of Arab history. The first section of the study deals with the relationship between the emerging nationalist movements and the outside world seeing it as a constructive force rather than as an obstacle to Western domination of the Arab world. The author continues by discussing the 'Taproots of Arab Nationalism' which are seen as coming from two streams of evolution, the first being the agitation for reform within the Ottoman Empire and the second the revivication of Islam.

KEDOURIE, ELIE
**Arabic Political Memoirs and Other Studies.**
*London: Cass. 1974.*
*viii, 326 pp., bibl., index, 22½ cms.*

A collection of essays only two of which are relevant to this study and these are considered in their relevant sections.
 Chapter 8. The impact of the Young Turk revolution on the Arabic-speaking provinces of the Ottoman Empire. Section 1b.
 Chapter 15. Sir Mark Sykes and Palestine 1915–16. Section 1c.

KEDOURIE, ELIE
**The Chatham House Version and other Middle Eastern Studies.**
*London: Weidenfeld & Nicolson. 1970.*
*vii, 483 pp., notes, bibl., index, 22 cms.*

A collection of studies by Kedourie on various aspects of the Middle East though all are not relevant to this study. The following contributions are of interest and will be found in the relevant sections:

\*Kedourie, Elie
**The impact of the Young Turk Revolution on the Arabic-speaking provinces of the Ottoman Empire.**
*In: Kedourie, Elie.*
*Arabic Political Memoirs and Other Studies, pp. 124–161.*

An examination of the impact of the Young Turk movement in the Arab provinces which begins with a study of the events leading up to the coup of 1908 dealing with the various reforms in the Empire and the rule of Abd al-Hamid. The initial effect of the events of 1908 was a series of coups by Young Turk sympathisers in the provinces consisting mainly of factions within the ruling institution both civil and military.

Reaction among the Arabs was somewhat different 'Whereas the majority of the latter (i.e. the Turkish population) generally approve of the modifications that are being introduced into the administration even though they may not be aware of the width of their scope, the Arabs are much pre-occupied about the reforms being in accordance with the principles of the Sacred Law'. A further effect was the decline in governmental authority and the erosion of social stability and this is substantiated by reports from British vice-consuls in the area who remarked in their reports on the deterioration of the Ottoman provincial government.

Kenny, L. M.
**Sati' al-Husri's views on Arab nationalism.**
*Middle East Journal. Vol. 7, No. 3, 1963, pp. 231–256.*

An examination of the philosophy of al-Husri's nationalism which was founded on the concept of Pan-Arabism based on secular principles with this being put forward as an alternative to regional nationalism. This philosophy was backed by a comparison between Arab and European nationalism drawing on the cultural and historical legacy of the Arabs as a foundation for the concept.

This article examines al-Husri's views through his writings and through the development of nationalism in the Arab world with the obstacles to its development being those placed in its way by Western imperialism.

KHADDURI, MAJID
**Aziz 'Ali Misri and the Arab Nationalist Movement.**
*In: Hourani, Albert, ed.*
*Middle Eastern Affairs Number Four (pp. 140–163).*
*(St. Antony Papers, No. 17.)*

Although an Egyptian nationalist Aziz ali Misri has a place in the general nationalist movement due to his early involvement in the Arab secret societies in Istanbul. Following his expulsion from Turkey, after personal differences with Enver Pasha, he fled to Cairo from where he left to join the Arab army at Rabigh. However, on the realisation that Hussein was seeking a complete break from the Ottoman Empire he attempted to enlist the support of other Ottoman Arab officers on seeking some form of compromise with the Turks on the basis of Arab autonomy within the Empire. The failure of this policy caused him to leave the revolt and to return to Cairo and from this point his involvement was more one of Egyptian nationalism.

KOHN, HANS
**General characteristics of nationalism in the Middle East.**
*In: Middle East Institute.*
*Nationalism in the Middle East, pp. 61–68.*

A survey of the development of the nationalist ideal in the Middle East which Kohn sees as having four strata forming the substance of today's Middle East nationalism. The first strata is seen as that brought about by Napoleon I which resulted in a revival in the Mediterranean bringing Egypt, Iran and Turkey into the arena of international diplomacy. The second, which was of lasting importance, was the penetration of the area by educational and religious missions in Lebanon and Syria and Kohn's judgement is that they should be regarded 'on the whole as the single most beneficial influence for the natives in the Middle East or anywhere else'.

KOHN, HANS
**A History of Nationalism in the East.**
*London: Routledge. 1929.*
*xi, 476 pp., bibl., index, 27 cms.*

A dated work but an extremely valuable contribution to the study of nationalism in the East. One section is of particular interest to this study:

Chapter IX. The New Arabia, pp. 266–318.

In this chapter Kohn considers the evolution of the nationalist movement in Arabia which assumed different forms from the nationalism of Turkey or Egypt. Arab nationalism evolved amongst two separate sections of the population on the one hand and the Bedouins and the inhabitants of Central Arabia and on the other the populations of the Mediterranean coast who were exposed to the influences of Europe.

Kohn considers the nationalism of Ibn Saud and that of Syria in its early forms, the disappointment following the policies of the Young Turks and the Arab Revolt. Also considered is the situation in Syria and Iraq after the war and the problems of Palestine and the mandate. Kohn lays particular stress on the two forms of nationalism, the religious based form of Ibn Saud and the Syrian form in which religion had not played such a significant part. It concludes that Arabia at that time was an example of nationalism in the primitive phase but was destined to advance to full realisation.

\*MacCallum, Elizabeth P.
**The Arab Nationalist Movement.**
*The Moslem World. Vol. XXV, No. 4, October 1935, pp. 359–374.*

The author considers the Arab awakening as a cultural and political force combining a revival of Arab learning with an adaptation of Western knowledge with the political aspect being an attempt to build up an area of independent Arab states. The movement began following the Napoleonic wars and the rule of Mohammed Ali in Egypt and his son Ibrahim Pasha in Syria followed by the spread of education in Lebanon and Syria through the Christian missionary schools.

The article continues by discussing the history of the movement beginning with the Arab National Committee of 1895 in Paris and the Arab role in the Young Turk revolution in 1908. Initially the Arab case was for a measure of autonomy within the Ottoman Empire but concessions were not forthcoming despite promises made by the Turks following the Arab Congress of 1911 in Paris. This failure led to the growth of the secret societies such as al-'Ahd with its military base and al-Qahtaniyah which was open to civilians and the gradual growth of a demand for complete independence.

MARDIN, SERIF
**The Genesis of Young Ottoman Thought:** A study in the
modernisation of Turkish political ideas.
*Princeton: Princeton University Press. 1962.*
*viii, 456 pp., bibl., index, 32 cms.*

Although this work makes very little mention of the Arab
provinces of the Ottoman Empire but its inclusion is justified by
the importance that the Young Turks and their policies had upon
the evolution of Arab nationalist thought.

MARMORSTEIN, EMILE
**The Fate of Arabdom:** A study in comparative nationalism.
*International Affairs. Vol. XXV, No. 4, October 1949, pp. 474–
491.*

This article is a discussion of the Arab nationalist movement as a
branch of the movement which began in 1848 in Europe with the
revolutions against the autocrats. In considering the development of nationalism in Central and Eastern Europe three clearly
defined stages are indicated, firstly the struggle for independence,
secondly the emergence of independent constitutional states and
the third the seizing of power by the dictators. In the comparison
Egypt, Iraq, Syria, Lebanon and Jordan are seen as in stage two
of this development. Comparisons are also made with the origins
of the independent Arab states which emerged from the Ottoman
Empire resembling the European states as both resulted from the
secession of national groups as a result of military defeats suffered
by the Empires. Comparisons are also made with the parts played
by language and by minority groups together with the solidarity
that nationalism brings between the emergent independent
countries.

MIDDLE EAST INSTITUTE
**Nationalism in the Middle East.**
*Washington: Middle East Institute. 1952.*
*iv, 68 pp., 23 cms.*

A series of addresses presented to the Sixth Annual Conference
on Middle East Affairs sponsored by the Middle East Institute in
March 1952. The addresses cover nationalism in the Middle East
in all its aspects and were given by experts in the field. Of the
seven addresses reproduced three are of direct relevance to this
study.
    Schroger, William D. 'Nationalism in the Arab World', pp.
      28–38.

Thomson, William. 'Nationalism and Islam', pp. 51–60.

Kohn, Hans. 'General characteristics of Nationalism in the Middle East', pp. 61–68.

Full assessments of each article will be found under the author's name in the relevant sections.

**\*Programme of the League of the Arab Fatherland, 1905.**
In: Anderson, M. S.
*The Great Powers and the Near East: 1774–1923.*
London: Edward Arnold. 1970.
pp. 148–149.

The foundation of the League of the Arab Fatherland in Paris in 1905 was an important stage in the development of Arab nationalism in Syria as it was the first explicit demand for separation of the Arab provinces from the Ottoman Empire.
The league's programme was as follows:

1. The separation of civil and religious power in the interests of Islam and the Arab nation.
2. The formation of an Arab Empire from the Tigris and Euphrates to the Suez Isthmus and from the Mediterranean to the Sea of Oman.
3. Government to be by a constitutional sultanate based on freedom of all religions and equality of all citizens before the law.
4. All interests of Europe to be respected including the concessions granted by the Turks.
5. The autonomy of Lebanon to be respected and the independence of the Yemen, Nejd and Iraq.
6. The throne of the Arab Empire to be offered to the prince of the Khedive family of Egypt who will declare himself in its favour.
7. The religious caliphate over the whole of Islam to be offered to that Sharif who will embrace its cause with an independent state of the Hedjaz with the town and territory of Medina as far as Akaba. He will enjoy sovereign honours and will hold moral authority over all the Muslims.

RAMSAUR, ERNEST EDMONDSON
**The Young Turks:** Prelude to the revolution of 1908.
*Princeton: Princeton University Press. 1957.*
*xii, 180 pp., bibl., index, 22 cms.*

Although not strictly relevant to this study this work is included because of the important nature of the Young Turk movement and its subsequent effect upon the Arabs. It was the Turkification

policies of the Young Turks which led to the gradual evolution of
Arabic thought from one based on Ottomanism to a concept of
Arabism.

*RESOLUTIONS OF THE ARAB-SYRIAN CONGRESS AT PARIS, 21 JUNE
1913
*In: Anderson, M. S.*
*The Great Powers and the Near East: 1774–1923, pp. 152–153.*

The Congress was composed almost entirely of representatives
from Syria and its call was for reform, decentralisation and
linguistic concessions and not for complete independence. This
latter demand was only sought by a few expatriates though in
1911 a secret society was formed in Paris to work for it.
  The following are the more important of the resolutions:

  1. Radical and urgent reforms are necessary in the Ottoman
     Empire.
  2. It is important to guarantee the Ottoman Arabs the exercise
     of their political rights by making effective their participation
     in the central administration of the Empire.
  3. It is important to establish in each of the Syrian and Arab
     vilayets a decentralised regime appropriate to their needs and
     aptitudes.
  5. The Arab language must be recognised in the Ottoman
     Parliament and considered as an official language in the
     Syrian and Arab provinces.
  6. Military service shall be regional in the Syrian and Arab
     vilayets except in case of extreme necessity.
  7. The Congress offers its sympathy for the reformist and
     decentralising demands of the Armenian Ottomans.
  8. The present resolutions shall be communicated to the
     Ottoman Imperial Government.
  9. These resolutions shall also be communicated to the powers
     friendly to the Ottoman Empire.

Also in: Hurewitz, J. C.
*Diplomacy in the Near and Middle East, pp. 268–269.*

*SA'ID, AMIN
**Al-Thawrah al' Arabiyah al-Kubra.**
*Cairo: Al-Holiby. 1935.*
*A translation of the Al-Ahd programme of 28 October 1913 taken
from pp. 46–47 of the above work.*
*In: Landen, Robert G., ed.*
*The Emergence of the Modern Middle East: Selected readings,
pp. 125–127.*

The programme was drawn up in response to the rise of Turkish nationalism and represented a move from the Ottomanism of the early twentieth century to a Pan-Arabism which varied in content from a cry for an Arab voice within a decentralised Ottoman state to Arab independence. Al-'Ahd was a secret society of some three hundred members comprising mainly Iraqi and Syrian officers in the Ottoman Army and including such figures as Nuri al-Sa'id. Although pressing for Arab rights within the Ottoman Empire its programme for a Turkish–Arab monarchy was never taken seriously but it was sufficient for it to be outlawed by the authorities and several of its members played significant roles in the nationalist movement during and after World War I.

The programme reproduced is as follows:

1. The Al-'ahd (The Covenant) Society is a secret organisation established in Istanbul with the object of gaining internal autonomy for the Arab countries in which they would remain unified to the Istanbul government in a system of government similar to the union of Austria and Hungary.
2. Al-'Ahd believes in the need to retain the Islamic caliphate as a holy trust in the hands of the Ottoman family.
3. The society believes Istanbul to be the head of the (Middle) East and if it is cut off by a foreign state, the (Middle) East will not live. Consequently, the society believes in protecting Istanbul from any peril.
4. Since the Turks have been the defenders of the border fortresses of the (Middle) East against the forces of the West for six hundred years, the Arabs must train to be the reserve forces for the border fortresses.
5. The members of Al-'Ahd must endeavour to act with integrity for countries cannot preserve their national political existence except with upright actions.

SAYEGH, FAYEZ A.
**Arab Unity:** Hope and fulfilment.
*New York: Devin-Adair Co. 1958.*
*xvii, 272 pp., notes, app., index, 21 cms.*

This work is a study of the concept of Arab unity in the modern day Arab world. However, in examining the problems facing Arab unity the author also examined the rise of the Arab nationalist movement from the time of Mohammed Ali and the Wahhabi movement and the rise of Arabism prior to the outbreak of World War I.

61

SCHROGER, WILLIAM D.
**Nationalism in the Arab World.**
*In : Middle East Institute.*
*Nationalism in the Middle East, pp. 28–38.*

This lecture begins by a consideration of what constitutes nationalism and a national identity from the political idea to the economic and territorial aspects. The lecture also considers the religious nature of nationalism in the Middle East considering Islam as a factor in unity and disunity in the Arab World. In essence nationalism is seen as having evolved in two distinct parts with the movements initially beginning at the top strata of society in terms of education and political experience with the support of the other layers of society until independence is achieved. The second part of the evolution is seen as the period following the attainment of independence as this unity seems to disappear and the problem becomes one of trying to develop an enthusiasm for national effort from the mass of the population.

SHARABI, HISHAM B.
**Nationalism and revolution in the Arab World.**
*London : Van Nostrand. 1966.*
*ix, 176 pp., illus., map, bibl., 21 cms.*

This book discusses the forces which have played a part in the evolution of the present independent Arab world. The work begins by discussing the concept of Arabism, the effect of Islam and the impact of Europe upon Islamic society. In considering the effect of European domination the work also considers the legacy of this domination dealing with the various types of influence and identifying four types; direct colonial domination, rule by protectorate, the mandate relationship and finally exclusive treaty relationship.

The third chapter of the work deals with the systems of power in the Arab world many of which were a direct result of the experience of European domination with independence coming as a result of post-war settlement, negotiated agreement or national uprising. After independence the states took on European facets of government which were alien in concept to the traditional society and the remainder of the work, which is not relevant to this study, deals with the reactions of these alien concepts and the resultant changes.

TUTSCH, HANS E.
**The Arab Quest for National Unity.**
*Swiss Review of World Affairs. April 1959, pp. 17–22.*

A great deal of this article is outside of the scope of this study though as an overall survey of Arab nationalism it is of interest. It deals in general terms, however, with the impact of Western civilisation, the Millet system of the Ottoman Empire, local nationalism and religious integration.

ZEINE, Z. N.
**The Central Islamic Lands in recent times:** The Arab lands. *In: Cambridge History of Islam. Vol. 1: 'The Central Islamic lands in recent times', pp. 566–594.*

The second part of this chapter deals with the question of Arab nationalism and makes two observations with regard to problems that arise in an understanding of the subject. The first of these being the problem of language as there is no real expression to convey the meaning of Arabism. The second is that writers on Arab nationalism are either Westerners with a Western concept of nationalism or from among the non-Muslim Near Eastern intellegientsia with their own concept of what Arab nationalism should be. Zeine then goes on to consider the growth of Arab nationalism towards the end of the nineteenth century, the transition from Ottomanism to Arabism and the influences of the Great Powers on political developments in the area.

## EUROPEAN INFLUENCES

DAVID, WADE DEWOOD
**European diplomacy in the Near East Question, 1906–09.**
*Illinois: University Illinois Press. 1940.*
*124 pp., notes, glossary, bibl., index, 26½ cms.*

Although this work does not deal with the Arab provinces its inclusion is justified because of the impact that the European powers had on the Turkish Empire, covering the period from 1906 to the Young Turk movement. This particular period of time was an important stage in the decline of the Ottoman Empire and in its relationship with the Arabs leading to the transition of Arab thought from Ottomanism to Arabism.

*GREAT BRITAIN: FOREIGN OFFICE, MISCELLANEOUS No. 3 (1939).
**Cmd. 5957.**
*Correspondence between Sir Henry McMahon, His Majesty's Commissioner at Cairo and the Sherif Hussein of Mecca, July 1915–March 1916, with map.*
*18 pp., map.*

The correspondence between McMahon and Hussein which preceded the declaration of the Arab Revolt against Turkey and were the cause of considerable controversy after the war regarding the promises made to the Arabs. In view of the importance of these letters the content of this work is fully described.

1. Hussein to McMahon 14.7.1915.
   Opening offer of support from Hussein to Great Britain.
   i  England to acknowledge independence of Arab countries within certain defined limits banded on the north by Mersina and Adana up to the 37° of latitude as far as the border of Persia, on the east from Persia to Basra, and the south by the Indian Ocean with the exception of Aden. Britain also to recognise the Arab Caliphate of Islam.
   ii Arab Government of the Sherif to grant England preference in all economic activities.

2. McMahon to Hussein 30.8.1915.
   A favourable response though considering the discussion of boundaries to be premature especially as Turkey was still the occupying power and supported by many of the Arabs.

3. Hussein to McMahon 9.9.1915.
   Further expression of support but unhappiness at the reluctance to discuss boundaries.

4. McMahon to Hussein 24.10.1915.
   Deals with Hussein's boundary question and agrees to all requests with the exception of Mersina and Alexandretta and part of Syria west of Damascus cannot be considered Arab.
   i   Subject to above and existing treaties with Arab chiefs Britain to support and recognise independence of regions described by Hussein.
   ii  Britain to guarantee Holy Places.
   iii Britain to advise Arabs and to assist in advising on independent forms of government but Arabs to use only British advisers.
   iv  Vilayets of Baghdad and Basra to have special administrative arrangements.

5. Hussein to McMahon 5.11.1915.
   i   Agreed to exclude Mersina and Adana but vilayet of Aleppo and Beirut were purely Arab despite Christian influence in Beirut.
   ii  Agreed to temporary British administration of Baghdad and Basra.
   iii Arabs could not enter the war until assured of British support.

6. McMahon to Hussein 14.12.1915.
   i   Notes agreement on Mersina and Adana.
   ii  Takes note of argument regarding Aleppo and Beirut but points out French interest which needs consideration.
   iii Arabs should give no aid to Turkey or Germany and no peace treaty would be signed which did not give the Arabs freedom from Germany and Turkey.
7. Hussein to McMahon 1.1.1916.
   Reaffirms Arab support for Britain against the Turks.
8. McMahon to Hussein 25.1.1916.
   Expresses pleasure at Arab support and understanding for French interests.
9. Hussein to McMahon 18.2.1916.
   i   One of Sherif's sons to command operations necessary for declaring the Revolt.
   ii  Eldest son to go to Medina to strengthen Syrian forces and to attack the Hedjaz railway.
   iii Requests for specific forms of aid including gold and guns.
10. McMahon to Hussein 10.3.1916.
   Britain acceded to above requests and gold sent with this letter. Remainder of supplies to be sent to Port Sudan. Further requested that no aid be given to Turks and urged that the selling of camels to the Turks by Ibn Rashid be stopped.

Map of the pre-war Turkish Administrative Districts comprised in Syria and Palestine.

GLUBB, JOHN BAGOT
**Britain and the Arabs:** A study of fifty years, 1908–1958.
*London : Hodder & Stoughton. 1959.*
*496 pp., maps, app., index, 21½ cms.*

This is a study of Britain's relationships with the Arabs beginning with the Young Turk movement in 1908 which also marked the beginning of the Arab national movement as a real force in the Arab World. The author begins by considering Britain's interests in the area which he defined as, not one of exploitation, but one of a need to achieve a presence to maintain the sea and land links with the Empire and this is linked with the decline of the Ottoman Empire and the power vacuum that this would leave in the area.

The work continues by considering the beginnings of Arab nationalism and the negotiations between Hussein and McMahon leading to the Arab Revolt against the Turks in 1916. This is examined in the light of the Sykes–Picot agreement together with the part played by the Arab Revolt in the Middle East War. The war in Mesopotamia is also dealt with followed by a consideration of the situation in Syria and Mesopotamia after the war during the period of the mandates and the problem of Palestine.

The remainder of the work is outside of the scope of this study though Appendix 1 reproduces Sherif Hussein's opening letter to McMahon with the second providing statistics of the main Arab countries.

KEDOURIE, ELIE
**Cairo and Khartoum on the Arab Question.**
*The Historical Journal. Vol. VII, No. 2, 1964, pp. 280–297.*

The problem of the Arab question in British diplomacy is examined in the light of its importance which, when compared to the great world issues, are seen as 'small and paltry transactions which, as luck would have it, have turned out, it is true, to be inopportune and profitless and the cause of much loss and tribulation'.

It is the aim of the article to 'trace this intimate conviction of sin to its earliest origins, to see whence it could have arisen, to elucidate the now forgotten transactions which engendered it, and the confusions and ambiguities which nurtured it. In order to achieve this the article examines the whole question of the promises to the Arabs in the light of the negotiators at Cairo and the British Officials at Khartoum faced with the problems of a large Muslim population open to the propaganda that Britain was involved in an anti-Muslim war.

\*KEDOURIE, ELIE
**England and the Middle East:** The destruction of the Ottoman Empire, 1914–1921.
*London: Bowes and Bowes. 1956.*
*viii, 9–236 pp., app., bibl., index, 21½ cms.*
*The Making of the Sykes–Picot Agreement.*

In this chapter Kedourie discusses the background to the Sykes–Picot agreement which was based on the understanding that following the end of the war the Ottoman Empire was to be broken up and shared amongst the Allies according to their spheres of influence. As early as 1915, however, the British Government had accepted the French interest in Syria and the French had also been advised of Britain's negotiations with the Sherif. The British government through Sir Henry McMahon and Sir Mark Sykes discussed the question of French claims to Syria with al-Faruqi whom they considered as a representative of the Arab leaders and a person of consequence in the counsels of the secret societies. After consultation with Hussein al-Faruqi reported to McMahon that in his opinion 'the occupation by France of purely Arab districts of Aleppo, Homa, Homs and Damascus would be opposed by Arabs with force of arms, but with this exception . . . they would accept some modification of the North Western boundaries proposed by the Sherif of Mecca'. It was on this basis that the Sykes–Picot agreement was negotiated and agreed upon.

It is argued by Kedourie that the Sherif of Mecca had in effect agreed to the Sykes–Picot agreement by accepting McMahon's undertakings prior to the declaration of the Arab Revolt. It has been said that al-Faruqi was not the accredited representative of the Arabs and that the English negotiators should not have taken his views into account. 'This was to reason after the event, but was no doubt all the more convenient that al-Faruqi had been killed in 1920 and could not refute such a contention.'

The second part of the chapter deals with the negotiations with Hussein to secure his participation in the war on the side of the Allies and links this with the development of the Arab nationalist movement within the Ottoman Arab provinces. The most effective nationalist organisations were the secret societies composed of Arab officers in the Ottoman army and these societies were more turbulent and extreme than the civilian ones and it was with these nationalist officers that Hussein found himself allied. 'A doctrine sustained them, with the aid of which they would oppose the arrangements of the Powers and the schemes of the statesmen; and no scruple or regard would stop them, for they had nothing to lose except their lives, and what they stood to gain was an empire or perhaps a few kingdoms. They were the first enemies of the Sykes–Picot agreement and their employment by the Allies the first step towards its destruction.'

KHAN, DR. RASHEEDUDDIN
**The Rise of Arab Nationalism and European Diplomacy: 1908–1916.**
*Islamic Culture. July 1962, pp. 196–206.*

The first part of the article deals with the gradual waning of the Ottoman Empire and the rise of Arab nationalism which gained momentum as a reaction against the Turkification policy of the Committee of Union and Progress. The nationalist movement gained its validity and popularity in the wake of Arab repression organised by the C.U.P. between 1909–1914. 'The suppression of Al-Ikha was to become the prelude to the growth of the first militant phase of Arab nationalism.'

MARLOWE, JOHN
**Arab nationalism and British Imperialism:** A study in power politics.
*London: The Cresset Press. 1961.*
*viii, 236 pp., bibl., index, 22 cms.*

In his introduction to the work the author feels that Arab nationalism, in a sense, can be regarded as a 'reaction to Western pressures, developed out of a growing consciousness of a common interest and of a common tradition'. The common interest is the building up of an economically and politically sound Arab world to safeguard itself against outside influences and the common tradition, though more difficult to define, conventionally consisting of a common origin, a common language and a common memory of a specific civilisation.

The work begins with a consideration of the beginnings of Arab nationalism which the author identifies with the landing of Napoleon in Egypt in 1798, the rise to power of Mohammed Ali and the gradual exposure of the Arab world to Western cultural, social and political ideas. The seed sown by Mohammed Ali was shaped in the future by the development of a specifically Arab consciousness among the Arabic speaking inhabitants of the Syrian vilayet of the Ottoman Empire.

MONROE, ELIZABETH
**Britain's moment in the Middle East, 1914–56.**
*London: Chatto & Windus. 1963.*
*254 pp., maps, notes, bibl., index, 22 cms.*

A useful work which examines the supremacy achieved by Britain in Middle East affairs for some forty years, how it was achieved, why it survived and why it eventually declined. The work is mainly concerned with Britain's actions in the Middle East but it is of relevance because of British involvement in the development of Arab independence especially in Iraq and Palestine.

The first section of the work is entitled 'Accident and design in war 1914–18' and this deals with the negotiations between Britain and Sherif Hussein. It considers in detail the correspondence between McMahon and Hussein and the motives of the British government in seeking Arab support in the area. The promises to the Arabs are compared with the Sykes–Picot agreement and the areas of agreement and conflict between the two undertakings are examined.

RUSTOW, DANKWART A.
**The Central Islamic Lands in Recent Times. The Political Impact of the West.**
*In: Cambridge History of Islam.*
*Vol. I. 'The Central Islamic Lands', pp. 673–697.*

Although not of direct bearing on this study this chapter is of interest because of the impact that the West had on the disintegration of the Ottoman Empire. From the middle of the nineteenth century the influence of the West had an important role to play in the developments in the region with the pressure being placed on the Turkish government and the educational and cultural influences of the Christian missionaries. This was followed by concrete involvement in World War I and subsequently through the administration of the mandates.
(Author entry only in Sections 1c and 2a.)

TIBAWI, A. L.
**American interests in Syria, 1800–1901.**
*London: O.U.P. 1966.*
*xv, 333 pp., bibl., index, 22½ cms.*

This work is based on documents, many of which are reproduced for the first time, and is a detailed study of American interests in the Syrian viyalet of the Ottoman Empire which includes present-day Syria, Lebanon and Israel. These interests are those in the cultural and religious fields which led to the establishment of schools, a Protestant College (now American University of Beirut), the printing of textbooks in Arabic and the creation of a native Protestant community.

The subject is studied against the background of the Ottoman administration and the rivalry between the Protestant missions and those of the Catholic Church in addition to the existing Arab institutions. These educational developments were to have far-reaching effects in the area as they brought the province into contact with Western culture and education and as a long-term result they brought into being an educated middle class with an intellectually based national consciousness. This is an extremely detailed study of this subject which was an important factor in the history of the province and the Arab national movement as a whole. It has an extensive bibliography of manuscript and archival sources, contemporary printed sources and secondary sources.

# ARAB CULTURAL REVIVAL

*Abu-Lughod, Ibrahim
**Arab rediscovery of Europe:** A study in cultural encounters.
*Princeton: Princeton University Press. 1963.*
*x, 188 pp., bibl., index, 21 cms.*

A study of the Arab awareness of the West from 1798 when Napoleon landed in Egypt to 1870 through the examinations and interpretations of the Arab chroniclers of the Napoleonic expedition, the second source is the development of the translation of Western material into Arabic which was initiated by Mohammed Ali. Finally there is the literature of the Arab travellers to Europe writing not only descriptive accounts but comments upon the political and social organisations which they had encountered.

During this initial period in the years up to 1870 contact with the West was mainly through the literary efforts of those Arabs who were in contact with the West. It is evident from these various writings that the Arabs had developed a deep respect for three main aspects of Europe, constitutionalism, education and social systems and the literary expression of Western society. This respect for European institutions extended to an acceptance superiority in all spheres except the religious in which the West was regarded as inferior. The author considers that the groundwork for the important developments from 1870 onwards was laid during this period thus helping to determine the future pattern of Arab society. 'Thus, any study of the "impact" of the West on that society must take as its starting point the perhaps small but nevertheless crucial contribution made by the Arabs themselves during this early period.'

Hourani, Albert
**Arabic culture: Its Background and Today's crisis.**
*The Atlantic Monthly. October 1956, pp. 125–131.*

Although the article is designed to provide the background to the Suez crisis, and as such a large amount does not concern this study, the examination of the Arabs' patterns of feeling and the development of a national consciousness is of relevance.

Initially the author considers the question of Islam in Arab life which gives the Arab a privileged position as the prophet had been an Arab, the language of the Koran was Arabic and Arabic is the main language of devotion and law. Secondly, language unites the Arab world and through the growth of education in the latter part of the nineteenth century came the revival of an interest in Arab history and literature.

The rise of an educated class was the result of increased trade with the West which also brought new ideas and techniques and Christian missionaries who set up schools and colleges. This was coupled with the development of the media of mass education, the popular press, the printing of books and later the development of radio and cinema. This led to the development of political parties, the political press and the social changes which 'also quickened political consciousness and gave it its first form, that of mass nationalism; and nationalism in its turn led to the emergence of a new sort of independent state'.

*HOURANI, ALBERT
**Arabic thought in the liberal age, 1789-1939.**
*London: O.U.P. (for the Royal Institute of International Affairs). 1962.*
*x, 403 pp., bibl., index, 21½ cms.*

This work is mainly concerned with the influence of English and French liberal thought on Arabic writers during the nineteenth and early twentieth century mainly in Egypt and the Lebanon. It examines the changes brought about by these influences, the attempts by the Ottoman government to reform in the face of the threat posed by Europe and the attempts to adopt these ideas to the needs of the Arabs.

The work has a chapter on Arab nationalism which considers the beginnings of Arab nationalism and the possibility of Mohammed Ali's Empire in Egypt being an Arab empire more than in terms of geographical location as expansion from Egypt would in the first instance be through the Arab countries. No evidence either written or policy wise seems to substantiate this possibility although it is felt that the words of his son Ibrahim Pasha seem to provide some signs of this idea 'I am not a Turk. I came to Egypt when I was a child, and since that time, the sun of Egypt has changed my blood and made it all Arab'.

The writer concludes that some nationalistic tendencies were in existence at that time but it is true that 'explicit Arab nationalism, as a movement with political aims and importance, did not emerge until towards the end of the nineteenth century as prior to this time the political activities of the Arabs were part of the general movements in the Ottoman Empire. This section also considers the rise of the Young Turks and the initial hopes for a measure of Arab autonomy within the Ottoman Empire. It also considers the rise of the Syrian secret society in 1875 composed of young

Christians of the Circle of Bustani which although short lived was the first signs of the awakening of political consciousness among the Syrian Christians. These hopes were dashed by the resultant policies of the Young Turks which were not liberal and the original Ottoman nationalism became purely Turkish nationalism. This section concludes by considering the influences of Arab writers on Arab nationalism after World War I and the gradual change in the format of this nationalism after 1930.

This is an excellent work which enables the reader to consider the fundamental thinking behind Arab nationalist feeling and its ultimate shape and direction. The bibliography is extensive, covering works in Arabic, works in other languages and periodicals excluding European and American titles well known to the specialist.

\*SHARABI, HISHAM
**Arab intellectuals and the West:** The formative years, 1875–1914.
*Baltimore: Johns Hopkins Press. 1970.*
*x, 139 pp., notes, index, 23 cms.*

An examination of the Arab awakening from the challenge presented to Arab society by the West on the social, political, economic and psychological levels and the effects of this challenge on the traditional culture of the Arabs and the attempts at adaptation. It considers the challenge from the intellectual consciousness of the Arab awakening during the first phase of the modernising process.

In the period in question the impact of Western civilisation and the gradual process of change was confined to Egypt and the Fertile Crescent and the roots it sent out were to be long lasting and important for the influences that they brought to bear on subsequent post-war events. The examination is not of the intellectuals contributions but '. . . in terms of their roles as commentators on and interpreters of their generation's experience'. The work is divided into the following topics:

1. The Emergence of the Arab Intelligentsia.
2. Theoretical foundations of Islamic Reformism.
3. The Ideology of Islamic Reformism.
4. The Structure of Christian Intellectualism.
5. The Social Ideology of Christian Intellectualism.
6. The Emergence of Muslim Secularism.
7. Arab Intellectuals and Political Action.
8. Arab Intellectuals and the West.

# OTTOMANISM TO ARABISM

AL-GARI, EMIL
**The Struggle of the Arab Nationalists against colonialism.**
*Cairo: Dar al Kahira. 1957.*
*98 pp., 21 cms.*

This work deals with the Arab position in the Ottoman Empire and the nationalist struggle against the Turks. It also deals with the effects of the increasing Western influence upon the Empire especially in relation to the impact of education and a popular press. The work concludes by dealing with the nationalist movement during World War I and the post-war mandates.

DAWN, C. ERNEST
**From Ottomanism to Arabism:** Essays on the origins of Arab Nationalism.
*London: University of Illinois Press. 1973.*
*xi, 212 pp.*

A collection of Professor Dawn's essays which are dealt with under their original publication details.

*DAWN, C. ERNEST
**From Ottomanism to Arabism:** The origin of an Ideology.
*Review of Politics. Vol. 23, No. 3, July 1961, pp. 378–400.*

This article discusses the transition from Ottomanism to Arabism which evolved in the nineteenth century and by 1918 was complete. Originally Ottomanism was a direct result of the realisation that the Empire had failed to keep pace with advances in Europe and it was from this realisation that Arabism evolved. The article discusses the ideology of Ottomanism which was based on a return to Islamism which would eventually prove that the East was superior to the West. This reference back to pure Islamism heightened the importance of the Arabs, their language and their past and this atmosphere together with the preoccupation with the impact of the West led to nationality being given a political content in addition to the religious one which was to end with Ottomanism ceasing to be a force amongst the Arabs.

EDWARDS, JOSIAH
**From Panarabism to Panislamism.**
*Contemporary Review. March 1932, pp. 343–351.*

The first part of this article deals with the pre-war attempts of the Arabs to obtain autonomy within the Ottoman Empire. The development of this demand is traced and the encouragement it received with the Young Turk movement of 1908 and the bitter reactions to the Committee of Union and Progress with its policy of Turkification leading to the move towards Arab independence.

*SAAB, DR. HASSAN
**The Arab Federalists of the Ottoman Empire.**
*Amsterdam: Djambatan. 1958.*
*xii, 322 pp., notes, bibl., 22 cms.*

This work deals with the attempts to further Arab nationalist aspirations within the framework of the Ottoman Empire which eventually led to the beginnings of Arab nationalism as a political force which took the place of Pan-Islamism and Constitutionalism. Much of the early part of this work falls outside of the scope of this study as it considers the early Arab Empire, the spread of Islam and the early Ottoman conquests. These considerations do, however, form the basis of the study of the rise of true nationalist movement of the twentieth century.

In considering the empire of Mohammed Ali, Saab concludes that it could not be considered an Arab Empire in the real sense of the word as he was never able to make a decision to become fully independent of the Sultan and in fact 'His expansionism took the modernistic Islamic dynastical form, the Ottoman form, the Arab form, without a definite adoption of any one of them'. The motivation of his son Ibrahim was on the other hand an attempt to awaken Egyptian and Arab consciousness though this was also doomed to failure due to pressure from the Great Powers.

The Wahhabi movement was considered to have a more lasting effect. Although Mohammed Ali was initially instrumental in defeating the movement on the instructions of the Sultan the movement was not destroyed completely. Although in the Nejd the movement had proved to be a unifying force welding together a multiplicity of tribes into one state at a later date it emerged as the initiator of a monarchical state which proved to be a factor in the future disintegration of Arab unity.

In considering the movement towards nationalism Saab begins by dealing with the hopes that were raised by the rise to power of the Young Turks and the proclamation of a new constitution but these hopes were dashed by the revival of the Turkish nationalistic spirit. In fact the disillusionment united all the Arab members of the Ottoman parliament by causing them to forget their differences in an attempt to further their common interests

74

which were, in the main, language and administrative autonomy within the Empire. These differences with the Ottoman parliament were heightened by the Turkish hostility to Arabic which took a religious, national and finally educational form of grievance.

It should be stressed that at this stage the move was not towards a break from the Ottoman Empire but reform within the framework of the Empire. The Arab Congress held in Paris in 1913 produced a general platform of Arab demands representing the wishes of representatives from Lebanon, Syria, Iraq and most of the Arab societies. The main requests were as follows:

1. A guarantee of the political rights of the Arabs through participation in the central government at Istanbul.
2. An autonomous administration for each Arab province.
3. The adoption of Arabic as an official language in parliament and in the Arab provinces.
4. The limitation of the military service of Arabs to the Arab provinces.

The work then considers two of the Arab associations which were working for this federal concept namely Al-Qahtaniya and al-'Ahd. Both societies had the same aims which were really a desire for complete autonomy for the Arab provinces within the Ottoman Empire and still retaining the Sultan as the titular head. These societies in company with the society El-Fatat attempted to achieve reform of the Empire but on the conclusion of the agreement between Sherif Hussein and Great Britain they broke with Istanbul and in the case of al-'Ahd this was significant as its membership was solely Arab officers of the Turkish army. On the realisation that reforms within the Empire were not possible the Arab nationalist leaders preferred to revolt against the Empire to achieve their aims. The work of these societies had represented the last Arab attempts to reintegrate the Turkish Empire through constitutional channels.

\*ZEINE, ZEINE N.
**Arab-Turkish relations and the emergence of Arab Nationalism.**
*Lebanon: Khayat's. 2nd ed. 1966.*
*156 pp., bibl., index, 21 cms.*

The third section of this work deals with the beginnings of the Arab nationalist movement and the growth of an anti-Turkish feeling.

3. Anti-Turkish sentiment in Arab Lands – Causes and Antecedents.

Anti-Turkish sentiment began to manifest itself during the latter part of the nineteenth century being the product of any national identity amongst the subject peoples although the desire for independent local government appeared in different parts of the empire especially in Egypt, Lebanon and Arabia. This chapter also considers the Wahhabi movement in Arabia, the rule of Mohammed Ali in Egypt and his brief control of Syria. It also deals with the anti-Turkish sentiment in Lebanon which was motivated by several factors such as Western education, the revival of the Arabic Language and Literature, the publication of Arab newspapers and most important of all the attitude of the Christian Arabs who considered themselves an alien island in a Moslem Empire.

4. Anti-Turkish Sentiment in Arab Lands II. The Reign of Abdul Hamid, 1876–1909.

This particular period was disastrous for the Ottoman Empire which was already in an advanced state of decay. The Empire was plagued by constitutional problems and all thoughts of reform disappeared under the tyrannical rule of the Sultan. At this stage two distinct lines developed the first being the secret societies formed by Lebanese Christians who wanted political reform and political independence and the Moslem factions who wanted reform within the framework of the Empire. This period also saw the rise of the Young Turks which brought a false sense of hope amongst the reformers in the Arab provinces which was soon to be dashed by the Turkification policy of the Young Turks.

5. The Emergence of Arab Nationalism I. Under the Young Turks, 1909–1914.

This chapter deals with the change of emphasis on the question of reform which as a result of the policies of the Young Turks changed from one of reform within the Empire to one of Arab autonomy. The Arab societies pressed for a truly representative central government in which all peoples would have equal status and for a large measure of autonomy for the Arab provinces. Any hopes that the Arabs had were destroyed by the pursuance of a policy of Turkish nationalism with its pro-Moslem aspects and the aim of imposing the Turkish language on the Empire.

# NATIONALISM AND ISLAM

\*Abu-Lughod, Ibrahim
**Retreat from the Secular path.** Islamic dilemmas of Arab politics.
*The Review of Politics. Vol. 28, No. 4, October 1966, pp. 447–476.*

In this discussion of the place of Islam in Arab politics and the moves towards a secular state the author begins by considering the first Ottoman Constitution of 1876 which for the first time defined the political community in non-religious terms. On the other hand the religious orientation of the State continued to be operative and this de facto secular orientation of society was to cause problems especially in the Arab states.

The dialogue between the secularists and the traditionalists continued in the Arab states with the latter drawing strength from the existing political institutions. This ideological struggle is seen in relation to the increasing impact of the West which was forcing the case for modernisation and creating the problem of the compatibility of this trend with an Islamic society.

Much of this article is outside the scope of this study as it deals with the period after the mandates. However, this is an important article as the subject is fundamental to the study of Arab politics at that time.

Al-Farugi, Isma'l Ragi A.
**On Arabism, Urubah and religion:** A study of the fundamental ideas and Islam at its highest moment of consciousness.
*Amsterdam: Djambate. 1962.*
*xi, 287 pp., index.*

'Urubah has been generally understood to be the Arab nationalist movement aimed at unifying the Arab states under one nation. This work offers a different interpretation regarding Arab nationalism as a Western import whereas Arabism is an historical concept being part of the "Arab stream of being". The author also equates "Urubah with Islam as he feels that Arab nationalism without Islam" . . . runs aground in ethical shallowness and superficiality.' The advocates of Islamism also come in for criticism as they fall into the same trap as the nationalists that of wishing to reconstruct society on the basis of a sole source of authority. Dr. Farugi feels that one has to take from the Qur'an and Arab history, by scholarship, those facets which are of value and to integrate these with Arabism which will then '. . . have found its ultimate and eternal goal'.

HURGRONJE, SNOUCK
**Islam and Turkish Nationalism.**
*Foreign Affairs (New York). Vol. 3, No. 1, 15 September 1924, pp. 61–77.*

The article discusses the whole basis of the Caliphate in its historical setting leading to the situation caused by the split between the Sherifian family of Hussein and the Ottoman Empire. The article then proceeds to a consideration of the Caliphate in the new situation and the possibility of support for Hussein in the Arab World, apart from the Hedjaz and Jordan, and concluding that it was unlikely to be forthcoming.

MORRISON, S. A.
**Arab nationalism and Islam.**
*Middle East Journal. No. 2, April 1948, pp. 147–159.*

This article discusses the relationship between Arab nationalism and Islam based on the view of Albert Hourani that 'The whole future development of the Arab countries depends on a change in the spirit of Islam: not its theoretical formulations, but the living creative spirit which moulds the life of the Islamic community'.

Although in its early stages the Arab revival tended to bridge sectarian differences later developments saw the movement passing more into the hands of the Muslims and thus became associated with the revival of Islam. This was inevitable because of the historical links between the Arab culture and Islam and even the Arab Revolt was partially motivated by religious zeal and with a demand for the restoration of the Caliphate to the Arabs.

*SAMRA, MAHMUD
**Islam and Arab Nationalism:** complementary or competitive.
*Middle East Forum. Vol. XIII, No. 2, 1966, pp. 11–15.*

This article begins by considering the term Arab and the concept of an Arab national consciousness and concludes that although a racial consciousness might have existed prior to the nineteenth century it could not be considered to be the same as the modern concept of nationalism. The ideas of nationalism began during the middle of the nineteenth century amongst the Christian Arabs but as the Muslims of Syria became educated they also became interested in nationalism and gradually assumed the leadership of the movement. The writer is of the opinion therefore that national consciousness amongst the Muslim Arabs began when the right of a Turk to be Caliph was called into question.

A contrary view was also expressed which put forward the

hypothesis that Islam was only perfect in its spiritual state and that it was necessary to separate this from politics if the Arab nations were to revive some of their former glory. At the Arab Congress in Paris in 1913 a Muslim delegate expounded on the conditions that the Arabs satisfied to be considered as a nation. 'According to the Germans, language and race form a nation: to the Italians, common history and traditions; and to the French the common political aspiration. If the Arabs are judged by all those theories then they form a nation. They all share in a common language, history, traditions and political aspiration. Thus according to all theories of nationalism, we have the characteristics of a nation. We are Arabs above all . . .'

THOMSON, WILLIAM
**Nationalism and Islam.**
*In: Middle East Institute.*
*Nationalism in the Middle East, pp. 51–60.*

Initially the discussion centres on the evolution of nationalism in Europe and the difference between this and nationality, as it was this form of nationalism as evolved in Europe which was taken as a model by the Eastern leaders.

The evolution of the independent Arab states of Jordan, Syria, Iraq and Lebanon are not seen as creations of Arab nationalism but as the results of Western intrigue. The problem of unity within the Arab countries is also discussed in relation to the diversive forms of government which existed within the Ottoman Empire and the problem of adopting Western ideals which conflicted with the social and cultural ideals of Islamic civilisation.

WILLIAMS, KENNETH
**Arabia and Islam.**
*Contemporary Review. January 1926, pp. 55–60.*

This article is mainly concerned with the impact of Islam, in the form of Wahhabism, on Arabia under the guidance of Ibn Saud. It deals with the invasion by Ibn Saud of the Hejaz due to his campaign against Sherifian corruption of the Holy Cities and the feud with Hussein which had begun before the outbreak of World War I. It deals with the success of the Wahhabi forces and the prospect of Britain once again assisting Hussein to maintain their influence in the area. It concludes by discussing the Wahhabi movement in general terms and in particular its impact upon Islam in Arabia and in other Islamic countries outside of Arabia.

# NATIONALISM IN SPECIFIC AREAS

*DAWN, C. ERNEST
**The Rise of Arabism in Syria.**
*Middle East Journal. Vol. 16, No. 2, Spring 1962, pp. 145–168.*

Initially Arabism and Ottomanism had as their central concern the vindication of Islam and the defence of the East against the West with the difference being that Arabism propounded the idea that the Arabs were a special people with special virtues and rights. In this article Professor Dawn discusses the rise of Arabism in Syria following the constitutional changes of 1908. The political nature of Arabism began with the formation of the secret societies with the members of the Arab nationalist movement being composed almost entirely of members of the Ottoman Decentralisation Society, al-Fatat and al-'Ahd.

Professor Dawn restricts his study to the provinces Syria and Aleppo which were to become part of the Syrian Republic for two main reasons, the first being that in that area Arabism eventually led to the formation of an elected body, the Syrian National Congress, and constitutional government. The second reason being the fact that more biographical material was available for that area than for the rest of the Arab world. In this context the part played by the Syrian Arabists before and during the war is discussed as is the development of the nationalist movement after the war. In the latter case the nature of the movement is discussed both in relation to its development and with regard to the participants and their background. The Arabists in Syria were those members of the elite who had no vested interest in the Ottoman state and following the collapse of the Empire they were joined by the Ottomanist Arabs who were left with no alternative to Arabism.

The article has appendices giving members of the Pre-1914 Arab Movement, the members of the nationalist movement between 1919–1920, age of members, education, family status, occupation and fathers' occupation.

ERSKINE, MRS. STEWART
**Palestine of the Arabs.**
*London: Harrap. 1935.*
*256 pp., illus., app., index, 21 cms.*

In considering the beginnings of the Arab nationalist movement in Palestine the study is, of course, related to developments in Syria because at this time Palestine was part of the Ottoman viyalet of Syria with Jerusalem as one of the sanjaks of the province.

This section also discusses the problems of the promises made to the Arabs through the McMahon–Hussein correspondence, the Sykes–Picot agreement between Britain and France and the Balfour Declaration regarding the Jewish National Home.

FOSTER, H. A.
**The Making of Modern Iraq:** A product of world forces.
*London: William & Norgate. 1936.*
*ix, 319 pp., illus., bibl., index, 23 cms.*

The initial part of this work dealing with the period prior to the mandate and the beginnings of Arab nationalism is very sketchy. The initial period of the mandate is, however, dealt with at some length as is the revolt against the British administration which was a result not only of opposition to the mandate but the external influences of dissidents in Syria and Iraqi officers demobilised from the Arab army.
See entry under reactions to the Mandate.

HITTI, PHILIP K.
**A short history of Lebanon.**
*London: Macmillan. 1965.*
*xi, 249 pp., maps, index, 20 cms.*

The granting of autonomy to Lebanon in 1867 was crucial to the future of the country as it opened the door to Western education provided by the Missionary societies of the Catholic and Protestant Churches and the resultant rise of an educated middle class. The evolution of the nationalist movement was initially of an intellectual nature and those involved were opposed to the Turkification policy of the Young Turks.

IRELAND, PHILIP WILLARD
**Iraq:** A study in political development.
*London: Cape. 1937.*
*510 pp., illus., maps, app., bibl., index.*

See Section 3a for annotation to this work.

JESSUP, HENRY HARRIS
**Fifty-three Years in Syria.**
*New York: Revell Co. 1919.*
*Vol. 1: 404 pp., illus., 23 cms.*
*Vol. 2: 428 pp., illus., app., 23 cms.*

The author served as a missionary in Syria with the Presbyterian

Church for a period of fifty-three years from 1856, a period which was crucial in the development of Syria under the increasing influence of Western interests and education.

Essentially of course this autobiography is largely concerned with the establishment and growth of the Christian missions in Syria but it is also interesting for the picture that it gives of the changes in Syrian society, the social problems of the area and the various massacres and persecutions which took place.

The appendices give details of the missionaries serving in Syria, sources used in compiling the history of the mission, the medical work of the mission and the Syrian Protestant College.

*LONGRIGG, STEPHEN HEMSLEY
**Iraq, 1900–1950:** A political, social and economic history.
*London: O.U.P. 1953.*
*x, 436 pp., app., bibl., map, index, 22 cms.*

In dealing with the war period Longrigg concentrates on the changes which World War I brought upon the country which had to undergo the traumatic experience of being ruled by a Western Christian country after four centuries of Ottoman Moslem rule. This section also deals with the British administration and the operation of the mandate together with the insurrection and the establishment of monarchical rule. It also deals with the problem of the minorities such as the Assyrians and the gradual progress under the mandate.

In his summary the author reviews the period from 1900 and concludes that the problems of Iraq can be attributed to the Arab character which was less able to adapt to the stresses of modern government, local nationalism and the heterogeneity of the people.

The work has an excellent bibliography covering both official and general works in Arabic and English together with an index to sources used.

OCHSENWALD, WILLIAM L.
**The Vilayet of Syria, 1901–1914:** A re-examination of diplomatic documents as sources.
*Middle East Journal. Vol. 22, Winter 1968, pp. 73–87.*

An introduction to the source documents of diplomatic correspondence which serve as a basis for research into the political history of the Middle East in the twentieth century. Mainly the guide is concerned with the quarterly reports of the British Consul from Damascus to Constantinople in the years 1900–1914, the contents of which 'suggest that a thorough-going review of diplomatic records may be productive of new data concerning conditions in Syria and, by implication, in other Arab parts of the Empire.

The article then provides an illustrative guide to the types of information that can be gathered from these reports, e.g. the Hedjaz railway, problems of the Druzes, corruption in the administration, etc.

PARFIT, CANON
**Mesopotamia:** The key to the future.
*London: Hodder and Stoughton. 1917.*
*39 pp., map, pamphlet.*

This pamphlet, by a Church of England missionary, is in three parts the first dealing with the early history of Mesopotamia, the second with the social and geographical character of the area and the last part the future prospects for the area. It is the latter part which is of relevance to this study.

This section deals with the economic prospects from agriculture and oil and discusses the benefits of British occupation which has proved to be one '. . . of prosperity and peace, while the Turkish domination is everywhere coincident with ruin and decay'. Also considered are German interests in the area through their interests in the railways and the attempts to declare a Jiddah to persuade the Arabs to serve with the Turkish armies. The removal of Turkish influence from the area is seen as essential to the freedom of the Arabs though this freedom must not be linked with European interference.

PHILBY, H. ST. JOHN
**The recent history of the Hedjaz.**
*Central Asian Society Journal. Vol. XII, July 1925, pp. 332–348.*

In his address Philby begins by considering the exploratory work of Richard Burton and the country and the people of the Hedjaz. From this base the address deals with the gradual deterioration of relations between Hussein and the Ottoman Government which led to the negotiations with the British and to eventual entry into the war on the side of the Allies.

SALEH, ZAKI
**Britain and Mesopotamia (Iraq to 1914):** A study in British Foreign Affairs.
*Baghdad: Al-Ma'aref Press. 1966.*
*350 pp., map, notes, bibl., index, 22 cms.*

An extremely detailed study the earlier part of which is not relevant by virtue of chronology, dealing with the early transit trade, Anglo-French rivalries at the beginning of the nineteenth century, and Anglo-Russian rivalry between 1830–1878.

The work is, however, a study of British foreign policy and not a history of Iraq, concentrating on the part played by the area in Britain's dealings with other European powers. Its interest to this study lies in the detailed negotiations regarding the Baghdad railway, the commercial exploitation of the area and its strategic relationship to India. Britain's dislike of Turkish neutrality was mainly concerned with her agreement to allow Germany to continue the Baghdad railway to Basra and following Russia's declaration of war on Turkey Britain followed suit. This move altered the pattern of Anglo-Iraq relations as prior to the war Britain had no imperialistic interest in the area.

'What followed was connected with Iraq under British occupation, under British mandate or independent. The war marked a neat turning point in the history of the land that was to be known as the Kingdom of Iraq, instead of Ottoman Mesopotamia.'

SALIBI, KAMAL S.
**The Lebanese identity.**
*Journal Contemporary History. Vol. 6, No. 1, 1971, pp. 76–86.*

A consideration of the Lebanon and the Lebanese identity which had begun to manifest itself around the middle of the nineteenth century. The article traces the development of the Lebanon from its early beginnings under the Ottoman Empire within which it had retained a large measure of autonomy with responsibility for maintenance of order, dispensation of justice and collection of revenue.

The Emirate lasted until 1841 when the co-ordinated opposition of Druzes and Christian feudal chiefs with British and Ottoman support brought it to an end though the idea of a separate Lebanese identity was still present amongst the middle class and especially among the Maronites.

This situation lasted until 1861 when civil wars between the Druzes and Maronites and the peasants and feudal chiefs resulted in the intervention of the Great Powers and especially Britain and France. The resultant settlement gave the Lebanon the status of an autonomous province to be governed by a non-Lebanese Ottoman Christian mutesarrif assisted by an elected administrative council and a locally recruited police force and civil service. This gave the Lebanese identity legal status and under this administration the Lebanese identity flourished as did the cultural and educational activities of the Protestant and Catholic missionaries with these assuming great importance in the developing of Arab national thought. Following the defeat of the Ottoman Empire in 1918 Lebanon came under the mandatory control of France gaining Republican status in 1926.

SPEIR, GEORGE N.
**Syria:** The raw material.
*Middle East Forum. March 1962, pp. 23–27.*

This is an assessment of a despatch on Syria written by T. E. Lawrence in 1915 for the Foreign Office which was first published in the *Arab Bulletin* of 12 March 1917 and subsequently in 'Secret Despatches from Arabia' in 1939. The first part deals with Syria as a geographical entity, the second with the cities in the area and the third part is an assessment of the national character-istics of the Syrians and a speculation as to their future politics. Lawrence's viewpoints are discussed in relation to the climate at the time and in relation to the contemporary situation in Syria coupled with the historic problem of its place within the Arab World. 'Syria,' said Lawrence, 'is essential for Arab self-determination. This is borne out by Syria's geographical position and its intellectual role in the field of Arab ideas.'

SPAGNOLO, J. P.
**French influence in Syria prior to World War I:** The functional weakness of imperialism.
*Middle East Journal. Vol. 23, 1969, pp. 45–62.*

This article discusses the influence of the French in the geo-graphical area of Syria based initially on the religious aspect which dated from the Crusades. During the latter part of the nineteenth century this was deepened by the establishment of the missionary schools and by support for the Christian minorities in relations with the Sublime Porte. The obverse side of this development was the restriction that this placed on French influence over the Muslims. 'They might well have reacted favourably to the same lay system of education with which French republicans had fought hard to endow themselves.'

Relations between the French and Syrians were marred by factors which were a functional weakness of imperialism partially because of France's global involvements . . . and second from the cultural barriers separating the imperialists from the object of their concern. These feelings were already clearly evident in the early relations between imperialist France and Syria prior to World War I.

TIBAWI, A. L.
**A modern history of Syria including Lebanon and Palestine.**
*London : Macmillan. 1969.*
*441 pp., plates, notes, bibl., index, 23 cms.*

The last section of part one of this work deals with the rise of the Arab nationalist movement. Hopes had been raised by the Young Turks which led to the forming of societies aimed at furthering the Arab cause within the framework of the Ottoman Empire though these hopes were to be dashed by the Turkification policy of the new order.

## BIOGRAPHICAL WORKS

*BIRWOOD, LORD
**Nuri As-Said:** A study in Arab leadership.
*London : Cassell. 1959.*
*xi, 306 pp., frontis., illus., maps, glossary, bibl., index, 22 cms.*

As this biography deals with the period of Nuri As-Said's life until 1958 and was in the press at the time of his assassination much of its content is outside the scope of this study but the early part of his life occupies at least half of the book.

The work begins with a consideration of Nuri As-Said's early life in Baghdad from his enrolment in a primary military school, through the military college at Istanbul and his subsequent service as an officer in the Turkish army. This period of service coincided with the period from the Young Turk movement of 1908 to the outbreak of war and it was during this time that he became a member of Al 'Ahd which was, at the time, working for Arab autonomy within the Ottoman Empire.

*CLEVELAND, WILLIAM L.
**The Making of an Arab Nationalist:** Ottomanism and Arabism in the life and thought of Sati' al-Husri.
*Princeton : Princeton University Press. 1971.*
*xvi, 21 pp., frontis., bibl., index, 22 cms.*

Although a study of one particular Arab nationalist this is also a study of the transition from Ottomanism to Arabism as part of the growth of the Arab nationalist movement. As with many of the first generation of nationalist leaders al-Husri was educated in an Ottoman school and became an imperial civil servant serving in the education department. This part of al-Husri's life forms the first section of this study dealing with his early life and his role as Arab adviser to the education department in Istanbul.

The second section deals with his role as the spokesman of Arab nationalism when the process of transition from Ottomanism to Arabism was complete. Following the defeat of the Sultan in 1908 he left Istanbul for Damascus and became Director of Education in the Syrian government and a close confidant of Faisal. Following the defeat of the Arab army by the French and the overthrow of the Arab government he followed Faisal into exile and thence to Iraq where he became Director General of Education following Faisal's 'election' as King of Iraq. He used this post to further the cause of nationalism through the medium of education and with his influence behind the political scenes.

The final part of the study deals with the nationalist thought of al-Husri with his concept of a nation and of Arab unity. In the evolution of the concept of pan-Arabism he was perhaps assisted by the fact that he owed allegiance to no country and therefore he had no regional loyalties. He was also a secular nationalist and his philosophy was an attempt to explore this form of nationalism as an alternative to regionalism. In this concept his approach was to the cultural and historical legacy of the Arabs based on a common language and history and he felt that if this cultural union could be achieved then political union would follow. 'He offered the dream of Arab unity, called for faith in the possibility and desirability of achieving that dream, and attempted to inculcate the values needed to give it reality. 'Arabism first . . . was truly his message.'

ERSKINE, MRS. STEWART
**King Faisal of Iraq.**
*London: Hutchinson & Co. 1933.*
*288 pp., illus., app., index, 23½ cms.*

The first section of this authorised biography deals with the awakening of the Arab national movement in Syria following the failure of the Young Turks to give the Arab provinces any measure of autonomy. During the period immediately following the outbreak of war between Britain and Germany Hussein was negotiating with McMahon regarding the possibility of the Arabs entering the war on the side of the Allies and Faisal was making contact with dissident Army officers in the Ottoman army at Constantinople and Damascus.

At first Faisal was a moderate in that he wanted Arab autonomy within the Ottoman Empire, however, this view changed following the repressive measures adopted by the Turks. 'On arriving at Mecca (1915) I explained all these circumstances to my father and told him of the desires of the Arabs; I also told him that, after having belonged to the Moderate Part, the changed situation and the prayers of the Arabs had influenced me to join them in begging him to take the lead of the Revolutionary Party. My father agreed, moved by the sufferings of the Arabs, and at the same time, hoping to assure their political future.'

\*Morris, James
**The Hashemite Kings.**
*London: Faber and Faber. 1959.*
*231 pp., illus., bibl., index, 22 cms.*

This is a biography of the Hashemite family only the first part of which is relevant dealing with King Hussein and his sons. The section of Sherif Hussein deals mainly with the Arab Revolt beginning with the negotiations with the British. 'On the one side stood the British, at once high principled and opportunist, harassed by their usual ethical self-questionings, but chiefly determined to win the war and safeguard their grand position in the world. On the other side stood the Hashemites, beguiling but exasperating, with intentions scarcely more altruistic, but with simplicities and naiveties that cast upon the British a perpetual sense of obligation.'

As soon as the Revolt was under way and British advisers had been attached to the Arab army, which was supported by British arms and money, the control of the Revolt slipped from Hussein's grasp and became vested in Faisal. 'Hussein noted with concern that the Amir Feisal was beginning to display an ominous spirit of independence: but he was six hundred miles away, could not enforce his formidable family authority (potent until his death), and was becoming powerless to interfere.'

Storrs, Ronald
**Orientations.**
*London: Nicholson and Watson. 1937.*
*xviii, 557 pp., illus., maps, index, 21 cms.*

The autobiography of a civil servant who held several posts of importance in the Middle East from the Ministry of Finance in Egypt to the Military Governorship of Jerusalem.

In 1914 Storrs was involved in the early negotiations with Hussein regarding the participation of the Sherifian forces on the side of the Allies. These were conducted through a go-between and in their early stages were purely exploratory as Hussein felt himself unable to break with the Turks at that time. In 1915, however, when Sir Henry McMahon was involved in the negotiations matters began to resolve themselves with a clearer commitment from the Arabs though in Storrs' opinion the demands of Hussein were too ambitious. 'It was at the time and still is my opinion that the Sherif opened his mouth and the British Government their purse a good deal too wide.'

# (c) THE ARAB REVOLT AND THE WAR IN THE MIDDLE EAST

## GENERAL WORKS

General works on the Middle East with references to the war in the Middle East and the Arab Revolt.

ALLEN, RICHARD
**Imperialism and nationalism in the Fertile Crescent:** Sources and prospects of the Arab–Israeli conflict.
*London: O.U.P. 1974.*
*x, 686 pp., maps, bibl., index, 20½ cms.*
*(Chapter X, pp. 221–259.)*

The chapter of relevance to this section is entitled 'The Middle East and the First World War' and deals initially with Turkey's entry into the war and the attempts to declare a jihad. This is examined in the light of British attitudes especially with regard to the effects of a jihad on the Muslim parts of the British Empire together with the complication that aspects of the Middle East were dealt with by different government departments.

The background to the Arab Revolt is also considered especially the negotiations between Britain and Hussein which led to the Arabs entering the war on the side of the Allies. 'Trusting apparently to Britain's sense of fair play, Hussein was prepared to shelve the problem of French interests until after the war, while making it plain that there could be no question of ceding any part of the Arab homeland to France or any other power.'

This chapter also deals with the part played by the Arab army in the Middle East War, the problems of the secret treaties and finally the Balfour Declaration. The problems following the immediate conclusion of the war were caused by the Arab provisional government in Damascus which met with immediate French opposition. The result was increasing unrest amongst the Arabs with revolt only being avoided by the issuing of the Anglo-French Declaration of 7 November 1918 promising national governments in those areas liberated from the Turks.

AL-MIYAHID, SHARIF
**Arab Nationalism:** A historical analysis.
*Pakistan Horizon (Karachi). 1963, pp. 37–46.*

Nationalism gained in momentum due to the dislike of the centralisation reforms of the Sublime Porte by Hussein which led to negotiations with Britain. On Turkey's entry into the war and declaring a Jihad Britain exploited this resentment to secure the support of the Arabs by dangling 'before the Sharif the concept of an indivisible Arab nation and kingdom from the Euphrates to the Nile'.

BEN-HORIN, ELIAHU
**The Middle East:** Crossroads of history.
*New York: W. W. Norton & Co. 1943.*
*248 pp., map, index, 21½ cms.*

The author deals with the problem of Arab unity and the problems which work against it namely Pan-Arabism versus Pan-Islamism. In this connection the author examines the Arab Revolt and the actual contribution made by the Arabs. The author concludes that the Arabs of Syria did little to achieve their own emancipation except for some of the Bedouin and a few Syrian officers who had deserted from the Turkish army.

COKE, RICHARD
**The Arab's place in the sun.**
*London: Butterworth. 1929.*
*318 pp., illus., maps, index, 22 cms.*

In the chapter on the Middle East War the author deals with the Arab Revolt and the political developments which were taking place between the Great Powers as to the future of the area after the war. The making of the Sykes–Picot agreement is discussed as is the conflict between this and the promises made to the Arabs. This latter point is also seen in the light of differing policies between the Arab Bureau who supported Sherif Hussein and the India Office who supported Ibn Saud.

FISHER, SYDNEY NETTLETON
**The Middle East:** A history.
*London: Routledge & Kegan Paul. 2nd ed. 1971.*
*xxx, 749 pp., maps, bibl., index, 22 cms.*

See Section 1a for annotation.
The chapter of relevance to this section is as follows.
Part IV. The Contemporary Middle East.
Chapter 28. Impact of World War I upon the Middle East.

LENCZOWSKI, GEORGE
**The Middle East in world affairs.**
*New York: Cornell University Press. 2nd ed. 1956.*
*xix, 576 pp., maps, bibl., index, 24 cms.*

Chapter two of this work deals with the war in the Middle East in general though the Sinai, Arabian and Mesopotamian fronts are considered separately. This section also examines the secret treaties and understandings between the Allies and British negotiations with the Arabs which led to the declaration of the Revolt and the problem of the Zionist aims regarding Palestine.

RUSTOW, DONKWART A.
**The Central Islamic Lands in recent times:** The political impact of the West.
*In: Cambridge History of Islam.*
*Vol. 1: The Central Islamic lands, pp. 673–697.*

See Section 1b for annotation to this work.

STEWART, DESMOND
**The Middle East:** Temple of Janus.
*London: Hamish Hamilton. 1972.*
*viii, 414 pp., bibl., index, 24 cms.*

In considering the Arab Revolt the author contrasts this with the stalemate in the Flanders trenches, the surrender in Southern Iraq and the ill-fated Dardanelles campaign. 'Thanks to an unclouded climate, a picturesque cast and the presence on the British side of a myth maker of genius, the Arab Revolt was to revive British morale.'

The author begins by considering the negotiations which led to the Arab Revolt beginning with the meeting between Kitchener and Abdullah in 1914 at which the possibility was raised though no promises were made by either side. This was followed by the McMahon–Hussein correspondence during which various commitments were entered into by both sides the interpretation of which was to plague post-war relations between Britain and the Arabs. The strength of the Revolt was furthered by the actions of Djemal Pasha as Governor of Syria who executed Arab members of dissident cells in Lebanon and Syria as this converted to rebellion any Arab waverers including Faisal and many Arabs in the Ottoman Army Corps.

## MIDDLE EAST WAR – GENERAL WORKS

\*FALLS, CYRIL
**Armageddon, 1918.**
*London : Weidenfeld & Nicolson. 1964.*
*x, 216 pp., illus., maps, notes, bibl., index, 21½ cms.*
*(Great Battles of History Series.)*

An account of the war in the Middle East with an examination of the Arab contribution in depth. The author begins by establishing the relationship between Lawrence and Allenby, which was one of mutual respect, and considers how this affected Arab participation in the campaign. Consideration is then given to the Arab role as the right flank of Allenby's army in the advance through Palestine which culminated in the capture of Damascus in October 1918.

A chapter is devoted to the position in Damascus following its capture with the attempt by the Arabs to set up an effective administration in the face of internal rivalries and opposing factions. Allenby followed the Sykes–Picot agreement by allowing French occupation of the zone allotted to them whilst insisting that they recognised Arab jurisdiction in the designated zone A, an arrangement which did not last as the French won the battle at the Peace Conference.

KLIEMAN, AARON S.
**Britain's war aims in the Middle East in 1915.**
*Journal Contemporary History. Vol. 3, No. 3, 1968, pp. 237–251.*

This article discusses the British war aims in the Middle East in relation to the Ottoman Empire and the problem of the Arab provinces. The policy rested on the sacrifice of Turkey and the strengthening of Arabia with the partition of the Arab provinces into spheres of influence. This examination is based mainly on the recommendations of the Bunsen Committee which although never officially implemented did influence the evolution of policy in the Middle East. It was this loss of opportunity to achieve a co-ordinated policy in 1915 which resulted in Britain pursuing conflicting policies following the end of the war.

**Turkey – A Past and a Future.**
*The Round Table. Vol. 7, 1917, pp. 515–546.*

The first part of this article deals with the position of Turkey prior to and during the war with a consideration of the possible outcome. The article then considers various aspects of the former Ottoman Empire and the areas of specific interest to this study are those dealing with Syria and Palestine and Mesopotamia.

*MacMunn, George and Falls, Cyril (compilers)
**History of the Great War, Military Operations, Egypt and Palestine from the outbreak of war with Germany to June 1917.**
*London: H.M.S.O. 1928.*
*xviii, 445 pp., illus., maps, refs., app., indexes, 22½ cms.*

MacMunn, George and Beck, A. F. (compilers)
**History of the Great War, Military Operations, Egypt and Palestine from June 1917 to the end of the war.**
*London: H.M.S.O. 1930 (in two parts).*
*Part 1: xxiii, 394 pp., illus., maps, refs., glossary, 22½ cms.*
*Part 2: 395–748 pp., illus., maps, app., indexes (part 1 & 2).*

This work is an official history of the war and is an extremely detailed account of the whole theatre of operations. It is extremely valuable for the general background that it gives to the Arab involvement and because it places the Arab Revolt in perspective.

Wavell, A. P.
**The Palestine Campaigns.**
*London: Constable & Co., 3rd ed., 1938.*
*xvi, 259 pp., maps, app., index, 21 cms.*

A good account of the Palestine campaign which stresses the value of the Arab Revolt in diverting Turkish forces to the Hedjaz to protect the railway and in protecting the right flank of Allenby's army on its advance through Palestine. The revolt also acted as a counter to German propaganda which was operating in Persia, Arabia and Afghanistan.

Weldon, Captain L. B.
**Hard Lying:** Eastern Mediterranean, 1914–1919.
*London: Herbert Jenkins. 1925.*
*ix, 246 pp., illus., index, 21½ cms.*

This is the autobiography of one of the officers on board one of the ships of the Royal Indian Marine transferred to the Royal Navy and used for the protection of the Suez Canal and coastal work in the Mediterranean.

Its inclusion in this work, apart from the general interest of naval actions in the area, is because of the section between pp. 142–159 which deals with the support given to the Sherifian forces in the Hedjaz and the capture of Akaba which was achieved by Naval forces and Arab troops before the main body of the Sherifian army led by Feisal and Lawrence arrived from the landward side.

# THE ARAB REVOLT

AJAY, NICHOLAS Z.
**Political intrigue and suppression in Lebanon during World War I.**
*International Journal of Middle East Studies. Vol. 5, No. 2, 1974, pp. 140–160.*

Prior to World War I, Lebanon was a part of the Ottoman Empire, but because of its position in relation to the Great Powers it had a certain degree of autonomy. However, the outbreak of war and the entry of Turkey into the hostilities led to its occupation by part of the Fourth Army Command under Djemal Pasha. A rift had already existed between the articulate population and the Turks due to the dissolution of the Committee of Reform and the closure of its headquarters. 'In peacetime the Turks had pursued a policy which, on the whole, alienated the bulk of the non-Turkish subjects. Now in wartime, these same subjects, unsympathetic to the Turkish cause, would be willing to help the enemy.'

The article then proceeds to discuss the Allied intelligence operation in Lebanon and the involvement of the local population together with the martyrs that these operations created and the repressive policy of the Turkish authorities culminating in a series of executions. However, these actions caused the populations to turn against the Turks and although the executions had gained short-term benefits for the Turks they 'were ultimately detrimental to the interests of the central government. In hanging the martyrs, Jamal Pasha' roused the revengeful hatred of the whole race'.

*ANTONOUS, GEORGE
**The Arab Awakening:** The story of the Arab nationalist movement.

*London: Hamish Hamilton. 1938.*
*xii, 13–471 pp., maps, app., index, 22 cms.*
*(Chapters Ten to Thirteen.)*

The Arab Revolt was declared on 10 June 1916 and this caused considerable consternation in Turkey and Germany so much so that it was kept a secret from the public for some weeks and attempts were made to discredit and belittle the event. The immediate significance of the revolt was that it 'had barred the road to the Red Sea and the Indian Ocean, and had interposed an obstacle to Turco–German southward expansion'. Following the capture of Wejh General Murray 'realised with a sudden shock that more Turkish troops were fighting the Arabs than were fighting him'.

The next section deals with the part played by the Arabs in the Middle East war which was concentrated upon bottling up the Turkish forces in the Hedjaz and acting as the right flank to Allenby's army on its advance through Palestine. The Revolt had its political significance as well especially following the capture of Akaba which '. . . became the tangible embodiment of the Revolt and a base for the political undermining as well as the military undoing of the Turkish power in Syria'.

The political campaign was based upon the propaganda that the Allied cause had become identified with the cause of Arab freedom though this was to have repercussions in the years to come. The chapter then concludes by dealing with the advance through Syria, the capture of Damascus and the occupation of Syria by the Allies and the setting up of an Arab provisional government under Faisal at Damascus.

ARENDT, HANNAH
**The Imperialistic character.**
*The Review of Politics. Vol. 12, No. 3, July 1950, pp. 303–320.*

The article discusses the character and quality of the administrators of the British Empire in India, Egypt and South Africa. 'The author of the imperialistic legend is Rudyard Kipling, its topic is the British Empire, its result the Imperialistic character (after all the only true character form of modern times). And whilst the legend has little to do with the realities of British imperialism it forced or deluded into its services the best sons of England.'

As part of this hypothesis the author considers the work of Lawrence casting him as an adventurer turned secret agent whose motives were destroyed by politicians. The Arab Revolt was

95

merely a useful device adopted by Britain as a means of securing her imperial dreams in the Middle East. Lawrence had to behave as if the Arab national movement was his prime interest and he took the part so well that he came to believe in it. 'He took great delight in a role that demanded a reconditioning of his whole personality until he fitted into the Great Game, until he became the incarnation of the force of the Arab national movement.'

This hypothesis is an important one if one compares it with the conclusions drawn by Knightley and Simpson in their 'Secret Lives of Lawrence of Arabia' and in the light of the Peace Settlement and Lawrence's subsequent writing on behalf of the Arab cause and his work with Churchill at the Colonial Office.

BELL, GERTRUDE
**The Arab War.**
*London: Golden Cockerel Press.*
*52 pp., 25½ cms.*

A series of articles written by Gertrude Bell between October 1916 and July 1917 for the Arab Bureau in Cairo which were published in the 'Arab Bulletin'. Its importance lies in the background information that it provides with regard to the situation in the Middle East at the time of the outbreak of the Arab Revolt.

CARRUTHERS, DOUGLAS
**Arabs in warfare.**
*London: Country Life. 1 April 1916, pp. 420–421.*

A discussion of the Arab's approach to war and in particular the possibility of armed action against the Turks. He considers the warlike attitude of the Arab on an inter-tribal basis and not in a concerted action against an outside enemy in a conventional war though he considers that in any action the nature of the terrain and their harmony with their surroundings gives them an advantage not easily matched. However, the author considers that the division of the Moslem world would take away the chief stimulus of a revolt that of a religious revival '. . . which alone really stirs them, and impels them to march to victory in spite of fearful odds, as they did in the days of their warrior prophet'.

Its value lies mainly in being a contemporary account of the attitude of British writers towards the Arab Revolt.

CLAYTON, GILBERT
**An Arabian Diary,** ed. by Robert O. Collins.
*Los Angeles: University of California Press. 1969.*
*xiv, 379 pp., app., bibl., index, 23½ cms.*

Although the Diary section is of interest in certain areas such as the mission to Ibn Saud the main relevance is the introductory essay. This deals with the work of Clayton at the Arab Bureau and its intelligence activities in connection with the Arab Revolt. It also deals with the decision to support the cause of Hussein and the necessity to placate Ibn Saud by means of diplomatic pressure and a small financial subsidy which only succeeded in securing his passive support during the war.

\*DAWN, C. ERNEST
**The Amir of Mecca al-Husayn ibn' Ali' and the origin of the Arab Revolt.**
*Proceedings American Philosophical Society. Vol. 104, No. 1, 15 February 1960, pp. 11–34.*

A discussion of the background to the Arab Revolt of 1916 which begins with an examination of the basis on which the Emir of Mecca ruled the Hedjaz as part of the Ottoman Empire and the problems faced in trying to administer the province. It considers the relationship between Hussein and the Sultan which was on the basis of mutual co-operation whilst the province was left largely disturbed. However, the proposed railway link to Mecca caused a deterioration in relations although Hussein still resisted overtures from the nationalists to lead a revolt against the Turks concentrating on strengthening his own position as Emir.

The article continues by considering the growing unrest in the area and the negotiations between Hussein and the British which were being conducted at the same time as Hussein was seeking a compromise solution with the Turks. The policy of centralisation favoured by the Young Turks placed a strain on relations which reached a new crisis point with Turkish demands for Sherifian participation in the War. Eventually Hussein was forced to choose between a continuance of his policy of Ottomanism which had successfully defended his position as Emir or support for the new force in the area that of the British whose victory could guarantee his position as Emir with overlordship of the surrounding area. 'The Hashemite conversion to Arabism, then, is an instance of the adoption of a new ideology by one element of the ruling class as an instrument of conflict with its rivals within that class.'

\*DAWN, C. ERNEST
**Ideological influences in the Arab Revolt.**
*In: Kritzeck, James and Winder, R. Bayly, eds.*
*The World of Islam.*
*London: Macmillan. 1960.*
*pp. 233–248.*

A consideration of the ideological influences in the Arab Revolt based on the political attitudes and ideas of Sherif Hussein and his son Abdullah both of whom played vital parts in the origins of the Revolt. The difference between the two men was that Hussein became a separatist only after he had failed to achieve his political ambitions within the framework of the Ottoman Empire whilst Abdullah was convinced of the necessity for revolt and had become an Arab Nationalist by the July of 1914.

The prime source of material on Abdullah's political ideas are his memoirs which appeared in 1945 but which Dawn concludes are based on his political ideas prior to 1916 and not those resulting from the experience of following years. The basic ideal expressed is that the Arabs must be considered a special people even before the coming of Islam but that this revelation enabled them to achieve complete nationhood and that this state would prevail as long as the teachings of the Koran were adhered to. This did not mean the expression of the idea of a sovereign state until the Ottomans began to replace fundamental Islamic institutions under the tanzimat reforms and more particularly the proposal to replace the caliphate with a western constitutional and nationalist regime. It was at this point that Abdullah considered that as true Moslems the Arabs had no choice but to rebel.

The source material for the political ideology of Hussein are the four proclamations issued between 10 June 1916 and 5 March 1917 the first in Egypt and the remaining three in Hussein's official journal al-Qiblah. Professor Dawn discusses the controversy of the authenticity of the first proclamation and concludes that the published version was the work of Hussein whilst the suppressed version with its tenets of Arabism is the work of Muhammed Rashid Rida the editor of al-Manor. In these proclamations Hussein's idea of nationalism embodied only the Hedjaz and not the Arab world as a whole and his reasons for the departure from a policy of compromise within the Ottoman Empire were the same as those put forward by Abdullah.

The main difference between the two men's concept of nationalism was that Hussein's was based on the conservative concept of tribal and family unity whereas Abdullah's was based on the theory of Arab pre-eminence among Muslims. Hussein held to the traditional Sunnite Islam whilst Abdullah advocated an Arab revival to reform Islam, though both were motivated by a desire to protect Islam and its institutions.

FARAN, CAESAR E.
**The dilemma of Arab Nationalism.**
*Die Welt des Islams. 1963, 8, pp. 140–164.*

Initially there was a possibility that the Arabs would side with the Turks following the declaration of a Holy War but 'When in the course of World War I Turkish authorities resorted to harsh suppressive measures against both Muslim and Christian Arab nationalists, the schism became irreconcilable'.

HART, B. H. LIDDELL
**T. E. Lawrence: through his own eyes and another's.**
*Southern Review. Vol. 2, No. 1, 1936, pp. 22–40.*

This article is included for the second part which is an evaluation of the Arab Revolt, the first being an examination of the *Seven Pillars of Wisdom*. The Revolt is examined in the context of the campaign in the Middle East and it is considered to be of great value in protecting Allenby's right flank and in occupying Turkish troops. The guerrilla tactics adopted by the Arabs are considered to have been ideally suited to the occasion as 'in view of the fact that the Turks had scantier reserves of materials than of men "killing engines" was a more deadly strategy than "killing Turks"'.

HURGRONJE, C. SNOUCK
**The Revolt in Arabia.**
*New York: G. P. Putnam's Sons. 1917.*
*vii, 50 pp., app., 19 cms.*

An account of the history of the Shereefate of Mecca and its place in the structure of the Ottoman Empire which was written shortly after the declaration of the Revolt. It also deals with the possible aims of the Revolt and the likely outcome, though this is dealt with very briefly. The proclamation of the Revolt by Sherif Hussein is produced as an appendix to the work.

IRELAND, PHILIP WILLARD
**Iraq:** A study in political development.
*London: Cape. 1937.*
*510 pp., illus., maps, app., bibl., index.*

See Section 3a for annotation to this work.

JOARDER, SAFUIDDIN
**Syria under the French Mandate:** An overview.
*Journal Asiatic Society of Pakistan. Vol. XIV, No. 1, pp. 91–104.*

The opening part of this article deals with the occupation of Damascus by the Allied army in October 1918 and the setting up of a provisional Arab Government under Faisal. The country was nearly in a state of anarchy having been ravaged by war and famine and with all aspects of the Ottoman Administration having broken down with many of the records having been removed by the officials who had fled the city.

Support for Faisal came from three main groups with the immediate support being from the Army officers from Syria, Iraq and Palestine who had served in Faisal's army. Secondly, Arab nationalism was strongly supported from areas with a predominance of Sunni Muslims such as Damascus, Homs and Aleppo. The third area of support came from the Bedouin tribes of the Hedjaz and Eastern Syria partly because of the subsidy from the British and because of Faisal's descent from the Prophet.

KEDOURIE, ELIE
**The Capture of Damascus, 1 October 1918.**
*In : Kedourie, Elie.*
*The Chatham House Version and other Middle Eastern Studies.*
*pp. 33–51.*
*Also in Middle Eastern Studies. Vol. 1, No. 1, October 1964, pp. 66–83.*

This chapter is a criticism of Lawrence's account of the capture of Damascus because of its inaccuracies and indeed Lawrence himself commented on the Damascus section of the *Seven Pillars of Wisdom* that 'I was on thin ice when I wrote the Damascus chapter and anyone who copies me will be through it, if he is not careful. S.P. is full of half truths here'.

Kedourie claims that the Australian War Diaries of the Australian Mounted Division substantiate the facts that the Turks had already abandoned Damascus and the Sherifian forces '. . . were allowed to occupy it and to claim that they had captured it'. The implication of such a move goes further than a criticism of Lawrence's account as it is seen as being '. . . instrumental in eroding the British position in Mesopotamia and in creating the bitter and tangled situation between British, French and Sharifians in Syria which General Gouraud resolved by force of arms at Khan Maisalun in July 1920'.

i. *T. E. Lawrence to His Biographer*, Robert Graves, p. 104.

\*KHAN, RASHEEDUDDIN
**The Arab Revolt of 1916–1918:** Political context and historical role.
*Islamic Culture. Vol. XXV, No. 4, October 1961, pp. 244–258.*

The Arab Revolt is seen as having acquired a political and romantic connotation in the contemporary Arab world. 'It was an episode of a powerful psychological value revealing national courage which historically should be taken as the first militant challenge of the nationally awakened but politically disorganised Arabs against the declining Ottoman authority.'

The article discusses the origins of the Revolt which eventually was declared in 1916 with the support of Britain. This support was forthcoming because the Revolt created a rift between the Arabs and Turks thus destroying Islamic solidarity and by creating civil war conditions in the Middle East it invalidated the call for Jehad and compelled the Turks to detach army detachments from the Canal area and Palestine to try and stem the Revolt.

\*KIRKBRIDE, SIR ALEC SEATH
**An Awakening:** The Arab Campaign, 1917–1918.
*Tavistock, England: University Press of Arabia. 1971.*
*vi, 134 pp., plates, map, app., index, 22 cms.*

The author spent a considerable period of time in the Middle East being attached to the Arab Army in February 1918 after a period in Army intelligence. After the war he became British representative in Transjordan followed by various posts in Palestine before becoming British Resident in Amman.

This book deals with the period from 1917 when the author was in the area collecting military intelligence for transmission back to Cairo. This was followed by attachment to the Arab army in company with Lawrence, Joyce and Stirling amongst others and the author provides an extremely interesting account of the activities of the Arab army.

The author examines the claim that the Revolt had little military value pointing out that the action tied up a large number of Turkish forces and that the disruption of communications around Deraa was a valuable and positive contribution to the advance of the British army from Jerusalem. Sir Alec is in no doubt that the result in the Middle East would have been the same without Arab assistance but only at a greater cost in British lives. 'Whatever the critics may say, the story of the Arab Revolt is one of success; but the sequel is not so happy. Looking back from a distance in time of over fifty years, I find it tragic that, after being regarded as liberators and allies, we should now be called colonisers and imperialists . . .'

KRESSENSTEIN, COLONEL BARON KRESS VON
**The Campaign in Palestine from the enemy's side.**
*Royal United Services Institute Journal. Vol. LXVII, August 1922, pp. 503–513.*

A description of the campaign in Palestine by the German Chief of Staff and later commander of the Turkish Eighth Army. It deals with the attempts by Djemal Pasha to capture the Suez Canal and Egypt in 1914 which was repulsed and the subsequent advances of 1916 by the Allied armies. It concludes with the taking of Jerusalem in 1917 by the British which was of little importance militarily '. . . but the moral effect of its capture, after having been in Turkish hands for seven hundred years, and following as it did so soon after the fall of Mecca, was a severe blow to the prestige of the Caliphate and of Turkey.'

LAW, SIDNEY
**The Revival of the Arab nation.**
*Fortnightly Review: New Series. Vol. 102, 1917, pp. 82–89.*

This article sees the outbreak of war against the Turks as a means of reviving the glories of the Arab nation. 'And as the result of this great war, which was intended to rivet upon Western Asia a militarism as deadening as that of the Sultan, and more formidable, Arabia will be released and revivified.' This approach is seen in relation to the situation in the Hedjaz where Hussein had revolted against the Ottoman government and to Mesopotamia which was being occupied by the Anglo-Indian army.

LAWRENCE, THOMAS EDWARD
**Emir Feisal, Creator of the Arab Army, A modern Saladin.**
*The Times (London). 7 August 1920, p. 9.*

The first part of a two-part article considering the career of Faisal and dealing with the creation of the Arab regular army into which he moulded the various tribes who abandoned their traditional rivalries as a result of his 'mediation, by reconciliation, by his personal appeals, by setting before the people in impassioned address the ideal of national union to win national freedom from the Turks'.

\*LAWRENCE, THOMAS EDWARD
**Evolution of a revolt,** ed. by Stanley and Rodelle Weintraub.
*London: Pennsylvania State University Press. 1968.*
*175 pp., illus., 22 cms.*

This work contains Lawrence's miscellaneous pieces which appeared as a series of newspaper and journal articles between 1918–1921, some of them anonymous. The text follows the format of the original publication, including captions, and where the pieces were signed, Lawrence's by-line and the accompanying identification of the writer. The title article 'Evolution of a Revolt' appeared whilst the *Seven Pillars of Wisdom* was being written in its revised form and the final version of the article formed part of the Subscriber's Edition of the 'Seven Pillars'. (See the entry for the article for annotation.)

The introduction is particularly valuable as it deals briefly with Lawrence's career prior to the Peace Conference but more extensively with his writings after the peace talks, especially those relating to his campaign supporting the Arab case. It also deals extensively with the writing of the *Seven Pillars of Wisdom* and its reliance on the *Arab Bulletin* reports, and Lawrence's hand-written notes and reports.

This is an extremely useful collection which shows not only the progress and pattern of the Arab Revolt but the campaign by Lawrence to secure the Arab's rights following the Peace Conference and the setting up of the mandates system.

\*LAWRENCE, THOMAS EDWARD
**The Evolution of a revolt.**
*Army Quarterly (London). Vol. 1, No. 1, October 1920, pp. 55–69.*

An examination of the military strategy of the Arab Revolt providing an explanation of the tactics adopted by the Arab armies in their struggle against the Turks. It was not possible to oppose the Turks using recognised military tactics and the essence of the Arab strategy had to be the stretching of the Turkish forces to breaking point without being drawn into a conventionally fought battle. 'Our victory lay not in battles, but in occupying square miles of country . . . We had nothing material to lose, so we were to defend nothing and to shoot nothing.'

In considering the criteria necessary for the success of the rebellion Lawrence expresses his thesis for success in terms which can be summarised as follows:

1. An unassailable base safe from attack and the fear of attack.
2. A sophisticated alien enemy with a disciplined army of occupation too small to dominate the country effectively.
3. A friendly population not necessarily totally active but with the non-active percentage being sympathetic.
4. The rebel force must be mobile and with endurance and good lines of supply.
5. The rebel force must have the equipment to paralyse the enemy's communication.

LAWRENCE, THOMAS EDWARD
**Oriental Assembly,** ed. by Arnold Walter Lawrence.
*London: Williams and Norgate. 1939.*
*xiv, 292 pp., illus., 22 cms.*

A collection of Lawrence's miscellaneous works with the exception of 'Crusader Castles', though not all are relevant to this study.

Of interest are the articles 'The Changing East', which first appeared anonymously in 1920, and which deals with the social and political changes taking place in the Middle East, and the 'Evolution of a Revolt' dealing with the development of the Arab Revolt. (See entries under the articles for annotations.)

This work also includes part of Lawrence's collection of war photographs, the exception being those in the Imperial War Museum, and these are of fringe interest as they form a useful pictorial background to the Arab Revolt.

\*LAWRENCE, THOMAS EDWARD
**Revolt in the Desert.**
*London: Cape. 1927.*
*446 pp., illus., map, 23½ cms.*

An abridgment of the *Seven Pillars of Wisdom* and the only version available to the general public until the complete work appeared in 1935. It is an easier work to read than the 'Seven Pillars', mainly because the reflective material and the personal insights have been omitted.

This work presents a straightforward account of the Arab Revolt from its inception to the taking of Damascus in October 1918. Although one must bear in mind the criticism of Lawrence that subsequent research has produced when reading this work it is still probably the best account of the military side of the Arab Revolt and the part played by the British officers attached to the Arab army.

\*LAWRENCE, THOMAS EDWARD
**Secret Despatches from Arabia.**
*London: Golden Cockerel Press. 1939.*
*173 pp., 25½ cms.*

Another collection of miscellaneous writings which appeared in the *Arab Bulletin*, which was issued in Cairo from 6 June 1916 to 6 December 1918. Some of the articles which first appeared anonymously are attributed to Lawrence as a result of annotations that appeared on his own copy. The contributions are significant in that they express the true views of Lawrence regarding the Arab Revolt, the personalities involved and the prospects for the future. The topics are extremely varied and range from the religious views of Hussein to the military operations against the Hedjaz railway and a guide to the British officers dealing with the Arabs entitled 'Twenty-Seven Articles'.

Of particular interest to this study is the contribution entitled 'Syrian Cross Currents' which deals with the Turkish occupation of Syria and the role of the Syrians in relation to the Arab Revolt. The article was extremely critical of the Syrians concluding that they were interested in their freedom provided it could be achieved by someone else and that 'They would so much rather the Judean hills were stained with London Territorials, dead for their freedom, to save them from the need of taking dangerous rides'. Lawrence also felt that 'a spontaneous rebellion in Syria is an impossibility: the local people will take no action until the front tide of battle has rolled past them'. (See Mousa, S. 'The Role of Syrians and Iraqis in the Arab Revolt' for the Arab view.)

All told there are thirty-eight articles reproduced in this work of varying length and content and many at variance in approach with public pronouncements on the subject and on Lawrence's later writings.

LODER, J. DE V.
**The Truth about Mesopotamia, Palestine and Syria.**
*London: Allen & Unwin. 1923.*
*221 pp., maps, index, 19 cms.*

A valuable work providing a useful account of Arab nationalism from the outbreak of the Arab Revolt though one must bear in mind that at the time of writing much of the official documentation on the subject was not available. The author provides an excellent introduction to the reasons for the Arab Revolt and the choice of Hussein as its leader.

LONGRIGG, STEPHEN HEMSLEY
**Syria and Lebanon under French Mandate.**
*London: O.U.P. 1958.*
*xii, 404 pp., maps, bibl., index, 21½ cms.*

See entry under Section 3c for annotation to this work as only the introductory section is relevant to the Arab Revolt.

MAC CALLUM, ELIZABETH P.
**The Arab Nationalist Movement.**
*The Moslem World. Vol. XXV, No. 4, October 1935, pp. 359–374.*

In considering the Middle East War the problems faced by the Arabs were threefold, firstly whether to accept British or French inducements to revolt against Turkey, or to accept German inducements to remain loyal. The result was the Revolt under the leadership of Hussein with the campaign being led by Faisal with the assistance of allied advisers one of whom was T. E. Lawrence.

The Revolt coupled with the advance of General Allenby on Damascus resulted in the defeat of the Turkish and German forces. In October 1918 Damascus was taken by allied troops and Faisal was established in Damascus with the Arabs confidently looking forward to the creation of an Arab kingdom of Syria.

McGILVARY, MARGARET
**The Dawn of a new era in Syria.**
*New York: Fleming H. Revell Co. 1920.*
*302 pp., illus., 21 cms.*

The author worked with the American Missionary Press in Syria arriving shortly before the outbreak of war and as an American was in a privileged position until the United States entry into the war.

This book provides an interesting insight into the social and economic condition in Syria during the war years with particular reference to the state of the ordinary people who were suffering not only from Turkish overlordship but from the allied blockade of the coastal ports. In this connection the author also discusses the relief work carried out to alleviate the famine conditions through the American Red Cross and using funds smuggled into Syria.

Conditions deteriorated following America's entry into the war which resulted in the arrest of several Americans and pressure on the American Missionary Press. The work ends by viewing the liberation of Syria from the Ottoman Empire and the resultant problems which needed assistance in economic and social areas and the backing of the Great Powers to secure her political future.

MEINERTZHAGEN, RICHARD
**Middle East Diary, 1917–1956.**
*London: The Cresset Press. 1959.*
*xi, 376 pp., index, 22 cms.*

Meinertzhagen was part of Allenby's Intelligence section from 1917 and this work represents extracts from his diaries, letters and recollections some of which are severely critical of the persons involved in the various events covered by the period of the book. In his assessment of the Arab Revolt Meinertzhagen deals sympathetically with the character of Lawrence but he is critical of his actions and the importance which was attached to the Arab Revolt.

*MOUSA, SULEIMAN
**The Role of the Syrians and Iraqis in the Arab Revolt.**
*Middle East Forum. Vol. XLIII, No. 1, 1967, pp. 5–17.*

This article discusses the claim that the Syrians and Iraqis had done nothing to bring about their freedom which was made by Lawrence in an article entitled 'Syrian cross-currents' (see entry for 'Secret Despatches from Arabia'), and in a letter home, dated 12 February 1917, in which he wrote: 'The time is not yet ripe to talk of Palestine, Syria and Iraq, for these three countries have made no attempt to liberate themselves, in spite of wholly favourable circumstances.'

The charges are discussed in the light of two major misconceptions the first being that the mass of the Arab people supported, in an active sense, the Arab secret societies, and the second the failure of Iraq and Syria to rise in spontaneous revolt against the Turks. The article details the part played by the Syrians and Iraqis in the campaign against the Turks and concludes that the majority of Faisal's northern army were mainly Syrians and Iraqis and it was this force which provided support for Allenby.

Mousa does, however, offer reasons as to why so many Iraqis and Syrians were unwilling to rise against the Turks:

1. The authority of the Turks had been established through force of habit and the lack of a national consciousness.
2. The strength of the religious link.
3. Local dissent among the Arabs. For example Ibn Rashid, Emir of Northern Nejd, supported the Turks because his enemy Ibn Saud, Emir of Southern Nejd, supported the British.
4. Fear of war damage.

PARKES, JAMES
**Palestine.**
*London : O.U.P. 1940.*
*32 pp., maps, 17½ cms.*
*(Oxford Pamphlets on World Affairs, No. 31.)*

See entry under Section 3c for annotation.

PAVEY, R. A.
**The Arab Revolt.**
*Marine Corps Gazette (U.S.A.). Vol. 40, No. 7, July 1956,*
*pp. 48–53.*

A discussion of the effects of the Arab Revolt from the military
aspect which was an influence on two fronts; that of tying up a
large number of Turkish troops in the Hedjaz as 'The Arabs
could keep the Turkish soldiers confined in the Turks' own base
by controlling the railroad and allowing just enough supplies to
get through to permit them to survive' and secondly by protecting
Allenby's right flank on the advance through Damascus.

PEAKE, F. G.
**A History of Jordan and its tribes.**
*Florida : University of Miami. 1958.*
*x, 253 pp., notes, maps, 27½ cms.*

The outbreak of the Arab Revolt saw all the activity concentrated
in the Hedjaz but following the arrival of Lawrence and the other
British officers the activity moved north into Jordan with attacks
on Akaba and Tafila though the latter could not be held in the face
of a superior force from Al. Qatrani. The situation was restored
somewhat by the British attacks in northern Jordan which drew
off Turkish forces from the south and enabled the Arabs to attack
Maan and to continue their raids on the Hedjaz railway which
succeeded in isolating Turkish troops for the whole of the war.
'All possibility of the Turkish troops in the Hedjaz being sent to
help in Palestine was from this time at an end and the Allied
advance against the latter could now begin.'

**Revolt in the Desert:** An Arabic version.
*The Near East and India. 28 April 1927, pp. 496–497.*

The article was prompted by the publication of an Arabic
edition of *Revolt in the Desert* translated by Abdul Masil Wazir.
The work was introduced by Nouri Pasha al Said and in view of

his part in the Arab Revolt this is reproduced in full in the article. In it Nouri al Said briefly recounts his role in the Revolt and the importance he attached to the part played by Lawrence and the other British officers attached to the Arab army. It is a complimentary introduction to Lawrence's book and gives an Arab view of the Revolt and the influence of the British advisers.

ROYAL INSTITUTE OF INTERNATIONAL AFFAIRS
**Great Britain and Palestine, 1915–1936.**
*London: Royal Institute of International Affairs. 1937.*
*111 pp., tables, notes, app., 22 cms.*
*(Information Department Papers, No. 20.)*

The pamphlet begins by very briefly giving the pre-war background to the Palestine situation before dealing with the war-time promises to the Jews and Arabs. In dealing with the McMahon promises to the Arabs it is considered regrettable that the British negotiators did not make clear from the start that Palestine was excluded from any agreement. It is also considered understandable that from the word of the letter from McMahon dated 24 October 1915 the Arabs should have interpreted Palestine as being within the independence area.

The section also deals with the Sykes–Picot agreement which provided for the division of the Ottoman Arab provinces between the Allies though this specifically excluded Palestine. 'With a view to securing the religious interests of the Entente Powers, Palestine, with the Holy Places, is separated from Turkish territory and subject to a special regime to be determined by agreement between Russia, France and Great Britain.'

This was followed in 1917 by the Balfour Declaration which formalised the concept of a Jewish National Home in Palestine. The motivation for this although partly altruistic was mainly because of the war situation as Lloyd George said in the House of Commons on 19 June 1936. 'It was important for us to seek every legitimate help we could get. We came to the conclusion from information we received from every part of the world that it was vital we should have the sympathies of the Jewish community.'

The situation was further complicated by the Anglo-French Declaration of 7 November 1918 which defined the war aims of the Allies and promised 'administrations deriving their authority from the initiative and free choice of the indigenous populations in Syria and Mesopotamia'. This declaration was seen as a qualification of the Sykes–Picot agreement by the Arabs and although the declaration omits Palestine the Arabs argued that 'they did not take it as such, the main reason which they give for their interpretation being that they did not use the name Palestine, and knew the whole region as Syria, and that the declaration was distributed throughout the whole of Greater Syria (i.e. including what is now Palestine) and Mesopotamia'.

It was hoped for a time, especially at the Peace Conference, that all these conflicting promises could be resolved and the promises to the Jews and Arabs implemented simultaneously.

SANDERS, GENERAL LIMAN VON
**The Turkish operations in Palestine, 19–23 September 1918.**
*Royal United Services Institute Journal. Vol. LXVI, May 1921, pp. 326–336.*

This article is taken from the book by von Sanders entitled *Funf Jahre Turkei* which deals with the author's activities in Turkey from 1913 as re-organiser of the Turkish army to its defeat in 1918. This excerpt deals with the period following February 1917 after Falkenhayn's failure to retake Jerusalem or hold Jericho and Sanders took over the Palestinian command.

SCHELTEMA, J. F.
**Arabs and Turks.**
*Journal American Oriental Society. Vol. 37, 1917, pp. 153–161.*

An article discussing the Arab Revolt in its historical context which aims at illustrating the fact that the discontent was not of recent growth. It discusses the relations between the two races as the Turks despised the Arabs because of their temperament and the Arabs and the Turks for their indolence and sluggishness of mind. 'Between Arab and Turk, physically and mentally in marked contrast, no attraction or accord was possible. Hence the sons of the shadowless desert under a cloudless sky, refractory already in their allegiance to the chiefs appointed by their common consent, proved superlatively troublesome to their intrusive Khalifs of the house of Ottoman.'

The article considers the history of the guardianship of the Holy Places in the Hedjaz and the various clashes both internally between the Arabs and with their Turkish overlords. Also considered is the rise of the puritan Islamic movement of the Wahhabi, its military defeat by the army of Muhammed Ali and its subsequent influence in Arabia. Scheltema considers that the declaration of the Arab Revolt in 1916 and the independence of the Hedjaz was to have far-reaching effects on the future outcome in Arabia.

SUGARMAN, SIDNEY
**The truth about T. E. Lawrence and the Arab Revolt.**
*Jewish Observer and Middle East Review. 12 September 1969,*
*pp. 17-20.*

An examination of Lawrence and the Arab Revolt which concludes that the Revolt was only an insignificant part of the war
and that its importance had been inflated because of Lawrence's
writings and the active encouragement that he gave to Lowell
Thomas' lectures. The whole conception of the Revolt with the
promises made to the Arabs to secure their support were at
variance with the aims of the interests of Britain and France and
'It is hardly surprising that we now have a Middle East consumed
by hatreds and frustrations and a deep, relentless urge to wipe
out imagined wrongs and fictitious injustices with blood'.

THOMAS, LOWELL
**With Lawrence in Arabia.**
*London: Hutchinson. 1925.*
*255 pp., frontis., illus., 21 cms.*

The famous biography of Lawrence written by a journalist whose
purpose was to publicise the war for the morale of the civilian
population in America. It is a highly entertaining account of the
Arab Revolt but lacks depth and examination of the underlying
political factors.

TIBAWI, A. L.
**A modern history of Syria including Lebanon and
Palestine.**
*London: Macmillan. 1969.*
*441 pp., plates, maps, notes, notes, bibl., index, 23 cms.*

The second part of this work deals with the Arab Revolt and the
negotiations with the Allies. The author deals with the
McMahon–Hussein correspondence and other British pledges as
they affected Syria and the point is made that many of the
resultant problems were caused by the shortcomings on both
sides mainly caused by the amateurism of the people involved in
the negotiations.

*TROELLIER, GARY
**Ibn Saud and Sherif Hussain:** A comparison in importance
in the early years of the First World War.
*The Historical Journal. Vol. 14, No. 3, September 1971, pp. 627–
633.*

This article discusses the question of British support in the Middle East for the Sherifian family under Hussein which in hindsight has been adjudged to be a mistake by some observers who believe that backing for Ibn Saud would have been more fruitful. Indeed Philby went even further by voicing the opinion that were it not for the death of Captain Shakespear the Arab Revolt might have taken a different course. In his 'Arabia' Philby wrote that Shakespear's death '. . . was a disaster to the Arab cause . . . Had he survived to continue a work for which he was so eminently fitted it is extremely doubtful whether subsequent campaigns of Lawrence would ever have taken place in the west . . .'

The article proceeds to discuss the hypothesis and concludes that this opinion is untenable and that Shakespear's death had no bearing upon the situation. Support for Hussein was determined in part by the religious and political importance of Hussein as the prospect of the war being declared a 'Jihad' could have had disastrous results in Moslem India. Secondly the Arab army was composed of Arab officers of the Ottoman army in Beirut and Damascus and the Arab tribes of the interior with each group responding to differing motivations. It seemed that Hussein and Abdullah were the best men to take advantage of this discontent as Abdullah had been involved in the Secret Societies in Syria and Turkey and Hussein as Emir of Mecca could rally the support of the desert tribes. These factors were reinforced by the fact that British influence in the Hedjaz seemed to provide added protection to Egypt from a Turkish attack and it also provided a defence to the troop corridor from India.

Ibn Saud, however, headed the Wahhabi movement which was looked upon by some Muslims with fear and disdain and he did not command the same authority as the Emir of Mecca. Politically, at this time Ibn Saud's influence did not extend beyond central and eastern Arabia and he had no direct contact with the Turkish army. Although he did neutralise the support of Ibn Rashid for the Turks this did not compare with that of Hussein who could neutralise four Turkish divisions between the Hedjaz, Asir and the Yemen. It is, the article concludes, only the subsequent career of Ibn Saud which could lead one to believe that British support was misdirected.

VICKERY, C. E.
**Arabia and the Hedjaz.**
*Journal Central Asian Society. 1923, Vol. X, pp. 46–67.*

The author deals with the Hedjaz in three sections the first being a general background regarding Arabia and Islamism which considers the religious background to the area with the holy city of Mecca making the area a place of pilgrimage. The second part of the article deals with the geography of the region and its government prior to the war which was based on the Sherifian family under the general over-lordship of the Ottoman Empire. Colonel Vickery then deals with the Arab Revolt in which he served as a member of the military mission, describing the capture of Wejh and the general development of the Revolt. Finally the author deals with the period from 1918 when he returned to the Hedjaz after a period in France to become British Agent to King Hussein describing the autocratical and tyrannical nature of the administration which was fraught with corruption.

In conclusion the article deals with the general situation developing in the region in which Colonel Vickery sees 'a growing power not of our forging, a power which eventually will overrun the very homes of those whom we have so openly and so prodigally supported'.

ZEINE, ZEINE N.
**Arab-Turkish relations and the emergence of Arab Nationalism.**
*Lebanon: Khayat's. 2nd ed. 1966.*
*156 pp., bibl., index, 21 cms.*

The final section of this work deals with the emergence of Arab nationalism during World War I.

6. The emergence of Arab Nationalism II. The War Years, 1914–1918.
This section deals very briefly with the war period without discussing the military aspects. The author considers the alliance between Turkey and Germany with regard to the relations between the Arabs and Turks and the prospect of a Holy War. Only brief coverage is given to the impact of Britain and France as neither country was directly involved in the Arab–Turkish relationship until the situation had already evolved.

# THE WAR IN MESOPOTAMIA

COX, PERCY
**Iraq.**
*United Empire. March 1929, pp. 132–144.*

The situation in Iraq prior to the outbreak of war was distinctly anti-British and this climate was seen as a threat to Britain's interests in Iraq and the Persian Gulf. Following Turkey's entry into the war an expeditionary force was sent to Iraq from India to occupy the country though this was only achieved at a tremendous cost in terms of men and equipment. As the British army occupied areas of country they were followed by the political officers who set up the administration necessary to fill the vacuum created by the retreating Turks.

After the signing of the armistice the British and French governments issued a statement of intent regarding the occupied territories stating that their aims were:

'The complete and final enfranchisement of the people so long oppressed by the Turks and the establishment of national governments drawing their authority from the initiative from free choice of native populations.'

ROTHWELL, V. H.
**Mesopotamia in British War Aims, 1914–1918.**
*Historical Journal. XIII, No. 2, 1970, pp. 273–294.*

An examination of British aims in Mesopotamia which can be divided into phases the first being controlled by the Government of India which supplied and controlled the troops with the attendant political officers being drawn from the Indian Government's Foreign Department. Initially the policy as advanced by Hardinge was one of annexation of Basra and whilst prepared to allow the inclusion of Baghdad in an Arab state he considered it essential that the Basra vilayet must be under British control.

In 1917, however, Mesopotamia ceased to be the Government of India's sole responsibility and the policy became more in keeping with general British policy as distinct from that of the Government of India. Eventually due to the significance of oil deposits in Mosul it was advocated that Britain must control the whole of Mesopotamia to secure a supply of oil for the Royal Navy from British controlled territory. It was this argument which won the day and official British policy pursued the aim of control over Mesopotamia with the inclusion of Mosul in the mandated territory.

SAUNDERS, HILARY ST. GEORGE
**Per Ardua:** The rise of British Air Power, 1911–1939.
*London: O.U.P. 1944.*
*xii, 356 pp., plates, maps, app., index, 22 cms.*

This work is included for the section on the Middle East War entitled 'The Desert Air: Middle East 1915–1917', (pp. 171–192). This deals with the part played by the Royal Flying Corps in the war in the Middle East both with the allied army and as a support force for the Arab army under Faisal. In addition this section considers the part played by aerial reconnaissance in the Middle East and in particular on the advance on Damascus.

WHITE, WILBUR W.
**The Process of change in the Ottoman Empire.**
*Chicago: University of Chicago Press. 1937.*
*ix, 315 pp., map, bibl., index, 23½ cms.*

In dealing with Iraq the author begins his study with the landing in 1914 of Indian troops into Mesopotamia. In the wake of this occupation army came the political officers whose duty it was to set up an administration to replace that of the Turks. The problem was heightened by the fact that it was not possible to adapt the existing Turkish administration as it had disappeared with the officials who had fled with the Turkish army.

The period immediately following the armistice saw the rise of nationalist feeling in anticipation of the Peace Conference with much of the action emanating from Ahd-al-Iraq formed by Iraqis in Faisal's army who sought an independent Iraq after the war.

WILSON, ARNOLD T.
**Loyalties: Mesopotamia.** Vol. I, 1914–17.
*London: O.U.P. 1930.*
*xi, 340 pp., plates, maps, bibl., index, 24½ cms.*

This first volume of Wilson's memoirs deals with the period of the military campaign in Mesopotamia. It provides an extremely detailed account of the military operations and in particular the contribution of, and the sufferings of, the ordinary soldier some 60,000 of whom perished in the campaign or in Turkish prison camps. As a political officer the author also deals with the work of his department in administering the areas won by the army. In this connection though it should be remembered that this was seen by the Indian government as an extension of the system of administration in the Indian Empire. Also as a representative of the India Office Wilson is very critical of the Arab Revolt and the work of the Arab Bureau.

# NEGOTIATIONS WITH THE ALLIES

*Busch, Briton Cooper
**Britain, India and the Arabs, 1914–1921.**
*London: University of California Press. 1971.*
*xii, 522 pp., maps, bibl., index.*

An extremely detailed account of the complex problems facing Britain in the Middle East during and after World War I. It discusses the involvement of Britain in the Arab Revolt and the course of Arab nationalism and how the Sykes–Picot agreement destroyed any possibility that the post-war settlement would leave Britain in a favourable light in the area. However, the author introduces the complicated element of the British government in India which did not favour the support of Arab nationalism due to the Indian involvement in Mesopotamia where the war was being fought against the Arab interests, and for which recompense was being sought . . . Also the government in India was interested in the Persian Gulf and in supporting Ibn Saud's position in Saudi Arabia.

This policy was in direct conflict with that being pursued from Cairo and London the cornerstone of which was the support of the Arab Revolt under Sherif Hussein. This conflict of policies was to play a major part in the formation of British policy in the Middle East and was only solved in 1921 when the responsibility for the Middle East was transferred to the Colonial Office.

It was the attitude of the India Office and the officials of the Indian government which handicapped the aid to the Arabs and the extent of future pledges as the insistence that Mesopotamia must be reserved for Britain was the direct result of Indian influence. The desire to hold Iraq weakened Britain's position in trying to deal with France over Syria and as long as the area was held by the two powers there could be no Arab unity. Even after the responsible department became the Colonial Office the legacy of India was still evident through the administration of Sir Arnold Wilson and Sir Percy Cox. In fact Professor Busch poses the hypothesis that to a certain extent India and Wilson might have been responsible 'for the incongruity of a grandiose declaration of Iraqi liberation, made in Baghdad in 1917, and the spectacle of the murdered political officers and besieged garrisons three years later'. This work shows that the role of India had a significance in Britain's relations with the Arab world during a crucial period to the lasting detriment of future relations with the independent Arab states.

The work has copious notes and an exhaustive bibliography.

FATEMI, NASROLLAH S.
**The Roots of Arab nationalism.**
*Orbis (Philadelphia). 1959, pp. 437-456.*

In considering the war the article deals briefly with this period concentrating solely on the contradictory promises made by Britain to the Arabs and to the French followed in 1917 by the Balfour Declaration, with optimism reawakened by the Anglo-French declaration of 1918. The disappointment of the nationalists is summed up by a quotation from Lawrence's *Seven Pillars of Wisdom* in which he declared that the Arab Revolt 'was an adventure which dared so much, but after the victory there came a slow time of disillusion and then a night in which the fighting men found that all their hopes had failed them'.

*FRIEDMAN, ISAIAH
**The McMahon–Hussein Correspondence and the question of Palestine.**
*Journal Contemporary History. Vol. 5, No. 2, 1970, pp. 83-122.*

A very detailed examination of the McMahon–Hussein correspondence in the light of official papers available for the first time in the Public Record Office. The article examines the background to the correspondence considering the situation in the Middle East at the time and the promises made by Hussein and the effect that these promises, if executed, could have had on the war against Turkey. It deals in depth with the opinions of the various personages both political and military concerning the backing of Hussein and the eventual realisation that the Sherif did not speak for the Arab world as a whole as he had claimed nor was the Revolt a popular uprising against the Turks.

Despite the localised nature of the Revolt and its initial set-backs the British Government, through the Arab Bureau, continued to support Hussein and the author discusses the reasons for this continued support which were, in the main, political with military reasons a poor second. The second half of the article deals with the question of Palestine in relation to the correspondence and the controversy following the peace settlement. The author discusses the opinions of the various British officials involved in the Middle East as represented in various official and private documents written at the time and in retrospect when the controversy over the Arab claim to Palestine arose. Amongst the authorities cited to substantiate the claim that Palestine was never included in the Arab areas are McMahon himself, Lieu-tenant-Colonel Clayton, Hubert Young and Hussein who had refused to join in the Arab opposition to the Balfour declaration. Further evidence is supplied by the failure of Faisal to use the correspondence to further the Arab cause at the Peace conference.

The work has extensive footnotes giving details of the official and private papers extant on the subject of the correspondence and on the question of Palestine.

\*Friedman, Isaiah
**The Question of Palestine 1914–18:** British–Jewish–Arab relations.
*London : Routledge & Kegan Paul. 1973.*
*xiii, 433 pp., notes, bibl., index, 22 cms.*

This work was originally designed as an article to supplement 'The Balfour Declaration' by Stein which was published in 1961. However, an examination of material in the Public Record Office led the author to believe that a more ambitious study was necessary. The prime aim of the work is to examine the motivations of British policy towards the Zionist Movement which although diverse were dominated by one main fear – that of stalemate in the war. In the event of a negotiated peace with Germany the fear existed, in 1917, that there was a possibility of a Turko-German protectorate of a Jewish Palestine and this could not be lightly dismissed.

The question of the Balfour Declaration is examined in relation to the Sykes–Picot agreement and the McMahon–Hussein correspondence and the author feels that, in the light of evidence now available, that these matters also call for revision. The assumption that the Sykes–Picot agreement was a 'product of greed' and 'a startling piece of double dealing' is called into question and Mr. Friedman concludes that these views are now no longer tenable. The agreement was considered necessary by the allies to make the Arab Revolt possible and the author maintains that there were no incompatibilities between the agreement and the pledges made to Hussein as these pledges were not of a unilateral nature. 'This controversial issue bedevilled Middle Eastern politics for over half a century, and still has . . . a political bearing. I have no axe to grind, but I am convinced from my close reading of the available documentary evidence, that the hands of the British Government were clean.'

The book has extensive notes to each chapter and a detailed bibliography listing unpublished sources, official publications, memoirs, etc., special studies, articles and pamphlets.

*GILBERT, MARTIN
**The Arab–Israeli conflict:** Its history in maps.
*London: Weidenfeld & Nicolson. 1974.*
*101 pp., maps, 25 cms.*

Part one is entitled 'Prelude to Conflict' and the following maps are of interest.
7. Britain's promise to the Arabs 1915.
8. The Allied plan for Palestine May 1916.
9. Britain and the Arabs 1917–1971.

GILLEN, D. Z.
**The Antecedents of the Balfour Declaration.**
*Middle Eastern Studies. Vol. 5, No. 2, May 1969, pp. 131–150.*

An examination of the reasons for the Balfour Declaration which were seen mainly as aimed at securing British interests in Palestine after the war and in securing Zionist support during the war. It was also a prudent move in the light of the possibility that the Turks would be persuaded by the Germans to offer similar concessions to secure Zionist support.

*HUREWITZ, J. C.
**Diplomacy in the Near and Middle East:** A documentary record.
*1535–1914. Vol. I.*
*London: Van Nostrand Co. 1956.*
*xviii, 291 pp., index, 23½ cms.*

**Diplomacy in the Near and Middle East:** A documentary record.
*1914–1956. Vol. II.*
*London: Van Nostrand Co. 1956.*
*xviii, 427 pp., index, 23½ cms.*

These two volumes consist of the documentary evidence necessary for an understanding of the diplomacy in the Near and Middle East during the years in question. In the main the documents are reproduced in full save for the preambles, provision for ratification and sections of the documents outside the geographical limitations of the area. The following are of relevance to this study:

Vol. I: Resolution of the Arab–Syrian Congress at Paris, 21 June 1913 (p. 268).
Vol. II: The Husayn–McMahon Correspondence, 14 July 1915–10 March 1916 (p. 13). British treaty with Ibn Saud,

26 December 1915 (p. 17). Tripartite (Sykes–Picot) agreement for the partition of the Ottoman Empire: Britain: France and Russia, 26 April–23 October 1916 (p. 18). Tripartite (Saint Jean de Maunenrie) agreement for the partition of the Ottoman Empire: Britain, France and Italy, 19 April–26 September 1917 (p. 23). The British (Balfour) Declaration of sympathy with Zionist aspirations, 4 June–2 November 1917 (p. 25).

\*INGRAMS, DOREEN
**Palestine papers 1917–1922:** Seeds of conflict.
*London: John Murray. 1972.*
*xii, 198 pp., illus., map, notes, index, 22 cms.*

An examination of the Palestine problem through the official documents, memoranda and letters available on the subject which are collected together in a chronological order and annotated by the compiler.

The work begins by dealing with the Balfour Declaration and the reasons for its existence. 'Negotiations seem to have been mainly oral and by means of private notes and memoranda, of which only the scantiest records are available, even if more exist.' The main motivation seems to have been to counter the Zionist pacifist propaganda in Russia so keeping revolutionary Russia in the war, the satisfying of a large Jewish population in America and the need to secure the support of world Jewry for the Allied cause.

The situation in Palestine in 1918 is examined following Allenby's successful liberation of the country and the fall of Damascus. It is evident from quoted material that the Arabs were uncertain as to the future one example being a report of General Clayton in January 1918 which stated that 'in Palestine task of restoring normal conditions and general relief at expulsion of Turks still precludes any great preoccupation in political questions, but local Arabs still evince some uneasiness at Zionist activity and fear a Jewish government of Palestine as eventual result . . .'

The Zionist Commission to Palestine is also considered in some detail as it was designed to establish good relations between the Jews and the Arabs and other non-Jewish communities in Palestine. The attempt was a failure and did nothing to allay Arab suspicions regarding the future and indeed the anniversary of the Balfour Declaration was marked by conflict between the Zionists and the Arabs.

KEDOURIE, ELIE
**Cairo and Khartoum and the Arab Question.**
*The Historical Journal. Vol. VII, No. 2, 1964, pp. 280–297.*

The problem of the promises to the Arabs is examined in the light of the Sykes–Picot agreement and the view expressed by Wingate that even if the promised Arab state became a reality 'I think it is in our power to erect such barriers as would effectively prevent it becoming the menace which the Indian Government appears to fear'. The article considers the implications of the Sykes–Picot agreement and compares it with the promises made to the Arabs and the continuing diplomatic overtures between the active participants in the Middle East though the Cairo officials were opposed to the agreement.

KEDOURIE, ELIE
**England and the Middle East:** The destruction of the Ottoman Empire, 1914–1921.
*London: Bowes and Bowes. 1956.*
*xiii, 9–236 pp., app., bibl., index, 21½ cms.*

Sir Mark Sykes and Colonel Lawrence.

Chapters three and four of this book deal with two of the personalities of the Middle East at the time of World War I, Sir Mark Sykes and T. E. Lawrence.

In considering the work of Sykes in the Middle East settlement Kedourie considers Sykes' background which initially meant support for the Ottoman Empire. This developed, however, following the advent of the Young Turks into support for Arab nationalism, subsequently changing to support for the Zionist movement as well. 'Sir Mark Sykes therefore conceived the Arab–Armenian–Zionist Entente and admonished the Arab leader in Cairo and the Hijaz to realise it. "If such an Entente becomes a public fact," he told the Sherif and his officers, "then your national movement becomes recognized in every country in the world".'

The chapter on T. E. Lawrence is a highly critical contribution as Kedourie considers that the Arabs were the least of Lawrence's concerns as his 'motives were strictly personal, to be sought only in his intimate restlessness and private torment. The poverty of his ideas matches only the passion with which he pursued their realisation.' This argument is reinforced by quotations from Lawrence's various writings and especially *Seven Pillars of Wisdom* which 'is a book which seeks to justify, and to prove right, not so much the Arab movement, as his own actions. He therefore chose whatever explanations seemed to offer the most convincing pretexts for his actions, however damaging they were to the cause he had adopted.'

KEDOURIE, ELIE
**Sir Mark Sykes and Palestine, 1915–16.**
*In: Kedourie, Elie*
*Arabic political memoirs and other studies, pp. 236–242.*
*(Also in Middle Eastern Studies, October 1970.)*

An examination of the views of Sir Mark Sykes especially with regard to Palestine in the eventual Peace Settlement. It is argued that Sykes was not a believer in the Sykes–Picot agreement as he was acting as an agent of his ministers and presenting their views. Sykes saw a need for Britain to occupy an area between the Sherif of Mecca and the French to safeguard the British Empire but the 1916 agreement gave Britain only a small area around Haifa with the remainder of Palestine being internationally administered. It was for this reason that the Zionist plan for Palestine became complementary to Sykes' plan for a British Palestine '... patronage of Zionism would be used to establish and maintain the British control of Palestine which Allenby's victory had made possible. And in the execution of this policy Sykes was certainly a key figure.'

KHAN, DR. RASHEEDUDDIN
**The Rise of Arab Nationalism and European Diplomacy, 1908–1916.**
*Islamic Culture. July 1962, pp. 197–206.*

The second part of this article deals with the Sykes–Picot agreement which is described as 'a classic piece of a treaty surreptitiously negotiated by the Entente powers for territorial aggrandisement in the period of their highest glory'. The terms of the agreement are discussed and it is considered that the Allied view that the agreement was a necessity of war is to be refuted as it was 'a tentative, yet important agreement to recast the political map of the Middle East'. Essentially the agreement is seen as 'a byword for classical diplomatic double dealing ... it was not only morally lamentable but also administratively absurd'.

*KHAN, RASHEEDUDDIN
**The Rise of Arab Nationalism and European Diplomacy, 1908–1916.**
*Islamic Culture. Vol. XXXVI, October 1962, pp. 244–258.*

This article concludes the section entitled 'The Arab Revolt of

1916–18' and deals in depth with the Hussein–MacMahon correspondence of 1915–1916, from which 'The charge of duplicity and breach of faith levelled against the British by the Arab stem generally from the genesis and substance of this momentous correspondence concluded two months before the Sykes–Picot agreement'.

Firstly the article deals with the background to the Sherifian negotiations with Britain through the early contacts with Lord Kitchener and Sir Ronald Storrs prior to Turkey's formal entry into the war. Consideration is then given in detail to the actual correspondence with criticism being levelled at both sides as 'a close examination of the trend and tenor of the correspondence reveals a continuous thread of evasive pledges by the British and compromises by the Sherif'. It is considered that the compromises and weakness of Hussein was a prime cause of the collapse of the Arab case after the war and the article is very critical of Hussein as it maintains that 'the Sherif played a reckless game which brought misery and frustration to his people . . . Probably his dynastic interests weighed more heavily with him than the realisation of the cherished dream of the Arabs for independence.'

'L'
**Downing Street and the Arab Potentates.**
*Foreign Affairs. January 1927, pp. 233–240.*

A discussion of the relationship between Britain and the Arab states though the various treaties and subsidies. The article considers the committee led by Churchill with Lawrence and Cox as two of its members which dealt with the subsidies paid to the Arab leaders. It then deals with the various leaders who were in receipt of the subsidies and the reasons for granting financial aid considering in detail the cases of Hussein and Ibn Saud.

LESLIE, SHANE
**Mark Sykes:** His life and letters.
*London: Cassell. 1923.*
*xi, 308 pp., plates, app., index, 24 cms.*

Only the part of this work dealing with the Great War is of relevance as this deals with the Sykes–Picot agreement which was concluded in 1916. 'The British policy in Syria was largely left to him (Sykes), though it was on the lines of Sir Maurice de Bunsen's Commission that the Sykes–Picot Treaty was based.' In fact Sykes resented the fact that the agreement bore his name. 'He was influenced by two principles. His hatred of oppression

urged him to do all in his power for the Arabs, the Jews, and the
minor nationalities . . .'

MONROE, ELIZABETH
**Britain's moment in the Middle East, 1914–1956.**
*London: Chatto & Windus. 1963.*
*254 pp., maps, notes, bibl., index, 22 cms.*

In the first section 'Accident and design in war, 1914–18' the war
in the Middle East is considered though the main area of concern
is with the political background and its relation to war as a whole.
In particular the author examines the campaign in Palestine in
the light of the emotive appeal of the Holy Land and the campaign in Mesopotamia in the light of the policy of the India
Office. These events are also linked to a consideration of the
political side of Britain's relations with the Arabs and Britain's
relations with France regarding the future of the area following a
successful conclusion of the war.

MONROE, ELIZABETH
**The origin of the Palestine problem.**
*In: Mansfield, Peter, ed.*
*The Middle East: A political and economic survey, pp. 47–66.*

Only the early part of this thematic study is of relevance as the
remainder is beyond the date of this study. The essay begins by
briefly outlining the period prior to World War I before dealing
in greater detail with the question of the McMahon–Hussein
correspondence and the various interpretations put upon the
agreement by each party. The Balfour Declaration is then considered and its apparent contradiction of the agreement with the
Arabs together with the complication of the Anglo-French understandings regarding the area following the end of the war.

SYKES, CHRISTOPHER
**Cross roads to Israel:** Palestine from Balfour to Bevin.
*London: Collins. 1965.*
*479 pp., illus., maps, app., bibl., index, 23½ cms.*
*(Chapter Two, pp. 29–57.)*

Only the early part of this work is of relevance dealing with the
period from the McMahon–Hussein correspondence which was
open to various interpretations as Britain always maintained that
the agreement did not include Palestine whereas the Arabs maintained that Syria was included in the agreement and that Palestine
was part of Ottoman Syria. The situation created by the Balfour
Declaration was considered by the Arabs to be a contradiction of

their agreement and the whole subject was further complicated by the existence of the Sykes–Picot agreement.

Attempts were made to reach an understanding between the Arabs and Zionists but these were a failure as Faisal was subject to pressures from his nationalist supporters causing him to withdraw from an understanding between himself and Weizmann. The escape clause was a codicil appended to the agreement by Faisal which stated that he would accept a Jewish presence in Palestine provided the Arabs gained their independence as promised. 'But if the slightest modification or departure were to be made, I shall not then be bound by a single word of the present agreement . . .'

**\*Tripartite (Sykes–Picot) Agreement for the Partition of the Ottoman Empire:** Britain, France and Russia, 26 April–23 October 1916.
*In (Woodward & Butler eds. Documents on British Foreign Policy, 1919–1939, 1st series. Vol. 4, pp. 241–251) and Hurewitz, J. C. Dipolomacy in the Near and Middle East, pp. 18–22.*

This deals with the agreement to partition the Ottoman Empire following the war which was the basis for subsequent Anglo-French discord and for much of the bitterness between the Arabs and Britain when this was compared with the Hussein–McMahon correspondence.

Basically the agreement provided for French interests in Syria and Lebanon, British interests in Mesopotamia and Palestine with international control over the Holy Places. In addition the two powers agreed to recognise and protect an independent Arab state or confederation of states in these areas. It was further agreed that these rights should not be ceded to a third power except to the Arabs unless with the agreement of the other power.

WOODWARD, E. L. AND BUTLER, ROHAN, EDS.
**Documents on British Foreign Policy, 1919–1939.**
*First Series. Vol. IV, 1919.*
*London: H.M.S.O.*
*xciii, 1,278 pp., maps, 25 cms.*

See entry in Section 2a on the Peace Conference for annotation.

# BIOGRAPHICAL WORKS

AARONSOHN, ALEXANDER
**With the Turks in Palestine.**
*London: Constable. 1917.*
*125 pp., 18½ cms.*

The story of a Palestinian Jew who served for a period in the Turkish army but who managed to purchase his release and eventually managed to escape to America. It provides an interesting account of the relations between the Jews and the Arabs whilst under Turkish rule and the treatment of both races by the Turkish army.

The author also provides a useful account of the effects of the German propaganda at the outbreak of the war with their attempt to gain Arab support for the Holy War. It also gives an insight into the change in Arab outlook following the Turkish failure to defeat the British army at the Suez Canal.

ABDULLAH I, KING OF TRANSJORDAN
**Memoirs of King Abdullah of Transjordan,** edited by Philip P. Graves.
London: Cape. 1950.
*278 pp., illus., refs., app., index, 20 cms.*

The outbreak of war saw no real involvement of the Arab provinces save for the tying down of British forces in Egypt and latterly to defend Iraq against British attacks. The situation in the Arab provinces was not helped by the fact that the regular troops, which in Iraq were nearly all Arabs, were withdrawn to defend Turkish provinces whilst their own country was overrun. It was against this background that the correspondence between Hussein and MacMahon began leading to the Sherifian forces joining the war on the side of the Allies in return for various post-war pledges.

The account then deals with the Revolt and the part played by the Arab forces concluding with the taking of Damascus in October and the installation of an Arab government under Faisal.

*ALDINGTON, RICHARD
**Lawrence of Arabia:** A biographical enquiry.
*London: Collins. 1955.*
*448 pp., illus., maps, bibl., index, 21 cms.*

Probably the most critical biography of Lawrence yet written which on its publication caused a great debate as to the validity of Aldington's conclusions. However, it did create the climate for a reappraisal of Lawrence which perhaps influenced later biographers, though it is not certain that all of Aldington's assertions were correct. The work is also critical of the Arab Revolt and of course of Lawrence's role. 'And one cannot escape the conviction that much of the history of the Arab war was simply political propaganda designed to prove that the Arabs had captured certain areas and towns (and therefore were obliged under British promises to be ruled by Lawrence's friend Feisal independently though perhaps not unsubsidised), though in fact the real work was done by English, Scottish, Anzac and Indian troops.'

The remainder of the biography continues in the same vein including the consideration of the Peace Conference and the question of the Cairo Conference but despite the highly critical nature of the work it is a useful study of the Middle East at this time.

BIRWOOD, LORD
**Nuri As-Said:** A study in Arab leadership.
*London: Cassell. 1959.*
*xi, 306 pp., frontis., illus., maps, glossary, bibl., index, 22 cms.*

In 1914 Nuri As-Said realised that he could no longer serve Turkey in its alliance with Germany and before he could be arrested he fled to Cairo and from there to Baghdad. After the outbreak of war he became an unwilling guest of the Indian Government for nearly a year until his transfer to Cairo in 1915. Whilst in Cairo he remained in contact with other Arab leaders until the outbreak of the Arab Revolt when he went to the Hedjaz with a number of Iraqi volunteers. The rest of the section is taken up with a description of the campaign in the desert until the fall of Damascus in 1918.

BRAY, N. N. E.
**A Paladin of Arabia:** The biography of Brevet Lieutenant-Colonel G. E. Leachman of the Royal Sussex Regiment.
*London: John Heritage. 1936.*
*xvi, 429 pp., illus., maps, 20 cms.*

As a political agent Leachman played a large part in establishing Britain's position in Mesopotamia especially after the disastrous events at Kut, though he was, at times, at variance with the attitudes of Philby.

During the revolt in Mesopotamia Leachman played a significant part in trying to bring about a settlement, as for two months he held the peace in the area of his administration before being assassinated by extremists. Although the efforts of Leachman and the other political officers were attacked by Lawrence in his letters to *The Times* Bray considers them unfounded as he knew little of the situation in Mesopotamia where unrest was being fermented by extremists operating from Syria using money supplied by Faisal.

*BRAY, MAJOR N. N. E.
**Shifting Sands.**
*London: Unicorn Press. 1934.*
*xii, 312 pp., frontis., illus., maps, index, 21½ cms.*

The author served with the Indian army prior to seeing service in Arabia and in his foreword he states that he wrote the book because of pressure from others who served with him during the Arab Revolt and because of the distorted view that had been presented of the Revolt by other writers.

The work is extremely critical of the Arab Revolt, its leaders, including Lawrence, and its tactics. Also criticised are the political undercurrents especially the Sykes–Picot agreement which was a direct contradiction of the promises made to the Arabs and should have been given to the Arabs and not concealed until after the war was over and the Arabs had served their purpose.

*DJEMAL PASHA
**Memoirs of a Turkish Statesman, 1913–1919.**
*London: Hutchinson. 1922.*
*302 pp., 22½ cms.*

These memoirs are of significance in considering the Turkish attitude towards Arab nationalism during the World War I. Djemal Pasha became Commander of the Turkish armies in Syria and Western Arabia and was responsible for the offensive against the Suez Canal and the subsequent repression of the Arabs in Syria. The repression was pursued with a single mindedness of purpose and direction and resulted in the execution of several high-ranking Syrian nationalists.

In this work Djemal Pasha seeks to justify his policy in Syria citing the interests of Turkey as his first consideration and secondly the fact that he considered the nationalists as traitors for whilst they voiced support for Turkey they were at the same time negotiating with the British to enter the war against Turkey.

The section dealing with the Arab Revolt falls on pp. 197–237.

EDMONDS, C. J.
**Gertrude Bell in the Near and Middle East.**
*Royal Central Asian Journal. Vol. LVI, Part III, October 1969, pp. 229–244.*

A great deal of this article is not relevant to this study as it deals with Gertrude Bell's travels in Arabia. However, the article also deals with her work in Iraq during the war as a member of the

Intelligence Branch of G.H.Q. Mesopotamian Expeditionary Force. In July 1916 she was transferred to the Political Department working closely with Sir Percy Cox and participating in the Civil Administration of the occupied areas.

Gertrude Bell's outlook was liberal in every sense of the word and much in sympathy with President Wilson's proposals for world peace, although initially she held the view that 'this country would be very easy to govern in the early stages . . . the stronger the hold we are able to keep the better the inhabitants will be pleased; they can't conceive an Arab Government, nor, I confess, can I'.

ERSKINE, MRS. STEWART
**King Faisal of Iraq.**
*London: Hutchinson & Co. 1933.*
*288 pp., illus., app., index, 23½ cms.*

The account of the Arab Revolt is a straightforward narration of the events from the initial uprising in the Hedjaz to the fall of Damascus. It also deals with the provisional Arab Government in Damascus which was fraught with problems as Faisal 'was surrounded by jealousy and discontent; jealousy expressed by the Syrians who resented the war-time followers of the Amir, Bedouin and Baghdadi, remaining in his suite and discontent because the situation was obscure'.

Further complication was caused by the French claim on Syria especially as it was believed that they were diametrically opposed to Arab independence. 'On one side, therefore, the Amir was faced by anti-French propaganda and on the other by the Central Syrian Committee which was formed under French influence and definitely opposed to the Sherifian party.'

*GARDNER, BRIAN
**Allenby**
*London: Cassell. 1965.*
*xx, 314 pp., illus., maps, bibl., index, 21½ cms.*
*(pp. 116–254.)*

The section of interest to this study begins with the section dealing with Allenby's period in the Middle East during the war. In this area the author considers Allenby's support for the Arab Revolt and the part played by the Arab armies on Allenby's right flank. The account deals with the taking of Jerusalem and the advance on Damascus which brought to a conclusion the Arab Revolt and the Ottoman Empire in the Arab provinces. In his last despatch of the war Allenby wrote of the Arab army:

'The Arab army has rendered valuable assistance, both in cutting the enemy's communications before and during the operations, and in co-operating with my cavalry during the advance on Damascus. By throwing itself across the enemy's line of retreat north of Deraa it prevented the escape of portions of the 4th Turkish Army, and inflicted heavy casualties on the enemy.'

GRAVES, ROBERT
**Lawrence and the Arabs.**
*London: Cape. 1927.*
*454 pp., frontis., illus., app., index, 20½ cms.*

This work is included for the account of the Arab Revolt and the Middle East War and because it was one of the two biographies authorised by Lawrence. Its value must be judged in the light of its reliance on 'Seven Pillars' and on Lawrence himself. It is for this reason that an examination of this work is not made in depth as it varies little from Lawrence's own writings.

HART, B. H. LIDDELL
**T. E. Lawrence in Arabia and after.**
*London: Cape. 1934.*
*490 pp., frontis., illus., maps, index, 22 cms.*

Originally conceived as a military study of the Middle East War this work became largely a study of the Arab Revolt and Lawrence's role. Liddell Hart feels that Lawrence's understanding of the war, and the tactics that he evolved, were far superior to many of the regular army officers though the importance of the Arab Revolt in relation to the campaign as a whole is not over-emphasised. Liddell Hart felt though that 'but for him [Lawrence] the Arab Revolt would have remained a collection of slight and passing incidents'.

KIRKBRIDE, ALEC SEATH
**A Crackle of thorns:** Experiences in the Middle East.
*London: John Murray. 1956.*
*viii, 201 pp., illus., map, index, 21½ cms.*

The author was a lieutenant in the British Army when in 1918 he was sent to examine the prospects of supplying the Arab army from Palestine instead of Egypt and to improve the collection of intelligence. It was from these beginnings that Kirkbride began his association with Lawrence and the Arab army with Kirkbride commanding the Iraqi artillery in the Hedjaz. On Lawrence

Kirkbride wrote that 'his undoubted courage and feats of endurance, combined with a flair for a rather flamboyant stage management of his warlike exploits, was just what was needed to impress and to appeal to the Arab mentality'.

*KNIGHTLEY, PHILIP AND SIMPSON, COLIN
**The Secret lives of Lawrence of Arabia.**
*London : Nelson. 1969.*
*x, 293 pp., plates, bibl., index, 23 cms.*

This is an important work in a consideration of the Middle East during this period and Lawrence's role in these events mainly because the authors had access to the Lawrence papers in the Bodleian Library, closed to public scrutiny until the year 2000, and because material in the Public Record Office relating to the period became available. As this is a biography a great deal of the book is not relevant to this study dealing as it does with the period prior to the Arab Revolt and his life following the Cairo Conference.

Prior to the outbreak of the Arab Revolt Lawrence was based in Cairo as an Intelligence Officer and he was subsequently involved in the abortive attempt to ransom Townshend's force besieged at Kut. However, this was not his only mission as he was charged with investigating possibilities of an Arab Revolt. 'According to Suleiman Fedi, a member of the Ottoman Parliament before the war, Lawrence asked him to collect a force and rebel against the Turks, promising him a virtually unlimited supply of gold to do this. Fedi declined the offer.'

The Arab Revolt began in June 1916 in the Hedjaz and Lawrence was attached to Emir Faisal's army as liaison officer to ensure that the Revolt ran in Britain's favour. Lawrence knew that the promises of freedom and independence he made to the Arabs were dead promises as Britain's imperial policy, 'a policy he has had in formulating – will make these promises "dead paper".' Despite this Lawrence attempted to work out a compromise whilst still carrying out his mission and his success is evidenced by the fact that Faisal linked his fortunes to those of Britain through the war.

This section on the Revolt also deals with the Sykes–Picot agreement the full impact of which was kept from the Arabs in case they should cease fighting. Lawrence and Hogarth attempted to undermine the agreement, not because of its betrayal of the Arabs, but because it gave the French rights in Syria which did not fit in with the plans of the Arab Bureau. 'In outright opposition to official policy, he was working on a scheme to get Faisal into Damascus before the Allies and establish him there, by force if necessary, as ruler of Syria. He hoped that his government, presented with a fait accompli, would come to its senses, renounce the Sykes–Picot agreement, and support Hussein, or preferably his son Feisal, as ruler of Syria under British protection.'

The Arab army moved into Damascus in October 1918 and a provisional Arab government was set up with Faisal at its head and Lawrence left the Middle East with the situation in Syria completely unresolved. Unrest was rife and Lawrence's sudden departure aroused even greater suspicion and an uprising was threatening the liberated areas. The result was the Anglo-French declaration which promised national governments in the liberated areas. 'It was not until the Peace Conference six months later that the Arabs began to suspect they had been sold short and that the declaration was not worth the ink in which it had been written.'

MONROE, ELIZABETH
**Philby of Arabia.**
*London: Faber. 1973.*
*332 pp., illus., maps, notes, bibl., index, 22½ cms.*

The earliest part of this biography that is relevant to this study is the chapter beginning with the period spent in Mesopotamia between 1915–17. Philby arrived in Mesopotamia in 1915 in response to a request from Sir Percy Cox for linguists to act as civilian administrators for the areas occupied as the army moved north towards Baghdad. It was Philby's task to study the finances of the occupied territory and to draw up a regular system of civil accounts, a task for which his work in the Indian Civil Service proved invaluable.

It was during this period that Philby first came into contact with Ibn Saud as he travelled to see him with a view to persuading Ibn Saud to take action against his rival Ibn Rashid of Hail who was cooperating with the Turks. The second part of the mission was to persuade Ibn Saud to act against Hussein whose support was being sought by the British through the Arab Bureau at Cairo. In 1917 Philby also travelled to Jidda to meet with Storrs and Hussein to try and settle this rivalry but Hussein was incensed at any mention of Ibn Saud causing Philby to telegraph Cox as follows:

'What he really wants is outward and visible sign of Saud's acceptance of his kingship, rather than any independent action as our ally . . .'

MORRIS, JAMES
**The Hashemite Kings.**
*London: Faber and Faber. 1959.*
*231 pp., illus., bibl., index, 22 cms.*

The section entitled 'The Sons' deals with the life of Faisal beginning with his part in the Arab Revolt, over which he had assumed active control as commander of the Arab army, though in theory the overall leadership was nominally in the hands of his father. The biography then traces the story of the Revolt from the original uprising in the Hedjaz through the capture of Akaba to the fall of Damascus. It is a straightforward narrative though to cover the full story this section must be read in conjunction with that dealing with Hussein.

MOUSA, SULEIMAN
**T. E. Lawrence:** An Arab view.
*London: O.U.P. 1966.*
*x, 301 pp., bibl., index, 22 cms.*

An important biography of Lawrence as it is the first full-length study of Lawrence by an Arab. The Arab Revolt is dealt with in great depth though it is also a highly critical study of the motives of Britain and Lawrence.

NUTTING, ANTHONY
**Lawrence of Arabia:** The man and the motive.
*London: Hollis and Carter. 1961.*
*256 pp., illus., maps, bibl., index, 22 cms.*

A biography of Lawrence which tends to follow the line that Lawrence himself took but it is useful for its account of the Arab Revolt and the Peace Conference.

ROLLS, S. C.
**Steel chariots in the desert.**
*London: Cape. 1937.*
*286 pp., illus., maps, 20 cms.*

An extremely readable account of the Arab Revolt by one of the armoured car drivers attached to Faisal's army and subsequently Lawrence's driver.

STITT, GEORGE
**A Prince of Arabia:** The Emir Shereef Ali Haider.
*London: Allen & Unwin. 1948.*
*314 pp., plates, bibl., app., 21½ cms.*

A biography of Sherif Ali Haider who was a direct descendant of the Prophet and a member of the same family as Hussein. His grandfather had been Emir of Mecca until 1865 when he was deposed by the Turks in favour of another branch of the family and the one to which Hussein belonged. This was part of the Turkish policy of playing off one branch of the family against another to ensure loyalty and obedience. It was not until 1916 when Hussein proclaimed the Arab Revolt that the Turks recognised Ali Haider as Emir but he was unable to establish his authority.

The book gives an insight into the intrigues which accompanied the politics of the Turkish Empire both in the Arab Provinces and in Istanbul. A useful account of the position of the Arabs in the Ottoman Empire following the Arab Revolt is also given and it illustrates the fact that the majority of the Arabs were not actively anti-Turkish and indeed many of them thought the conflict of little concern to them. In dealing with the period following the armistice the work deals with the attempts of Ali Haider to maintain a position of authority within the Arab world and the way in which the Turkish government repaid his loyalty during the war. The value of this work is enhanced by the extracts from the Emir's diaries upon which the biography is largely based.

STORRS, RONALD
**Orientations.**
*London: Nicholson and Watson. 1937.*
*xviii, 575 pp., illus., maps, index, 21 cms.*

During the war Storrs spent a period as Political Liaison Officer at Baghdad and this period is dealt with by extracts from the author's contemporary diaries in which he describes his meetings with, and impressions of, Arnold Wilson, Gertrude Bell, Philby and Sir Percy Cox. Following the fall of Jerusalem to the forces of Allenby he was transferred to Jerusalem to become Military Governor.

The next section of the biography deals with this period up to the appointment of Sir Herbert Samuel as High Commissioner. This period saw the beginnings of the implementation of the Balfour Declaration and the growing unrest amongst the Arab population resulting in various civil disturbances. In the main this situation is dealt with from the British aspect and the problems of the administration though it is apparent that Storrs had sympathy for both sections of the community.

# Section 2

# The Peace Settlement and its consequences

This section deals with the period following the armistice covering the Arab case at the Peace Conference, the rivalry between Hussein and Ibn Saud, Arab reactions to the plans for Palestine and the Cairo Conference of 1921.

## (a) Arab case at the Peace Conference and the resultant settlement.

This section considers the aspirations of the Arabs regarding the Peace Conference in the light of the McMahon–Hussein correspondence and the conflicting interests of France together with the abortive King–Crane Commission and the resultant settlement.

The Arab case at the peace conference was based on the promises made by Britain in the McMahon–Hussein correspondence which is dealt with in section 1c on the Arab Revolt. These promises were, however, complicated by the Sykes–Picot agreement and during this period the two agreements became intertwined. The Sykes–Picot agreement itself is an essential study and this is to be found under the heading 'Tripartite (Sykes–Picot) Agreement for the partition of the Ottoman Empire: Britain, France and Russia, 26 April–23 October 1916' with the text being reproduced in Woodward and Butler's *Documents of British Foreign Policy, 1919–39*, 1st series, Vol. IV, and Hurewitz, J. C. *Diplomacy in the Near and Middle East*. The substance of the agreement is also illustrated by the explanatory map showing the proposed spheres of influence of Britain and France.

The complexity of the situation is further added to by the 'Anglo-French Declaration to the Arabs' of November 1918 which, in Arab eyes, qualified the terms of the Sykes–Picot agreement and this can be seen if one examines 'Amir Faysal's Memorandum to the Supreme Council at the Paris Peace Conference' which was presented on 1 January 1919. The Arab case regarding this situation can best be judged by the articles by Rasheeduddin Khan entitled 'The Peace Settlement, Arab Diplomacy and

Anglo-French power politics: 1918–20' which examines the situation in detail and A. L. Tibawi's 'Syria in the McMahon Correspondence: Fresh evidence from the British Foreign Office Records'. The question is also considered by Nevakivi in *Britain, France and the Arab Middle East, 1914–1920* though this work is more concerned with the interaction between the two powers rather than with the Arab cause itself. Antonius' work on the Arab nationalist movement is also of relevance here especially with regard to the position of Faisal.

To provide a study of the Arab case as part of the general peace settlement these are several works on the Peace Conference which do not form part of this study except in a related way. However, of special interest are Stephen Bonsal's study *Suitors and Supplicants* which deals with the small nations at the Peace Conference, Harold Nicolson's *Peacemaking 1919* and the biographies of T. E. Lawrence by Aldington, Graves and Liddell Hart.

### (b) The rivalry between Hussein and Ibn Saud.

This section considers the conflict between Sherif Hussein of the Hedjaz and Ibn Saud of the Nejd, a situation which was apparent before the Arab Revolt but which had been shelved during the war by British support for Hussein and the payment of a subsidy to Ibn Saud in return for his neutrality and cessation of hostilities against the Hedjaz. The end of the war, however, saw a gradual worsening in relations between Hussein and Britain and his refusal to sign a treaty opened the way for Ibn Saud to move against Hussein and to occupy the Hedjaz thus taking over administration of the Holy Places.

Of particular interest in this section is Elizabeth Monroe's *Philby of Arabia* which deals in depth with the conflict between the two rulers and the two British Government departments involved. The subject is treated in similar vein by Powell in *The Struggle for power in Moslem Asia* in which he stresses that Hussein's survival rested on the subsidy paid to Ibn Saud. Presenting the Hashemite case are the memoirs of Abdullah I, King of Transjordan with the British view, being presented by Gilbert Clayton's *Arabia and the Arabs* and *An Arabian Diary* and Sir Ronald Storrs' autobiography *Orientations*.

### (c) The Arab position in relation to the Palestine Mandate.

This section considers the question of Palestine and the Arabs from the British military administration to the granting of the mandate and the question of Transjordan. In this period of limbo the area was under the control of a British military administration followed by a Civil administration with Sir Herbert Samuel as High Commissioner.

The Arab case and the problems of the Balfour Declaration can be examined through the Balfour Declaration itself and the Foreign Office 'Report of a committee set up to consider certain correspondence between Sir Henry McMahon and the Sherif of Mecca in 1915 and 1916'. The Arab case is also argued in an article by Sharif al-Miyahid entitled *Arab Nationalism: a historical analysis* and the pamphlet produced by the Arab Office of Jerusalem entitled 'The Problem of Palestine: Memorandum presented to the Anglo-American Committee of Enquiry' which although arguing the case following World War II does relate largely to the period of this study.

The question of the Arab–Jewish discussions to achieve an understanding is dealt with by Jon Kimche in *Palestine or Israel: The untold story of why we failed 1917–1923: 1967–1973* and in articles by Yosef Lumtz and M. Perlemann both of whom deal with contacts between the Arab nationalists and the Zionists.

The view of the British administration is put by Ashbee in *A Palestine Notebook, 1918–1923*; Sir Ronald Storrs in *Orientations* and most clearly by Kimche's work already mentioned. The official documents regarding this period are contained in Butler and Bury's *Documents on British Foreign Policy, 1919–39*, 1st series, Vol. XIII, and extremely useful as a visual interpretation is Martin Gilbert's *The Arab–Israeli conflict: Its history in maps*.

The situation in Transjordan is not so well represented as it did not assume real significance until the Cairo Conference being administered in a loosely organised manner and excluded from the terms of the Balfour Declaration. Events in Transjordan during this period are covered by Peake's article 'Transjordan' and in Philby's article of the same name; by White in *The Process of change in the Ottoman Empire* and briefly by Kirkbride in *A Crackle of Thorns* which is mainly concerned with the period following the Cairo Conference.

### (d) The Cairo Conference.

The Cairo Conference held in March 1921 was an attempt by Churchill to tidy up the problems of the Middle East which had not been resolved by the Peace Settlement. It was concerned with three main areas, the need to reduce financial and military commitments in Iraq, the problem of Palestine and Transjordan and the position of Sherif Hussein in the Hedjaz.

The major contribution to this study is Aaron Klieman's *Foundations of British policy in the Arab World: The Cairo Conference of 1921* which deals with the subject in depth considering the background to British policy in the Middle East, the conflicting promises made to the Arabs and the French, the Peace Conference and the settlement, and the continuing problems of the Middle East. The actual conference is also considered in some detail as are the solutions arrived at and an assessment made as to the success or failure of the conference. The official account is represented by the Colonial Office 'Report on the Middle East Conference, Cairo and Jerusalem, March 12th to 30th 1921'. Other more general accounts are to be found in the various biographies of T. E. Lawrence.

The question of Iraq is dealt with in several contributions amongst which are Sir Percy Cox's article entitled 'Iraq'; Mrs. Erskine's biography of Faisal and H. A. Foster's *The Making of modern Iraq: A product of world forces* with personal observations in Volume II of the 'Letters of Gertrude Bell'. A detailed discussion of the subject is provided by two articles by Rasheeduddin Khan 'Mandate and the creation of the Hashemite Monarchy in Iraq: 1919–1921'. Further studies are those of Elie Kedourie's *England and the Middle East: The destruction of the Ottoman Empire, 1914–1921* which has a section on Mesopotamia covering the period 1918–21 and Powell's *The struggle for power in Moslem Asia*. Opposition to Faisal's candidature is dealt with in Elizabeth Monroe's biography *Philby of Arabia* which considers the administrative structure in Iraq and the opposition of officials such as the Minister of the Interior, Seyyid Talib.

The situation in Palestine and Transjordan is dealt with in Baha Uddin Touka's *A short history of Transjordan*. This aspect of the conference is also considered by Desmond Stewart in his *Middle East: Temple of Janus* and by Alec Seath Kirkbride in *A Crackle of Thorns*. Also of interest are the various biographies of T. E. Lawrence cited in this section.

The problem of Sherif Hussein was relatively minor when measured against that of Iraq and the Palestine–Transjordan questions as his presence was no longer crucial to British policies in the Middle East. All of the biographies of Lawrence deal with the question as does Desmond Stewart in *Middle East: Temple of Janus* and Storrs in *Orientations*, more specific, however, is the article by Gaster entitled 'Lawrence and King Hussein; the 1921 negotiations'.

In all these aspects of the Cairo Conference, however, the one indispensable work is that by Klieman which must form the basis for any study of this event which was of great importance as is stressed by Klieman. 'And in its recognition of the importance of the Middle East for any global power and for world politics it has not been equalled since, not by Great Britain nor by the United States.'

# (a) ARAB CASE AT THE PEACE CONFERENCE AND THE RESULTANT SETTLEMENT

## GENERAL WORKS

*ALLEN, RICHARD
**Imperialism and nationalism in the Fertile Crescent:**
Sources and prospects of the Arab–Israeli conflict.
*London: O.U.P. 1974.*
*x, 686 pp., maps, bibl., index, 20½ cms.*
*(Chapter 10, pp. 247–259.)*

The Peace Conference was a disaster in so far as the Arab cause was concerned and in this section the author deals with the Conference itself, the conflict between Faisal and the French and the Zionist lobby at Versailles. The subject of the King–Crane Commission is also dealt with though its recommendations were never presented. The conference finally agreed on a settlement which satisfied the Allies but did little for the Arab cause.

'Whatever reasons of state, ambition, or confused purposes governed the actions of the Allies, and particularly the British, in these crucial years, the treatment of the Arab peoples during and after World War I – and the consequences for the Jewish return to the Holy Land and for Western standing in the Middle East – lay a heavy burden on those responsible, and one in which their descendents can take no pride.'

BEN-HORIN, ELIAHU
**The Middle East:** Crossroads of history.
*New York: W. W. Norton & Co. 1943.*
*248 pp., map, index, 21½ cms.*

FISHER, SYDNEY NETTLETON
**The Middle East:** A history.
*London: Routledge & Kegan Paul. 2nd ed. 1971.*
*xxx, 749 pp., maps, bibl., index, 22 cms.*

See Section 1a for annotation.
The chapter of relevance to this section is as follows:
Part IV. The Contemporary Middle East.
Chapter 29. The Middle East at the Paris Peace Conference.

IZZEDDIN, NEJLA
**The Arab world:** Past, present and future.
*Chicago: Henry Regnery Co. 1953.*
*xvi, 412 pp., illus., index, 24 cms.*

This work includes a consideration of the political implications of the Arab Revolt and in particular the Sykes–Picot agreement in relations between the Arabs and the Allies at the Peace Conference. Consideration is also given to the evolving of the Mandate system which came out of the peace settlement and is considered as a betrayal of the Arab cause by the Great Powers and in particular Britain and France.

\*LENCZOWSKI, GEORGE
**The Middle East in world affairs.**
*New York: Cornell University Press. 2nd ed. 1956.*
*xix, 576 pp., maps, bibl., index, 24 cms.*

Chapter Three deals with the Peace Settlement and begins by summarising the contradictory claims and attitudes assumed by the participants dealing with the conflict between Britain and France, the claims of the Arabs, the Zionist case and the position of the Americans, together with other claims not relevant to this study. The King–Crane Commission is also discussed but the report was never presented to the Peace Conference being buried in the archives of the American delegation.

The question of the assignment of the mandates was left to the San Remo Conference of 1920 but the Arab cause was lost once the principles of the mandate system had been accepted by the Allies. The result was that France assumed responsibility for Syria and Britain assumed responsibility for Iraq and Palestine.

RAPPARD, W. E.
**The Practical working of the mandates system.**
*Journal British Institute International Affairs. September 1925, pp. 205–226.*

This article does not deal with any specific mandate but is a consideration of the system in general terms. The system was designed to provide an administration for countries not able to govern themselves with the eventual aim that the people should be guided and trained until they were fit to govern themselves and to merit independence.

The article also considers the work of the mandate commission and dwells at some length on Article 22 of the Covenant of the League of Nations under which the mandates were set up. The author stresses that if they are to be regarded as a success the countries administering the mandates must be conscious of their international obligations and their obligations to the peoples of the country being administered.

RUSTOW, DONKWART A.
**The Central Islamic lands in recent times:** The political impact of the West.
*In: Cambridge History of Islam.*
*Vol. 1, The Central Islamic lands, pp. 673–697.*

SAYEGH, FAYEZ A.
**Arab unity: Hope and fulfillment.**
*New York: Devin-Adair Co. 1958.*
*xvii, 272 pp., notes, app., index, 21 cms.*

STEWART, DESMOND
**The Middle East:** Temple of Janus.
*London: Hamish Hamilton. 1972.*
*viii, 414 pp., bibl., index, 24 cms.*

In considering the Peace Conference it is stressed that the Sykes–Picot agreement and the Balfour Declaration were bitter blows to the Arabs but the dependence of the Hashemites on Britain meant that all they could do was press for the fulfilment of the wartime pledges. Faisal was refused official recognition as a delegate to the peace conference by the French and in the negotiations that followed Britain decided that the oilfields of northern Iraq, which France was prepared to exchange for British support over Damascus, were more important than supporting Faisal's claim to Syria.

Britain was also tied by the question of the Zionist designs in Palestine and the need to protect the Suez canal and the communications with India. This led to Britain being given the mandate for Palestine despite Arab protests that this had been promised as part of the independent Arab States. The Syrians attempted to oppose French control over Syria but despite the evidence of the King–Crane Commission the French were given the mandate for Syria which it had to assume by force.

TIBAWI, A. L.
**A modern history of Syria including Lebanon and Palestine.**
*London: Macmillan. 1969.*
*441 pp., plates, maps, notes, bibl., index, 23 cms.*

# THE PEACE CONFERENCE–GENERAL WORKS

ARAKIE, MARGARET
**Broken sword of justice.**
*London: Quartet Books. 1974.*
*195 pp., bibl., index, 21½ cms.*

An examination of the American role in dealing with the Palestine question much of which is irrelevant to this study by nature of period. The earlier part of this study is of interest, however, as it considers the background to the situation prior to the Peace Conference and the King–Crane Commission. The report of the commission was shelved as neither America nor Britain would accept a mandate for Syria and the French refused to give up their claim. 'But although it officially remained a deal better, it was, in the view of some experts, not without influence in strengthening the British Government's subsequent tendency to restrict and moderate Zionist aspirations.'

\*BONSAL, STEPHEN
**Suitors and Supplicants.**
*New York: Prentice Hall. 1946.*
*xvi, 301 pp., app., index, 23 cms.*

The author was attached to the Peace Conference and this is an account of the arguments and pleas put forward by the small nations including the Arab states. The section covering the Arab case appears on pages 32–51, though this should also be linked to the presentation of the Zionist viewpoint pages 56–57.

LEBOW, RICHARD NED
**The Morgenthau Peace Mission of 1917.**
*Jewish Social Studies. Vol. 32, October 1970, pp. 267–285.*

A consideration of the peace mission by Morgenthau which aimed at concluding a separate peace with Turkey which, amongst other things, would have secured the autonomy of the Arab provinces. It is considered that the motive was one of anti-Zionism as a separate peace would have dashed the hopes for a Jewish National Home in Palestine. Although Morgenthau was a Jew he saw the Zionist movement as a purely political movement which 'threatened to undermine the status of Jews in those states where they had been accorded citizenship'.

The proposal was doomed to failure due to doubts about Morgenthau's possible support for Germany, the Zionist opposition as represented by Weizmann and the dangers inherent in peace talks with Turkey. 'The road was clear for a closer alliance between Britain and Zionism and for the publication of a declaration of sympathy with Zionist aspirations.'

LOUIS, WILLIAM ROGER
**The United Kingdom and the beginning of the Mandates System, 1919–1922.**
*International Organisation. Vol. XXIII, No. 1, Winter 1969, pp. 73–96.*

Not all of this article is of relevance as it deals with the mandates as a whole and not just with the Middle East. However, the general introductory section examining the nature of the mandate system is of interest as are the concluding sections dealing with the meaning of the mandate system and its legacy.

The author deals with the class A mandates in the Middle East relating to Syria, Iraq, and Palestine, the first two complicated by the Zionist problem. In this area concern was not so much for the inhabitants but for the interests of America, France and Britain each with differing policies to pursue. Indeed two quotations will serve to illustrate this point, the first being a memorandum from Churchill to Balfour on 21 October 1921 which stated '. . . we are committed in Palestine to the Zionist policy against which ninetenths of the population and an equal proportion of the British officers are marshalled.'

The second quotation is from a memorandum by Balfour in which he discusses the question of consulting the wishes of the inhabitants with regard to the three possible mandatories for Syria. 'Are we going "chiefly to consider the wishes of the inhabitants" in deciding which of these is to be selected? We are going to do nothing of the kind. England has refused. America will refuse. So that, whatever the inhabitants may wish, it is France they will certainly have. They may freely choose; but it is Hobson's choice after all.'

MANUEL, FRANK E.
**The Palestine question in Italian Diplomacy, 1917–1920.**
*Journal of Modern History. Vol. 27, No. 3, September 1955, pp. 263–280.*

A discussion of the attempts made by the Italians to gain equal participation in the government of an internationalised Palestine based upon the Treaty of London where the principle of fair shares among the Allies in the dismemberment of Turkey had been asserted. However, the Sykes–Picot agreement of the following year, 1916, had divided the Arab provinces of the Ottoman Empire between France and Britain without reference to Italy. After the Balfour Declaration in 1917 the Italians actively supported the Zionist cause and only acquiesced regarding the mandate following assurances over the custody of the Holy Places.

\*Monroe, Elizabeth
**Britain's moment in the Middle East, 1914–1956.**
*London: Chatto & Windus. 1963.*
*254 pp., maps, notes, bibl., index, 22 cms.*

Section two of this work is entitled 'Together at the Peace, 1919–22' and deals with British and French rivalries at the Peace Conference over the Middle East settlement and the conflict between the wishes of the two powers and the Arab case. The result was a compromise between the two powers which left the Arab aspirations severely curtailed as the British troops evacuated Syria leaving the French to occupy the Lebanon with Faisal holding the inland towns. In return Britain added the oil-bearing provinces of Mosul to the mandate for Iraq and these agreements were confirmed by the San Remo Conference in 1920 as was the British mandate for Palestine.

Monroe, Elizabeth
**The Round Table and the Middle Eastern Peace Settlement, 1917–1922.**
*Round Table. Vol. 60, November 1970, pp. 479–490.*

A consideration of the influences brought to bear by the *Round Table* in Britain's attitudes towards the Peace Settlement in the Middle East. Part of the attitude can be realised from a series of articles in the journal by Lionel Curtis which argued that 'for the derelict territories severed from Turkey, some democratic guardian state must be responsible to the League of Nations for ensuring equality of opportunity for outsiders, for fitting the people to govern themselves, and for precluding forced labour and the raising of troops other than for local duties'.

As the peace conference developed and the influence of the Americans increased the influence of the *Round Table* group waned and it fell back on the role of attempting to pick out the points that mattered and telling the truth about what was going on.

\*Nevakivi, Jukka
**Britain, France and the Arab Middle East, 1914–1920.**
*London: Athlone Press. 1969.*
*xiv, 284 pp., maps, app., bibl., index, 22½ cms.*

The book deals exclusively with the relationship between Britain and France in the Arab Middle East from the outbreak of World War I until the San Remo Conference of 1920. Essentially the work is outside the scope of this study as it deals only indirectly with the Arab nationalist movement but its inclusion is justified by the direct bearing that the policies of these two countries both separately and jointly had on the nationalist cause in the Middle East.

The work begins with an introductory section covering the position of Britain and France in the Middle East prior to 1914 leading into an examination of the war period up to the Sykes–Picot agreement. It continues by dealing with the final period of the war to the armistice of 1918 during which the Sykes–Picot agreement was subjected to a great deal of questioning especially by the Arabs in relation to the promises from Britain and the Balfour Declaration.

The question of the peace settlement is dealt with at some length especially the Arab position in Syria and its conflict with the aims of France. It is made clear that the Arab question had involved the peace conference in a series of attempted political compromises to achieve some agreement between Faisal and the French but rapprochement was not easy as Faisal was not willing to compromise and in this attitude he was backed by Colonel Lawrence. The question of Syria caused a strain in relations between the two countries not made easier by the attitude of Clemenceau who 'was archaic and blind in his incomprehension of the force of the new nationalism in the east'.

Nevakivi then deals with the failure of Faisal in Syria caused as much by his failure to reach agreement with the French as by the Arab nationalists' attitude to his apparent ineffectiveness and willingness to place Syria under the mandatory power. Indeed in a conversation with an American peace delegate Lawrence is reported to have said 'the Arab National Movement feeds on an opposition and would fall to pieces in six months without it; hence the French are probably helping it'.

The work ends by considering the re-establishment of the entente after the provisional settlement in 1919 and the San Remo Conference on 1920. In dealing with the San Remo Conference the author also deals with the armed rising of the Iraqi nationalists in protest, a move assisted by the Iraqi-born officers in Damascus who were members of 'al Ahd. Nevakivi's conclusion is that British policy in the Middle East was hampered by the need to try and satisfy three conflicting promises made to the French, Arabs and Jews, and that the entente with France caused resentment from the Arabs causing endless damage to the reputation of the two countries in the Middle East.

The book is well indexed and has an extremely detailed bibliography which lists primary sources official and unofficial, published and unpublished and private papers both published and unpublished, secondary published sources and details of personal interviews given to the author. The appendices reproduce the Anglo-French agreement of 1916, the Anglo-French declaration of 7 November 1918 and the Aide-Memoire in regard to the Occupation of Syria, Palestine and Mesopotamia pending the decision in regard to mandates of 13 September 1919.

NICOLSON, HAROLD
**Peacemaking, 1919.**
*London : Constable. 1933.*
*ix, 378 pp., frontis., illus., 22½ cms.*

This work is a consideration of the Peace Conference as a whole and consequently much of the work is not relevant to this study. Book one is in narrative form and is an examination of the Peace Conference in retrospect, whilst Book Two is entitled 'As it seemed then' and is a series of extracts from Nicolson's diaries covering the period from January 1919 until the Treaty of Versailles.

**The Outlook in the Middle East.**
*The Round Table. Vol. X, December 1919, pp. 55–97.*

This article is divided into three parts the first of which deals with the postponement of the peace settlement following the armistice with Turkey. It considers the reasons for the delay, the main one being the problem of the distribution of the mandates and the problems of ratification of any treaty by America.

The second part of the article considers the responsibilities of the British Commonwealth in the area resulting from the mandates which were likely to be granted to Britain. Consideration is given to the problems of administering the affairs of Mesopotamia, and the attendant problems of Russia and Persia, the problem of Palestine and the Zionist cause.

The final part deals with British policy in relation to Islam and in the context of relations with post-war Turkey and the effects that these would have on Moslem India. The solution of the problem of a large Moslem population in a Christian Commonwealth is seen as a challenge which, if achieved, could have a lasting influence throughout the world.

*Papers Relating to the Foreign Relations of the United States
**The Paris Peace Conference, 1919,** XII.
*Washington: 1947.*
*pp. 749–750.*

This is part of the report of the King–Crane Commission which was sent by President Wilson in 1919 to investigate the wishes of the Syrians and Palestinians with regard to the mandates. It is an essentially impartial statement of the position with the main points being as follows:

1. A freer expression of opinion was made to the authors as Americans than would have been made to a mixed commission.
2. An intense desire for unity of all Syria and Palestine and for as early independence as possible.
3. Repulsion to being made a mere colony of any power and against any kind of French mandate, except in the Lebanon where sections asked for independence with French collaboration.
4. America regarded as first choice for the mandate because of her lack of territorial ambition.
5. The same conditions should hold for Iraq as for Syria.
6. If America should decline then England should be approached but deny all rights and refuse all assistance to France.
7. Vigorous opposition to Zionist plan and Jewish immigration.
8. Complete independence of Mesopotamia and outright opposition to the Sykes–Picot agreement and Balfour Declaration.
9. Political rights should be no less than under Turkey.
10. Arabs considered the Syria–Palestine problem extremely important and recommended strong support for King Faisal.

**Tentative recommendations for President Wilson by the Intelligence Section of the American Delegation to the Peace Conference, 21 January 1919.**
*In: Hurewitz, J. C.*
*Diplomacy in the Near and Middle East, pp. 40–45.*

Only the section of the report relating to the Near and Middle East has been reproduced and Hurewitz points to the pervasive British influence apparent especially with regard to the Territorial aspects as American interests at this time were purely cultural. The sections reproduced are those relating to Constantinople and the Straits, Turkey, Armenia, Mesopotamia, Syria, Palestine and Arabia. In the section dealing with Palestine it was recommended that a separate state of Palestine be established initially under the mandatory control of Great Britain and that it should become a Jewish state.

TOYNBEE, ARNOLD J.
**The World after the Peace Conference:** Being an epilogue to the *History of the Peace Conference of Paris* and a prologue to the *Survey of International Affairs, 1920–1923.*
*London: O.U.P. (for British Institute of International Affairs). 1925.*
*iv, 91 pp., map, 24½ cms.*

A survey of the world after the Peace Conference which attempts to put the changes which took place after the war into an historical perspective and into a probable future. The work considers the form of Middle East nationalism, the manner in which it developed and its probable development.

In a work of this length any treatment can only be sketchy and of course the work is intended to be introductory to the more detailed survey. It does, however, provide a valuable statement of the position at the outbreak of war, the immediate post-war changes and the prospects for the future.

## THE PEACE CONFERENCE – PROBLEM OF THE ARAB PROVINCES.

**\*Amir Faysal's 'Memorandum to the Supreme Council at the Paris Peace Conference', 1 January 1919.**
*In: Hurewitz, J. C.*
*Diplomacy in the Near and Middle East, pp. 38–39.*

The memorandum presented by Faisal to the Peace Conference which purported to speak for Arab Asia, a claim challenged by Ibn Saud and other Arab rulers in the Arabian Peninsula. The memorandum was presented and amplified by Faisal when he appeared before the Supreme Council with T. E. Lawrence and other members of the Hedjaz delegation.

**\*THE ANGLO-FRENCH DECLARATION TO THE ARABS, 7 NOVEMBER 1918.**
*In: Anderson, M. S.*
*The Great Powers and the Near East: 1774–1923, pp. 166–167.*

This declaration was issued a month after the fall of Damascus and was regarded by the Arabs as superseding the Sykes–Picot agreement but this was not the view of the Allies, especially the French. It thus represented a further complication in the tangled web of contradictory obligations entered into by the Allies prior to the Peace Conference.

The declaration expressed the views of the Allies regarding the liberated Arab provinces with the prospect of freely chosen national governments. 'In order to carry out these intentions France and Great Britain are at one in encouraging and assisting the establishment of indigenous Governments and administrations in Syria and Mesopotamia, now liberated by the Allies, and in the territories the liberation of which they are engaged in securing, and recognising these as soon as they are actually established.

*ANTONIUS, GEORGE
**The Arab Awakening:** The story of the Arab nationalist movement.
*London: Hamish Hamilton. 1938.*
*xii, 13–471 pp., maps, app., index, 22 cms.*
*(Chapter XIV, pp. 276–324.)*

The peace settlement was complicated by the Sykes–Picot agreement which is described as 'a shocking document' and by the Balfour Declaration together with other aspirations of the Allies. The settlement was an imposed one as it 'violated both the promises specifically made to them (i.e., the Arabs) and the principles which the Allies had enunciated as the foundations of the future Peace'. The position faced by Faisal was an impossible one as he was fighting the Arab cause in the face of opposition from the French, compromise from the British and Zionist pressure over Palestine. This caused difficulties for Faisal in Syria as the nationalists wanted him to take a stand against the French over Syria and against Britain over the Zionists and Palestine.

The King–Crane Commission is seen as a significant expression of Arab feeling which represented the true desire of the Arabs for the future of Syria. The report was never presented to the conference and the principles of the mandate system were agreed with the assignment of the mandates deferred to the San Remo Conference.

*BUTLER, ROHAN AND BURY, J. P. T. EDS.
**Documents on British Foreign Policy, 1919–1939.**
*First Series. Vol. XIII, The Near and Middle East.*
*January 1920–March 1921.*
*London: H.M.S.O. 1963.*
*lxxxiii, 747 pp., 24½ cms.*

The section of interest to this study begins on page 215 and covers Arabia, Syria and Palestine from 12 February 1920 to 7 January 1921.

The entries are far too detailed to list separately but the subjects covered are of interest to this subject and deal, in general terms, with the situation in Syria at the time of the French occupation, the situation in Palestine prior to the Mandate and the rivalry between Hussein and Ibn Saud.

EDWARDS, JOSIAH
**From Panarabism to Panislamism.**
*Contemporary Review. March 1932, pp. 343–351.*

The Arab cause was dashed by the terms of the Peace Settlement and the San Remo Conference which conflicted with the promises that the Arabs considered had been made to them as a condition of entry into the war. However, the article considers that although the Arab dream was '. . . equally due to Allied propaganda, responsible and irresponsible' and that the 'largely Arab, population of these territories had a case and some legitimate grievances against both the Mandatories and their method of administration' the Arab world had been torn by traditional feuds and needed a strong peace settlement and subsequent rule to bind them together.

FARAH, CAESAR E.
**The Dilemma of Arab nationalism.**
*Die Welt des Islams. 1963, 8, pp. 140–164.*

The Arab nationalists had joined the war on the Allies side on the basis of full independence and unity following the war on the basis of the Hussein–McMahon correspondence, 'When the time of fulfilment came in 1919–20, Fertile Crescent Arabs gained no independence and, worse yet, lost whatever regional unity they had enjoyed under the administration supplied by the Ottomans.' This parcelling out being the result of mandates given by the League of Nations based largely on the Sykes–Picot agreement of 1916.

This also presented a problem to the nationalist movement as any semblance of unity that had been enjoyed was dissipated in the intensified struggle to combat the new system. 'Localism, ethnic and sectarian separatism were emphasised through what may be regarded as a deliberate policy on the part of the mandate authorities to weaken the nationalist cause.'

HOWARD, HARRY N.
**An American experiment in peacemaking:** The King–Crane Commission.
*The Moslem World. Vol. XXXII, No. 2, April 1942, pp. 122–128.*

The Supreme Council shortly after the opening of the Peace Conference had adopted a resolution calling for the partition of the Ottoman Empire and the adoption of a mandate system for those people who were to be trained for political independence. It was suggested by the Americans that because of the Anglo-French military occupation of Syria it was impossible to obtain '. . . an accurate statement of the Syrian point of view except by an examination on the spot by commissioners authorized by the Peace Conference'.

The projected commission as an international unit did not materialise as the British did not go although they offered all assistance and the French made no attempt to assist or to participate. In the end the commission consisted only of the Americans who arrived in Palestine on 10 June 1919. Regarding Palestine the commission found that no 'British or American official here believes it is possible to carry out the Zionist programme except through the support of a large army', in Syria they found complete opposition to any French presence having found 'unexpectedly strong expressions of national feeling'.

The report was presented to the American Commission to Negotiate Peace on 28 August 1919. It was urged that a mandate should be established in Syria with Faisal as the monarch and including the area of Palestine with a modified Zionist programme with the area to be under American or British administration. The mandate for Mesopotamia to be offered to Britain in strict fulfilment of the spirit of the Anglo-French Declaration of 9 November 1918.

*HOWARD, HARRY N.
**The King–Crane Commission.**
*Beirut : Khayats. 1963.*
*xiv, 369 pp., maps, bibl., app., index, 21½ cms.*

An extremely detailed account of the King–Crane Commission which makes use of the private papers of Henry Churchill King and other papers of members of the commission and their advisers.

The work begins by considering the background to the Paris Peace Conference as it affected the Middle East dealing first with the secret treaties between the Allies and their conflict with the promises made to the Arabs. Consideration is then given to the opening of the Peace Conference and the position taken by the Great Powers with the decision being taken to accept the mandate system as a basis for settlement.

The conflicting aspirations at Paris between the Allies and the Arabs led to the decision to call for a commission of enquiry to resolve the problem. The next section of the book deals with the setting up of the commission and the problems associated with it which led to the American members going on their own.

Consideration is then given to the Commission's work in Palestine and Syria dealing first with the problem of Zionism in Palestine and producing a majority viewpoint which felt that the express wish of the Arabs was to be part of a United Independent Syria and this applied to both Moslem and Christian Arabs alike. The Commission found that it was only the Jewish population who favoured the establishment of a Jewish National Home.

The question of Syria forms a large section of the work due to the complicated nature of the problem. It deals with members' initial impressions of the question of Syria and in particular with the Syrian Congress of July 1919 which firmly laid down the political aspirations of the Arabs. The Commission dealt at length with the position of France in Syria and concluded that it was evident that a French mandate would not be acceptable to the Arab population as a whole except amongst the Arab Christian community in the Lebanon.

The remainder of the work deals with the problems of Turkey, the evolvement of an American policy for the Near East, the Treaty of Lausanne and an assessment as to whether or not the King–Crane Commission was worth while.

The appendix reproduces the recommendations of the Commission.

HOWARD, HARRY N.
**The Partition of Turkey:** A diplomatic history, 1913–1923.
*New York: Howard Fertig. 1966.*
*486 pp., maps, notes, index, 23½ cms.*

This work deals with the break up of the Ottoman Empire following World War I and although much of this is outside the scope of this study certain sections are of relevance.

This work considers the results of the Peace Conference in relation to the Ottoman Empire including the break up of the Empire in the Middle East. The settlement in the area is examined in the light of the Sykes–Picot agreement, the McMahon–Hussein correspondence and the dealings between the India Office and Ibn Saud.

*Hurewitz, J. C.
**Diplomacy in the Near and Middle East:** A documentary record, 1914–1956. Vol. II.
*London: Van Nostrand Co. 1956.*
*xviii, 427 pp., index, 23½ cms.*

The main annotation to this work will be found under Section 1c, however, the following are of relevance to this section.

British and Anglo-French statements to the Arabs, January–November 1919 (p. 28).

Amir Faysal's memorandum to the Supreme Council at the Paris Peace Conference, 1 January 1919 (p. 38).

Summary record of a secret meeting of the Supreme Council at Paris to consider the Sykes–Picot agreement, 20 March 1919 (p. 50).

Resolution of the General Syrian Congress at Damascus, 2 July 1919 (p. 62).

Ingrams, Dorren
**Palestine papers 1917–1922:** Seeds of conflict.
*London: John Murray. 1972.*
*xii, 198 pp., illus., maps, notes, index, 22 cms.*

The question of Palestine in the Peace Settlement is dealt with in chapters entitled 'Who shall have Palestine', 'The Peace Conference' and the 'King–Crane Commission'. The crux of the situation was that the Zionists, realising that they could not expect immediate control, pressed for a British trusteeship, the Arabs wanted an independent Arab Palestine possibly forming part of a larger Arab state whilst the French had ideas of a greater Syria which included Palestine. Britain wanted a buffer state between Egypt and a French Syria and she also wished to keep her promises to the Zionists whilst the Americans favoured some form of international control.

The conflicting aims detailed above are examined as is the work of the King–Crane Commission whose task it was to investigate the wishes of the inhabitants of the area. Its proposals and findings were never presented to the Peace Conference and the prospects for an amicable agreement were as far away as ever. The Peace Conference came to an end without any agreement over the future of the Turkish territories in the Middle East but it was assumed that Britain would have the mandate for Palestine and the French the mandate for Syria and Lebanon.

154

KEDOURIE, ELIE
**The Chatham House Version.**
*In: Kedourie, Elie*
*The Chatham House Version and other Middle Eastern Studies,*
*pp. 351-394.*

This chapter discusses the view of the recent history of the Middle East as put forward in the publications of the Royal Institute of International Affairs and although each publication has a disclaimer as to the opinions expressed '. . . the books and other publications dealing with the Middle East which, for some three decades, came out under the auspices of the Institute, are seen on examination to have in common not only a publishers' imprint, but also assumptions, attitudes, and a whole intellectual style which make it possible to speak of the Chatham House Version'.

In particular Kedourie examines the viewpoint of Arnold Toynbee and especially the feeling of guilt regarding the Arabs and Britain's dealings with them. One example is Toynbee's opinion regarding Syria and Palestine which he felt had been unconditionally promised to Hussein and that therefore the Balfour Declaration was incompatible with this promise. This view took no account of the fact that Hussein was informed that all promises were subordinate to their commitments to France and Russia. The question of Toynbee's influence is taken further to demonstrate how this guilt complex influenced other writers for the Institute.

*KEDOURIE, ELIE
**England and the Middle East:** The destruction of the Ottoman Empire, 1914-1921.
*London: Bowes and Bowes. 1956.*
*xiii, 9-236 pp., app., bibl., index, 21½ cms.*
*The Unmaking of the Sykes-Picot Agreement.*

This chapter of Kedourie's work is devoted to the events which caused the Sykes-Picot agreement to be called into question. It is considered that the decline of the agreement began in 1917 with the fall of Baghdad when the British Government through Sykes invited the people to 'unite with your kinsmen in the North, East, South and West' and even further by the July 1918 statement of the military Governor of Jerusalem which 'proclaimed that the Arab Movement would bring back the ancient lustre of past Arab greatness'.

Further official statements refuting the agreement came in

June 1918 in a reply from Wingate to Hussein, following publication of the agreement by the Bolsheviks, in which he wrote that Djamal (i.e. Djamal Pasha) 'has ignored the fact that the subsequent outbreak and the striking success of the Arab Revolt, as well as the withdrawal of Russia, has long ago created an altogether different situation'. The Declaration to the Seven issued in July 1918 although mainly directed against the ambitions of Hussein also disowned the agreement by implication.

The latter part of the chapter deals with the events following the capture of Damascus and the establishment of a provisional Arab Government. An attempt to solve the resultant deadlock between Britain and France was the proposed commission to Syria which the French decided not to participate in and Lloyd George then decided not to send any British representatives which meant that the American Commissioners went on their own. 'The Sykes–Picot scheme was dead. Its doom was announced in the declarations made to Hussein and the Seven Syrians in the last months of the war; it was irreparably damaged by the events which took place at the capture of Damascus; and its fate was sealed by Lloyd George's policy at the Peace Conference in the first half of 1919. There was nothing to replace it.'

\*KHAN, RASHEEDUDDIN
**The Peace Settlement, Arab Diplomacy and Anglo-French power politics, 1919–1920.**
*Islamic Culture. Vol. XLII, No. 2, April 1968, pp. 57–73.*

The early part of the article deals with the Arab case at the Peace Conference which was affected by the position at the time of the armistice with Faisal installed in Damascus, Iraq occupied by the British, conflicting promises and agreements and the question of Palestine. The Arab case foundered on three antagonistic trends, British interests in Iraq and Palestine, French interests in Syria and Lebanon and Zionist designs in Palestine. The situation was further complicated by disagreements between Lloyd George, Clemenceau and Wilson over interpretations of agreements made and the future pattern envisaged by the Great Powers after the armistice.

At the same time as the Arab case was being discussed at the Peace Conference nationalist feeling was running high in Syria and Iraq which did not assist Faisal in the presentation of the Arab case. 'Suspicion about Faisal was growing all round. The French accused him of perfidy, the British were disturbed by his double-talk and his own people were dubious of his secretive moves and underhand dealings.'

*KHAN, RASHEEDUDDIN
**The Peace Settlement, Arab Diplomacy and Anglo-French power politics, 1919–1920.**
*Islamic Culture. Vol. XLIII, No. 3, July 1968, pp. 133–150.*

The second part of this article deals mainly with the unrest among the Arab army officers in the light of the developments at the Peace Conference. 'The fact was,' as Miss Bell had put it, 'the Mesopotamians in Faisal's army . . . were at the root of the nationalist agitation.'

The policy as evolved in Paris, despite the findings of the King–Crane Commission, saw British interests secured in Iraq, Britain installed in Palestine but with increased Zionist pressure and France secure in Syria and Lebanon.

At the same time Faisal had been holding discussions with Weizmann over the question of Palestine and signed an agreement regarding the possibility and need for Arab-Jewish co-operation in Palestine though Faisal added the proviso that '. . . he would abide by the terms of the agreement only on condition that the Arabs obtained their independence as demanded in his memorandum of January 1919'.

The problem of Syria was not solved by the Peace Settlement as it was obvious that the nationalists were not going to co-operate with the French over the mandate. The result was that the French assumed control over Syria by force and Faisal was forced to flee to Palestine. 'On July 25, 1920, with the French in control of Damascus, Faisal banished from the throne, and the nationalist movement almost disbanded, the cherished dream of Arab freedom and unity in the Jezirat ul-Arab and Al-Hilal ul Khasib changed into a nightmare through which it was to pass during the succeeding three decades.'

KNIGHTLEY, PHILIP AND SIMPSON, COLIN
**The Secret lives of Lawrence of Arabia.**
*London: Nelson. 1969.*
*x, 293 pp., plates, bibl., index, 23 cms.*

Lawrence attended the Peace Conference as a member of the British Delegation to be used to influence Faisal in accepting whatever was decided at the Conference, though Faisal's attendance at the Conference was achieved only after differences with the French. 'His prime object was to make Faisal cling to the British and come to believe they were his only real friends.' The Arab case at the conference was destined to fail because of the desire in Britain for demobilisation, the need for troops in Syria to go to real trouble spots and the desire for oil which led to the need to barter with the French for Mosul.

In this section the authors deal with the relationship between Lawrence and Faisal, the confrontation between the Allies, the rivalry between British Government departments and the impact of the Zionist cause on the Peace Conference. The result was inevitable and Faisal was obliged to accept the Anglo-French agreement over Syria and the mandate was assumed by force. 'It is not difficult to imagine the bitterness that Lawrence must have felt in seeing – as Hogarth had put it when he left Paris in disgust – "all this fiasco and the melancholy consummation of four years' work".'

LAWRENCE, THOMAS EDWARD
**Emir Feisal II.** The Sykes–Picot Treaty, Impatient Arabs. *The Times (London), 11 August 1920, p. 9.*

In the final part of the article Lawrence deals with the ultimate downfall of Faisal which followed the falling away of Arab support for his leadership. After the fall of Akaba the composition of the Arab army had changed being primarily composed of Syrian tribesmen and villagers as the Bedouin had returned to the Hedjaz, thus when Faisal refused to resist the French occupation of Syria he was at odds with his own supporters.

Faisal was attempting to pursue a middle of the road policy regarding the French, the troubles in Mesopotamia and the Palestinian Arabs' complaints regarding the Jews. This attempt at moderation alienated his supporters who wished him to take arms against the French in Syria, the British in Mosopotamia and the Jews in Palestine 'and he must feel it rather ironic that his downfall came by the very violence he had promised not to use'.

LAWRENCE, THOMAS EDWARD
**Evolution of a revolt,** ed. by Stanley and Rodelle Weintraub. *London: Pennsylvania State University Press. 1968.*
*175 pp., illus., 22 cms.*

See entry under the section 'The Arab Revolt and the war in the Middle East' for annotation.

LAWRENCE, THOMAS EDWARD
**Four pledges to the Arabs.**
*The Times (London), 11 September 1919, p. 11.*

A letter from Lawrence regarding British promises to the Arabs and to the French discussing Britain's promise to King Hussein, dated 24 October 1915; the Sykes–Picot agreement of May 1916;

the British statement to seven Syrians at Cairo on 11 June 1917; and finally the Anglo-French Declaration of November 1918. Quotations from these documents are used to substantiate the claim that Britain broke her pledges to the Arabs to satisfy the demands of the French and her own imperial interests.

MARMORSTEIN, EMILE
**A note on Damascus, Homs, Homa and Aleppo.**
*In: Hourani, Albert, ed.*
*Middle Eastern Affairs Number Two. pp. 161–165 (St. Antony's Papers, No. 11).*

In the Hussein–McMahon correspondence certain areas were to be excluded from any future Arab state because they could not be considered purely Arab and amongst these were the portions of Syria lying to the west of these districts. It is the author's contention that this paragraph was the work of Sir Mark Sykes and his evidence for this rests on *The Caliph's Last Heritage* by Sykes which was published in 1915 and was an account of the period between the conquest of Alexander the Great and the capture of Baghdad by Suleiman the Magnificent. It is Sykes' commitment to the Crusades that causes the author to argue that this emotional involvement led Sykes to dictate that the Muslims should receive no more territory than that held by them at the height of the Crusaders' power.

ORMSBY-GORE, HON. W.
**The Organisation of British responsibilities in the Middle East.**
*Journal Central Asian Society. Vol. 7, Part 3, 1920, pp. 83–105.*

This article begins by surveying the background to the situation in the Middle East with the author drawing on his experiences with the Arab Bureau to set the scene. The author then deals with the situation in the area with Britain in control of Palestine, Iraq and Transjordan all of which brought a measure of responsibility but which has to be matched with the enormous financial burden of administering and policing the area.

The essence of this article, however, is not the military aspect of the problem but that of the organisation of the administrative developments of the region and political relationships with the people. In this context the article examines the problems in Iraq, Palestine, and Transjordan faced by the British Government and the proposed administration together with the Hedjaz which was under the control of Sherif Hussein. The whole picture is seen by Ormsby-Gore as being the need to consolidate the new Arabic

Empire with possibly a new Civil Service and even a new ministry with responsibility for the area. The author could see no future for a federation under Hussein and that if Faisal became a ruler of Syria it must be on the basis of complete independence from the Hedjaz.

POWELL, E. ALEXANDER
**The Struggle for power in Moslem Asia.**
*London: John Long Ltd. 1925.*
*320 pp., maps, index, 22½ cms.*

A sympathetic treatment of the Ottoman Empire and its constituent provinces with a marked animosity towards the interference of the European powers. In dealing with the position in Syria it is stressed that the French presence was a direct result of the Sykes–Picot agreement and contrary to the promises made by the Allies regarding independence which was to be the result of an Allied victory.

The Peace Conference dashed Syrian hopes as the Supreme Council decided 'that the Syrians had not yet reached a stage of development where they could be entrusted with independence and that they must be placed under the tutelage of more advanced nations . . .' This despite the fact that the King–Crane Commission found opposition to any French presence and of the petitions that they received 73.5% asked for complete independence. Even when the Syrians were convinced that the mandate was inevitable it was requested that it be given to America and, if she refused, to Britain but not to France but this was dashed by America's refusal to accept any responsibilities in the Near East. As a result the mandate was given to France and this was confirmed by the San Remo Conference in 1920.

**\*Recommendations of the King–Crane Commission on Syria and Palestine, 28 August 1919.**
*In: Hurewitz, J. C.*
*Diplomacy in the Near and Middle East, pp. 66–74.*

Initially the Commission was to consist of representatives from Britain, France and America but the French refused to nominate representatives and the British named theirs and then withdrew with the result being that the commission consisted only of the two American representatives and their staffs.

In considering the Syria question the Commission favoured an American mandate but failing that a British one of short duration though sufficient to ensure the success of the new state whose boundaries should be preserved according to the wishes of the majority of the people. The problem of Palestine is dealt with at great length and the commission came to the conclusion that it was not possible to adopt the Balfour Declaration in view of the opposition of the Arab peoples but that a modified plan could be put into operation with Palestine as part of Syria with a limited amount of Jewish immigration to preserve the Arab identity.

The commission recognised that these proposals would result in French disagreement and suggested that if a gesture was needed to preserve cordial relations they should be given a mandate over Lebanon, not enlarged, but this was not recommended as a solution.

**Summary record of a secret meeting of the Supreme Council at Paris to consider the Sykes–Picot Agreement, 20 March 1919.**
*In : Hurewitz, J. C. Vol. 2.*
*Diplomacy in the Near and Middle East, pp. 50–59.*

The meeting resulted from the Anglo-French dispute over the Sykes–Picot agreement which had begun with the French insisting on a strict interpretation of the agreement whilst Britain needed a laxer attitude to reconcile various differences within the British Government and the problems of the separate promises to the Arabs and the Jews. The result of the meeting was an agreement to set up a commission to go to Syria to investigate the problem and if necessary to extend its survey beyond Syria if the need arose.

**Syria:** The Present and the Future.
*Scottish Geographical Magazine. Vol. XXXII, August 1916, pp. 378–383.*

A review of 'La Syrie de demain' by Nadra Moutran which has as its main theme the argument that the only hope for Syria lay in the establishment of a French protectorate. The review deals mainly with the part of the book which discusses the contemporary situation in Syria and in particular the Turkish administration and its effects upon the social and economic life of the Syrians.

\*TIBAWI, A. L.
**Syria in the McMahon Correspondence:** Fresh evidence from the British Foreign Office Records.
*Middle East Forum. Vol. XLII, No. 4, 1966, pp. 5–32.*

This article is based on the hitherto unavailable British documents which became available to historians in 1966. At the outbreak of war the Syrian coast was blockaded by the British and foreign trade was brought almost to a standstill, conscription had a disastrous effect upon agriculture, and the requisition of animals and the cutting of trees for fuel led to a very critical situation in Syria. This deterioration led to politically minded Arabs seeing this as an opportunity to secure a better future than that offered by the Ottomans.

This move amongst the Arabs was parallel to the policy of Britain which aimed at securing the support of an Arab movement either openly or indirectly. The article, however, considers the attitudes of the British politicians in their negotiations with the Arabs and the various promises which were given and concludes that although these were open with regard to the Arab peninsula and the Holy Places they were less overt with regard to the north-western frontiers. It is also apparent from the documents consulted by the author that the negotiations between McMahon and Hussein were conducted in the full knowledge that no concessions to the Arabs would be secured from France and that the outlines of the Sykes–Picot agreement were in being at least six months before the two men met to work out the detail. The resultant agreement is considered by Tibawi to be more representative of Sykes' views than of Picot's as 'Sykes was indeed another example of an individual proving himself stronger than the institution he served. He was surely more than an adviser, for in the long run British policy in the Arab land was decided along the lines he advocated and not along those lines broadly defined by Grey (British Foreign Secretary) and his professional advisers.'

**Tripartite (Sykes-Picot) Agreement for the Partition of the Ottoman Empire: Britain, France and Russia, 26 April–23 October 1916.**
*In: Woodward and Butler, eds.*
*Documents on British Foreign Policy, 1919–1939. First series. Vol. 4, pp. 241–251,*
*and*
*Hurewitz, J. C. Diplomacy in the Near and Middle East, pp. 18–22.*

See Section 1c for annotation to this work.

WHITE, WILBUR W.
**The Process of change in the Ottoman Empire.**
*Chicago: University of Chicago Press. 1937.*
*ix, 315 pp., map, bibl., index, 23½ cms.*

The question of Syria was complicated by the Sykes–Picot agreement and the fact that the Arab army under Faisal had participated in the fall of Damascus in October 1918 and the subsequent assumption of power by Faisal. The Peace Settlement brought home the fundamental problems regarding the future of Syria and although the King–Crane Commission had reported opposition to any French presence no real results came of the mission. Feeling was further intensified by Faisal's acceptance of the throne of Syria in March 1920.

*WOODWARD, E. L. AND BUTLER, ROHAN, EDS.
**Documents on British Foreign Policy, 1919–1939.**
*First Series. Vol. IV, 1919.*
*London: H.M.S.O.*
*xciii, 1,278 pp., maps, 25 cms.*

The section of relevance to this study falls on pp. 241–634 and deals with the 'Policy of His Majesty's Government in regard to Syria and Palestine before the First Conference of London. May 30 1919–February 12 1920'.

The entries are far too detailed to list separately but the subjects dealt with are as follows:

King–Crane Commission.
Palestine as a National Home for the Jews.
Arab opposition to the Sykes–Picot agreement especially French presence in Syria and Britain's refusal to accept a Syrian mandate.
Faisal's visit to Paris and Lawrence's appointment as adviser.
French occupation of Syria.
Relations between Britain and Hussein and Hussein and Ibn Saud.

ZEINE, Z. N.
**The Central Islamic lands in recent times:** The Arab lands.
*In: Cambridge History of Islam. Vol. 1: The Central Islamic lands in recent times, pp. 566–594.*

This chapter is in two parts the first dealing with political developments from 1918–48. The first section considers in general terms the political developments in the region following the end of World War I dealing with the Arab hopes for independence, the granting of the mandates and the effect that this had on relations between the Arabs and the Western powers.

# BIOGRAPHICAL WORKS

Aldington, Richard
**Lawrence of Arabia:** A biographical enquiry.
*London: Collins. 1955.*
*448 pp., illus., maps, bibl., index, 21 cms.*

See main entry under 'The Arab Revolt and the war in the Middle East' for annotation.

Birwood, Lord
**Nuri As-Said:** A study in Arab leadership.
*London: Cassell. 1959.*
*xi, 306 pp., frontis., illus., maps, glossary, bibl., index, 22 cms.*

After the fall of Damascus Nuri As-Said remained with Faisal and was one of the members of the Arab Commission which went to Versailles to present the Arab case. The result, however, was indecisive and it was not until 1920 that the situation was resolved by the San Remo Conference which gave the mandate for Syria to France. Following the defeat of the Arab army by French troops and the expulsion of Faisal, Nuri As-Said followed him into exile.

Bray, N. N. E.
**A Paladin of Arabia:** The biography of Brevet Lieutenant-Colonel G. E. Leachman of the Royal Sussex Regiment.
*London: John Heritage. 1936.*
*xvi, 429 pp., illus., maps, 20 cm.*

See annotation under entry in 'The Arab Revolt and the war in the Middle East'.

Erskine, Mrs. Stewart
**King Faisal of Iraq.**
*London: Hutchinson & Co. 1933.*
*288 pp., illus., app., index, 23½ cms.*

Faisal represented his father at the Peace Conference though any hopes for Arab independence were soon to be dashed as he was rebuffed by the French who intended to take up the conditions of the Sykes–Picot agreement. Although an Allied Commission to consider the future of Syria was promised and in fact set up as the American King–Crane Commission its recommendations were shelved as neither America nor Britain were prepared to accept a mandate for Syria.

In the absence of any immediate solution to the problem the Syrians took matters into their own hands and declared Faisal King of Syria. In April 1920 the San Remo Conference conferred the mandate for Syria to France and in October General Gouraud arrived as French High Commissioner. Unrest was in the air and Faisal protested at the occupation of the country and appealed for the mandate to be withdrawn. The result was an ultimatum from the French, the occupation of Damascus by force and the deposing of Faisal, resulting in his having to take refuge in Palestine.

GRAVES, ROBERT
**Lawrence and the Arabs.**
*London: Cape. 1927.*
*454 pp., frontis., illus., app., index, 20½ cms.*

An account of the Arab case at the Peace Conference which relies on Lawrence for much of its substance. (See the entry under 'The Arab Revolt and the Middle East War' for a fuller annotation.)

HART, B. H. LIDDELL
**T. E. Lawrence in Arabia and after.**
*London: Cape. 1934.*
*490 pp., frontis., illus., maps, index, 22 cms.*

In considering the question of the Peace Conference this work presents a straightforward account of the proceedings. However, one must remember that the aim of the work is to present a biography of Lawrence and therefore events at the Peace Conference and behind the scenes are dealt with in this light.

*MEINERTZHAGEN, RICHARD
**Middle East Diary, 1917–1956.**
*London: The Cresset Press. 1959.*
*xi, 376 pp., index, 22 cms.*

After working in the intelligence section of Allenby's staff the author became part of the British peace delegation to the conference at Paris covering the Middle East and the Zionist cause. Following the peace settlement he became Political Officer for all the occupied territory including Syria, Palestine and Transjordan until resigning from the army in 1925.

This is a very useful work for a study of this period especially as, being in the form of a diary, it provides comments and assessments made at the time of the events. It is of less interest to this study from the question of the Arab case at the Peace Conference in relation to Palestine as Meinertzhagen was a supporter of the Zionist cause.

*Morris, James
**The Hashemite Kings.**
*London: Faber and Faber. 1959.*
*231 pp., illus., bibl., index, 22 cms.*

The Peace Conference found the Arabs free from Turkish control but caught in the more complex web of international politics with the problems of the secret treaties, the McMahon–Hussein correspondence and the Balfour Declaration. Faisal attended the conference as an envoy of the Grand Sherif with instructions to remain firm on the agreement that Hussein had secured from the British, 'independence for all the Arab countries, with the reservations hazily accepted in the McMahon correspondence. Nothing less than full independence would do. There was to be no shilly-shallying with limited autonomy, spheres of influence, National Homes, or the newfangled notion of mandates. A bargain was a bargain.'

Faisal did his best but he was out of his depth as the sole consideration was the settlement of conflicting ambitions between the allies. Britain and France agreed to a modification of the Sykes–Picot agreement with France having the run of Syria in return for Britain having control of northern Iraq, where oil was expected to be found. The King–Crane Commission was ineffective and the pressure of Zionism and international politics meant that the Arab cause was to be sacrificed in return for a general settlement. The result was that Faisal left the conference in April 1919 and was proclaimed King of Syria and his brother Abdullah King of Iraq by the nationalists.

Arab opposition to the Peace Settlement was to no avail as the San Remo Conference confirmed the French mandate for Syria and Britain was given Iraq, Palestine and Transjordan with the proviso that the Balfour Declaration should be honoured. 'Few of the Arab aspirations were fulfilled. Few of the British pledges were, in Arab eyes anyway, honoured.'

Mousa, Suleiman
**T. E. Lawrence:** An Arab view.
*London: O.U.P. 1966.*
*x, 301 pp., bibl., index, 22 cms.*
*(Chapter VIII, pp. 213–256.)*

The Arabs anticipated that the Peace Conference would bring the fulfilment of their independence aims but it was only after a dispute between France and Britain that Faisal was even allowed to present their case. It was a lost cause from the beginning as the

French insisted on implementing the Sykes–Picot agreement and Britain needed French agreement to secure the oil deposits in northern Iraq. Even the King–Crane Commission was a failure as the report was never presented to the Peace Conference. 'Arab hopes were shattered because President Wilson had failed to curb the imperialistic spirit of Britain and France.'

NUTTING, ANTHONY
**Lawrence of Arabia:** The man and the motive.
*London: Hollis and Carter. 1961.*
*256 pp., illus., maps, bibl., index, 22 cms.*

A biography of Lawrence which tends to follow the line that Lawrence himself took but it is useful for its account of the Arab Revolt and the Peace Conference.

TOYNBEE, ARNOLD J.
**Acquaintances.**
*London: O.U.P. 1967.*
*viii, 312 pp., illus., index, 22 cms.*

The essay on Lawrence deals mainly with his activities at the Peace Conference in Paris and his conflict with the French whilst acting as Faisal's representative. '. . . in Paris Lawrence had, I think, already realised that, however many tactical successes he might achieve in his campaign on behalf of the Arabs, he was not going to win his war. Independence for the ex-Ottoman Arabs was not an issue over which Britain was going to break with France.'

# (b) RIVALRY BETWEEN HUSSEIN AND IBN SAUD

## GENERAL WORKS

*ANTONIUS, GEORGE
**The Arab Awakening:** The story of the Arab nationalist movement.
*London: Hamish Hamilton. 1938.*
*xii, 13–471 pp., maps, app., index, 22 cms.*
*(Chapter XV, pp. 325–349.)*

Hussein was at a disadvantage following the Peace Settlement as he had been excluded from the deliberations and his dreams of ruling an Arab Empire had been dashed. Hussein's only strength was the moral justice of his case but this was of little consequence at the tables of Versailles or San Remo. It was only support from Britain which had maintained Hussein's position during the war and kept Ibn Saud neutral.

Hussein was unable to handle relations with his neighbour as he assumed that his leadership of the Revolt gave him political ascendancy over his neighbours. The question was complicated by the long-standing border dispute between the two rulers which Hussein had attempted to solve with high handedness and disregard for Ibn Saud's position. 'For whatever grounds he may have had for crediting his neighbour with acquisitive designs, he should have foreseen the provocative effect of his attitude on the ruler of Najd who had a far more powerful army at his disposal than Hussein possessed or could muster.'

The position of Hussein was weakened after the Cairo Conference as he refused to enter into a treaty with Britain and the unsuccessful protracted negotiations led to Hussein being regarded as a ruler who was no longer of any consequence. As a result the invasion of the Hedjaz in 1924 by the Wahhabi forces was allowed by Britain and Hussein was forced to abdicate in favour of Ali. Defeat was inevitable, however, and by December 1925 Ibn Saud controlled the Hedjaz. Hussein was an exile in Cyprus and Ali an exile at Faisal's court in Baghdad.

BEN-HORIN, ELIAHU
**The Middle East:** Crossroads of history.
*New York: W. W. Norton & Co. 1943.*
*248 pp., map, index, 21½ cms.*

BENOIST-MECHIN, JACQUES
**Arabian Destiny.**
*London: Elek. 1957.*
*x, 298 pp., illus., maps, bibl., index, 21 cms.*

Although this book is about Ibn Saud of Saudi Arabia it is included because of the relationship between Hussein and Ibn Saud and the position of the two leaders in relation to British interests in the Middle East. This work deals with British negotiations between Ibn Saud which prevented him from attacking Hussein at the time of the declaration of the Arab Revolt.

The work also deals in detail with the peace conference from which Ibn Saud was excluded and the subsequent waning of Hussein's power which resulted in the Wahhabi conquest of the

Hedjaz and the eventual creation of the Saudi Arabia of today. The conclusion reached is that British support should have been given to Ibn Saud and not to Hussein though this is a view in hindsight and must be contrasted with the religious position of Hussein as Emir of Mecca and the strategic value placed on the Suez Canal and Egypt to which an ally in the Hedjaz offered additional protection.

BUTLER, ROHAN AND BURY, J. P. T., EDS.
**Documents on British Foreign Policy, 1919–1939.**
*First Series. Vol. XIII, The Near and Middle East, January 1920–March 1921.*
*London: H.M.S.O. 1963.*
*lxxxiii, 747 pp., 24½ cms.*

See the section on the Peace Settlement for annotation.

WOODWARD, E. L. AND BUTLER, ROHAN, EDS.
**Documents on British Foreign Policy, 1919–1939.**
*First Series. Vol. IV, 1919.*
*London: H.M.S.O.*
*xciii, 1,278 pp., maps, 25 cms.*

See entry under Section 2a on the Peace Conference for annotation.

## SPECIFIC WORKS

CLAYTON, GILBERT
**Arabia and the Arabs.**
*Journal Royal Institute of International Affairs. January 1929, pp. 8–20.*

The greater part of this article is not relevant to this study by nature of geography but of interest is the section dealing with the rivalry between Hussein and Ibn Saud. The article briefly sketches in the background to the situation in 1916 before dealing with the situation during the war. Following the defeat of the Rashids in 1921 relations between the Nejd and the Hedjaz reached a critical stage due to the obstinacy of Hussein in his dealings with Ibn Saud and also '. . . King Hussein by his arrogance and the reactionary nature of his rule had alienated many of his people and undoubtedly weakened his own position'.

Relations deteriorated even further until in 1925 Ibn Saud invaded the Hedjaz and the Hashemite dynasty was overthrown with the area being absorbed into Ibn Saud's kingdom.

CLAYTON, GILBERT
**An Arabian Diary,** edited by Robert O. Collins.
*Los Angeles: University of California Press. 1969.*
*xiv, 379 pp., app., bibl., index, 23½ cms.*

This introductory section considers the roots of dissent between Hussein and Ibn Saud which were accentuated by the support given to Hussein by Britain through the Arab Bureau whilst the Indian Office favoured Ibn Saud. The rivalry was suppressed during hostilities by use of diplomatic pressure and financial subsidies.

The resentment merely smouldered during the war and at the end of hostilities Hussein attempted to re-occupy Al Khurma but his forces were easily defeated by the Ikhwan. The Cairo Conference merely added to Ibn Saud's fears as he saw the creation of Hashemite rule in Iraq and Transjordan thus surrounding the Nejd with potential enemies. The results were sporadic raiding by the Ikhwan into Iraq and Transjordan which were dealt with by the British forces and some measure of understanding was reached between Sir Percy Cox and Ibn Saud.

The end of the conflict between Hussein and Ibn Saud was in sight and the corruptions and inefficiency of the Hashemite rule in the Hedjaz contributed to its collapse. Through his own follies such as his refusal to sign a treaty with Britain, his failure to become a member of the League of Nations and his treatment of the pilgrims led to the withdrawal of the British subsidy and in 1924 the invasion and occupation of the Hedjaz by Ibn Saud resulting in the creation of the state of Saudi Arabia.

GLIDDEN, HAROLD W.
**Arab Unity:** Ideal and reality.
*In: Kritzeck, James and Winder, R. Bayly, eds.*
*The World of Islam.*
*London: Macmillan. 1960.*
*pp. 249–254.*

Developments after the war illustrate the fact that the desire for Arab unity was confined to the Hedjaz and the area north of the Arab Peninsula with opposition from, amongst others, Ibn Saud. The rivalry between Ibn Saud and Hussein was not only confined to the question of unity but was concerned with Hussein's control over the Holy Places which conflicted with the puritanical Islam of the Wahhabi movement.

The move to found an Arab Caliphate was defeated by the incompatability between Hussein and Ibn Saud which eventually resulted in the taking of the Hedjaz by the forces of Ibn Saud. Arab unity was never a reality as far as Arabia was concerned and until this could be achieved it would be internal Arab tensions rather than foreign intrigue which would be the real obstacle.

HOWARD, HARRY N.
**The Partition of Turkey:** A diplomatic history, 1913–1923.
*New York: Howard Fertig. 1966.*
*486 pp., maps, notes, index, 23½ cms.*

In dealing with the period following the peace settlement and the granting of the mandates this work also considers the rivalry between Hussein and Ibn Saud. This problem is seen in the light of the differing British policies in the area with the Foreign Office and the Arab Bureau having supported the Sherifian cause whilst the India Office had supported the cause of Ibn Saud.

The result of this rivalry was to be the conquest of the Hedjaz by the forces of Ibn Saud and its incorporation into what is now Saudi Arabia whilst Hussein was forced into exile having been abandoned by the British Government.

*LAWRENCE, THOMAS EDWARD
**Secrets of the war on Mecca.**
*Daily Express (London). 28 May 1920.*

An article dealing with the conflict between Hussein and Ibn Saud which had lain dormant during the war as a result of Britain's support for Hussein and the subsidy paid to Ibn Saud. It was Ibn Saud's aim to stamp out the corruptness of the Hedjaz society and to impose on the area the Wahhabi brand of Islam which caused the great powers some concern with the problem being complicated by the fact that in Britain the Foreign Office, the War Office and the India Office adopted different attitudes. Lawrence felt that a policy of trying to reconcile the differences between Hussein and Ibn Saud could only be of a temporary nature because of the religious aspect and that if a solution were to be found it would 'involve that most difficult thing, agreement between three government departments'.

PHILBY, H. ST. JOHN
**Lawrence of Arabia:** the work behind the legend.
*Review of Reviews (London). June 1935, pp. 15–17, map.*

The main thread of this article is the discussion of the basic mis-conception of British policy regarding the revolt of the Arabs against the Turks, that of supporting the Sherifian family instead of Ibn Saud. In 1914 Ibn Saud had already begun to harass the

Turks whilst Hussein had done nothing but talk about the prospect and balancing this against the concessions that would be made to Hussein following the war.

According to Philby this attitude alone should have been enough to secure support for Ibn Saud and the Arab Bureau in Cairo made a basic mistake in advocating support for the Sherifian family. The article concludes that the only monument to the Arab Revolt, as conceived by the Arab Bureau, were the destroyed remains of the Hedjaz railway. 'El Orens, Destroyer of Engines, as he was known to the Turks, earned his nickname.'

PHILBY, H. ST. JOHN
**The recent history of the Hedjaz.**
*Central Asian Society Journal. Vol. XII, July 1925, pp. 332–348.*

The rift between Hussein and Ibn Saud is dealt with briefly and, as one would expect, the treatment is sympathetic to the claims of Ibn Saud. Although the rival claims to Khurma were an excuse for armed conflict the dispute's origins were evident in 1916 and were only solved by the successful invasion of the Hedjaz by Ibn Saud in 1925.

*POWELL, E. ALEXANDER
**The Struggle for power in Moslem Asia.**
*London: John Long Ltd. 1925.*
*320 pp., maps, index, 22½ cms.*

In this chapter entitled the 'Danger in the Desert' the author discusses the differing treatments accorded to Hussein and Ibn Saud by the British Government in their intrigues against the Turks. Comparisons are then drawn between the role of Hussein in the Hedjaz with his exploitations of the Holy Places of Islam and the rule of Ibn Saud with his strict adherence to the Wahhabi interpretation of Islam.

Following the end of the war it seemed as if the pan-Arab ideal with the Hashemites having the thrones of the Hedjaz, Transjordania, Iraq and Syria was to be achieved resulting in an Arab Empire under British control and protection. This failed because of the conflict between Hussein and Ibn Saud with this feud making an Arab federation an impossibility, though other factors also were instrumental in destroying this concept. Hussein, however, was not content to remain quietly in the Hedjaz and in 1918 his forces made raids into the Western parts of the Nejd but in May of the following year his forces were soundly defeated by the Wahhabis and only British intervention prevented them marching on Mecca.

The conflict did not cease and various border disputes continued to flare up and in 1921 Ibn Saud told Sir Percy Cox that unless Hussein were kept in order he would be compelled to retaliate. The enthronement of Faisal in 1921 exhausted Ibn Saud's patience as he was now surrounded by enemies but any move on his part was stifled by Britain addressing him as King of the Nejd and paying him a subsidy of £60,000 per year in monthly sums in arrears. 'The truth of the matter is that King Hussein will remain on his throne only so long as Ibn Saud receives sixty thousand pounds of British money every year.'

## BIOGRAPHICAL WORKS

ABDULLAH I, KING OF TRANSJORDAN
**Memoirs of King Abdullah of Transjordan,** edited by Philip P. Graves.
*London: Cape. 1950.*
*278 pp., illus., refs., app., index, 20½ cms.*

Following the Arab Revolt Abdullah deals with the problem of the Wahhabis and in particular the question of Khurma where the local Sherif had adopted the Wahhabi creed and persecuted any of the tribes that would not share in his conversion. The attempt to bring the Sherif to task was a failure and the Hashemite forces were soundly defeated with Abdullah only just escaping with his life.

\*HOWARTH, DAVID
**The Desert King:** A life of Ibn Saud.
*London: Collins. 1964.*
*252 pp., illus., bibl., index, 21 cms.*

This biography of Ibn Saud is included for the picture it presents of the rivalry between Hussein and Ibn Saud as this aspect and period of Ibn Saud's life is dealt with in some detail. Howarth considers that the choice of Hussein was a fundamental error which was proved to be so by events after the Peace Conference. Also dealt with is the religious aspect of the question with the disciplined form of Islam as practised in the Nejd in direct conflict with the decadence of the Hedjaz and the unfit guardianship of the Holy Places in the eyes of the Wahhabi movement.

\*MONROE, ELIZABETH
**Philby of Arabia.**
*London: Faber. 1973.*
*332 pp., illus., maps, notes, bibl., index, 22½ cms.*

The rivalry between Ibn Saud and Hussein caused problems for the two British Government departments interested in the Middle East with the Foreign Office through the Arab Bureau supporting Hussein and the India Office Ibn Saud. Such was the intensity of the rivalry that it was necessary for one condition of the subsidy given to Ibn Saud to be that he refrained from attacking the Hedjaz. Indeed during 1917 Philby travelled to Jidda to see Hussein but he failed to find any solution to the problem.

In 1918 the Emir of Khurman who was supported by Hussein had turned Wahhabi and so Hussein sent a force to occupy the oasis but it was routed by the Ikhwan who made no distinction between religion and politics. This clash did not result in any serious developments as Philby used all his persuasion to move Ibn Saud into attacking Hail and Ibn Rashid though many of the king's advisers wished the army to be used to attack Mecca. Further trouble arose over Khurma in 1919 when Abdullah's army sent to take the oasis was heavily defeated. Philby was sent to mediate as Britain did not wish Hussein to be defeated but his services were not required as Ibn Saud did not follow up his advantage.

The defeat of Hussein and the incorporation of the Hedjaz in what is now Saudi Arabia was achieved following the taking of Mecca in 1924 whilst Philby was in England having resigned his post in Transjordan.

*MORRIS, JAMES
**The Hashemite Kings.**
*London: Faber and Faber. 1959.*
*231 pp., illus., bibl., index, 22 cms.*

The conflict between Hussein and Ibn Saud, mainly over the administration of the Holy Places and the treatment of pilgrims, had been neutralised during the war by British support for Hussein and by payment of a subsidy to Ibn Saud to secure his neutrality regarding the Turks and the Hedjaz.

After the end of the war Hussein was embittered by what he saw as the cynicism of British foreign policy and he refused to sign a peace treaty at all. Following the Cairo Conference Lawrence went to Jidda to meet with Hussein to tidy up the relationship with the Sherif and to ensure that his influence was limited to the Hedjaz. Negotiations were a failure as Hussein refused to recognise the mandate systems, he refused to condone the Balfour Declaration or Faisal's negotiations with Weizmann and he refused to sign a treaty with Britain. Once this protection was removed the Hedjaz became vulnerable to Ibn Saud and in 1924 his forces successfully invaded the Hedjaz and Hussein left for an exile in Cyprus.

STORRS, RONALD
**Orientations.**
*London: Nicholson and Watson. 1937.*
*xviii, 557 pp., illus., maps, index, 21 cms.*

Although Storrs does not deal directly with the rivalry between Hussein and Ibn Saud he does consider the reasons for the downfall of the Sherifian rule in the Hedjaz. Hussein had become less and less of a practicable ruler 'regarding the mere suggestion of anything he did not wish to do as an attack on his honour and his sovereign rights'. Discussions with Hussein were protracted and often inconclusive as 'time after time the King would go back on agreements made after hours of discussion the day before'.

This led to a withdrawal of British support in any real sense and exposed Hussein to the attentions of Ibn Saud and, having rejected a treaty of friendship with Britain, he had nothing to fall back on when the Wahhabis invaded the Hedjaz in 1925.

# (c) ARAB REACTION TO THE PALESTINE MANDATE

## *GENERAL WORKS*

*ALLEN, RICHARD
**Imperialism and nationalism in the Fertile Crescent:**
Sources and prospects of the Arab–Israeli conflict.
*London: O.U.P. 1974.*
*x, 686 pp., maps, bibl., index, 20½ cms.*
*(Chapter 11, pp. 260–293.)*

The final section of interest to this study is that entitled 'British rule in Palestine: The Early Years'. This deals with the period immediately following the capture of Jerusalem and Palestine to the early years of the mandate where the situation although not satisfactory was under some measure of control. This period saw the implementation of the Balfour Declaration and the conflict between the Jews and Arabs on the one hand and on the other the two separate communities with the British administration.

BEN-HORIN, ELIAHU
**The Middle East:** Crossroads of history.
*New York: W. W. Norton & Co. 1943.*
*248 pp., map, index, 21½ cms.*

MACDONALD, J. RAMSAY
**Zionism and Palestine.**
*The Contemporary Review. Vol. CXXI, April 1922, pp. 434–440.*

An examination of the problems in Palestine which Ramsay MacDonald feels are directly due to the crude duplicity resulting from the encouragement given to the Arab Revolt, the promises to the Jews and the Sykes–Picot agreement which the Arabs will never forgive. 'Our treatment of the Moslem has been a madness.' The article then examines the problems of Jewish immigration and the character and nature of the Jews and the contribution that they made to Palestine and the effect that they could have on the future of the country.

This leads to an assessment of the problems created by the immigration of the Jews many of which are considered to be the result of propaganda and misunderstanding. MacDonald, however, sees hope for Palestine despite these problems and the initial friction between the two peoples. 'But these are matters of detail. A policy which, whilst keeping Palestine open to a Jewish "return" not only protects an Arab in his rights but sees that he shares amply in the increased prosperity of the country, is certainly not doomed to failure.'

MONROE, ELIZABETH
**Britain's moment in the Middle East, 1914–56.**
*London: Chatto & Windus. 1963.*
*254 pp., maps, notes, bibl., index, 22 cms.*

In considering the question of Palestine in the section 'The years of good management, 1922–45' the author is really concerned with the British viewpoint and the problems of Zionism. This is seen in the light of Arab opposition to anything short of Arab domination over the Jewish minority and the situation was further complicated by the fact that this opposition was seen as 'local non-co-operation, and never as a manifestation of the wider kind of Arab nationalism that was at work also in Syria'.

PARKES, JAMES
**Palestine.**
*London: O.U.P. 1940.*
*32 pp., maps, 17½ cms.*

See entry under Section 3c for annotation.

\*Peake, F. C.
**Transjordan.**
*Journal Royal Central Asian Society. Vol. XXVI, 1939,
pp. 375–396.*

Colonel Peake served with Lawrence in the Hedjaz and following
the war he formed the police force in Transjordan which was
subsequently to become the Arab Legion, as a result his knowledge of the area, from the British viewpoint, is considerable. The
author begins by sketching the historical importance of the area
from its earliest history and the development of the trade routes.
The author then goes on to deal with the area during the Arab
Revolt and the part played by the Sherifian forces and their
British advisers.

The article then considers the position in the area following the
cessation of hostilities with the setting up of an Arab administration in 1919 though this fell into decay with the protracted negotiations at Versailles and the Zionist problems and pressures in
Palestine. The situation in Transjordan was very delicate and the
British Administration in Palestine was obliged to set up an
administration and to raise a police force to restore order. Feisal's
expulsion from Syria raised further problems as Abdullah
arrived at Amman in 1920 to lead an army against the French.
This conflict was averted by the Cairo Conference in 1921 which
granted Abdullah the governorship of the area.

\*Philby, Hon. H. St. J. B.
**Transjordan.**
*Journal Central Asian Society. Vol. II, No. 4, 1924, pp. 296–312.*

Initially the article considers the area in ancient history when the
country was part of Palestine and the Promised Land but this was
altered by the Balfour Declaration which created Palestine and
Transjordan out of the vilayet of Syria. The state of Transjordan
began life in April 1921 when Abdullah became Governor of the
country though the arrangement was not without problems
mainly due to Arab opposition to the French mandate over Syria,
resulting in various raids over the border.

These problems increased and it seemed as if the solution
arrived at in Cairo had been a failure. Churchill sent Lawrence
out to survey the problem and to suggest a solution. The result
of Lawrence's visit was the sacking of all the British staff with the
exception of Peake and the appointment of Philby as adviser to
Abdullah. In May 1923 the British granted Transjordan its

independence with Abdullah as ruler and Philby as British representative to administer the £150,000 grant in aid. Philby then goes on to describe the maladministration of the independent state which resulted in conflict between Philby and Abdullah thus destroying the progress made under Lawrence. Once again Britain had to appoint staff from Palestine with that administration controlling the financial and political situation. Philby concludes, 'I am fully conscious that the history of Transjordan, as I have given it to you today, is a record of personal failure. I have failed, and can only say that circumstances proved to be altogether too strong for me when first Lawrence and then Mr. Churchill himself vanished from the scene.'

\*Royal Institute of International Affairs
**Great Britain and Palestine, 1915–1936.**
*London: Royal Institute of International Affairs. 1937.*
*111 pp., tables, notes, app., 22 cms.*
*(Information Department Papers, No. 20.)*

The granting of the Mandate to Britain was a protracted process due to the complications of the question of France in Syria and Italy's insistence on a treaty with Turkey thus delaying the granting of the mandate until 1923. Faisal was prepared to accept 'the effective superposition of a great trustee but not all Arabs held this view and many denied the validity of the mandate because it conflicted with the wartime promises made to the Arabs by McMahon. Transjordan although included in the mandate for Palestine was excluded from the terms applicable to the Holy Places and the implementation of the Balfour Declaration.

The next section considers the two communities in Palestine dealing firstly with the political contrasts and then with the social and economic differences between the communities.

Stewart, Desmond
**The Middle East:** Temple of Janus.
*London: Hamish Hamilton. 1972.*
*viii, 414 pp., bibl., index, 24 cms.*

At the time of the Cairo Conference the question of Palestine was raised and Abdullah records in his memoirs that 'The people of Palestine', he claims to have told Sir Herbert Samuel and Churchill, 'refute the Balfour Declaration and insist on the retention of the Arab character of Palestine. We shall not agree to the annihilation of the Arabs for the sake of the Jews.' Churchill attempted to reassure the Arabs whilst meeting a delegation at Jerusalem in 1921 by assuring them that Jewish immigration would only be allowed as long as it did not conflict with the political and economic freedom of the Arab population.

The feelings of the Palestinian Arabs were very clear as they were opposed to any extensive Jewish immigration or any eventual Jewish control. One of the major objections was religious as Palestine contained shrines sacred to both Moslem and Christian Arabs and neither considered the Jews as suitable guardians of the Holy Places. Indeed in 1919 when dealing with this question the King–Crane Commission stated that 'in fact, from this point of view, the Moslems, just because the sacred places of all three religions are sacred to them have made very naturally much more satisfactory custodians of the holy places than the Jews could be'.

SYKES, CHRISTOPHER
**Crossroads to Israel:** Palestine from Balfour to Bevin.
*London: Collins. 1965.*
*479 pp., illus., maps, app., bibl., index, 23½ cms.*
*(Chapter 3, pp. 58–75.)*

In considering the Arab reaction to the question of Palestine after the Peace Conference Sykes deals with the outlook of Faisal based on the discussions he had with Weizmann in 1918. In his memorandum to the Peace Conference on 'The Arabs of Asia' Faisal said of Palestine that '. . . the enormous majority of the people are Arabs. The Jews are very close to the Arabs in blood, and there is no conflict of character between the two races, . . . They [the Arabs] would wish for the effective super-position [*sic*] of a great trustee, so long as a representative local administration commended itself by actively promoting the material prosperity of the country.'

However, Faisal's position was insecure and he was the leader of the Arabs only for as long as he represented their wishes 'or so long as he received agreeable pledges on their behalf, but as soon as he said or did otherwise, or received discouraging modification of pledges, he was a foreign Bedouin chief'. Faisal's position was not helped by the leak of the agreement with Weizmann and as a result he was accused of being in the pay of the Zionists which led to his adopting an anti-Zionist position. Following his exile in July 1920 the Weizmann agreement disappeared as well with the result that Arab-Jewish relationships suffered a set back and the future pattern of opposition between the two peoples was to develop along these lines.

WHITE, WILBUR, W.
**The Process of change in the Ottoman Empire.**
*Chicago: University of Chicago Press. 1937.*
*ix, 315 pp., map, bibl., index, 23½ cms.*

The Palestine situation was complicated by the vagueness of the McMahon–Hussein correspondence, the Balfour Declaration of 1917 and the question of the Holy Places. Following disturbances among the Arab population prior to the granting of the mandate to Britain the news of the mandate was ill received as one of the conditions was that the Balfour Declaration was to be implemented resulting in Jewish immigration and conflict between the two peoples and each in turn with the British administration.

Transjordan was a different problem as it was to have been part of the Arab territory but following Faisal's removal from Damascus it was included in the Palestine mandate. This was short-lived, however, as in April 1921 Abdullah was made Emir of Transjordan and the area was withdrawn from the Jewish homeland provisions of the mandate.

## *OFFICIAL DOCUMENTS*

*****The British (Balfour) Declaration of sympathy with Zionist aspirations 4 June–2 November 1917.**
*In: Hurewitz, J. C.*
*Diplomacy in the Near and Middle East, pp. 25–26.*

Reproduction of the text of a letter from the French Foreign Minister Jules Conbon to Sokolow dated 4.6.1919 giving an assurance that France would assist in the Zionist cause in Palestine.

Reproduction of Official Zionist formula dated 18.7.1917 presented to the British Cabinet by Baron Rothschild which was later modified and presented as the Balfour Declaration of 2 November 1917 and this is also reproduced.

BUTLER, ROHAN AND BURY, J. P. T., EDS.
**Documents on British Foreign Policy, 1919–1939:**
*First Series. Vol. XIII. The Near and Middle East, January 1920–March 1921.*
*London: H.M.S.O. 1963.*
*lxxxiii, 747 pp., 24½ cms.*

See the section on the Peace Settlement for annotation.

*****Great Britain, Foreign Office, British State Papers Cmd. 5974:** Report of a committee set up to consider certain correspondence between Sir Henry McMahon, (His Majesty's High

Commissioner in Egypt) and the Sherif of Mecca in 1915 and 1916.
*London: H.M.S.O. 1939.*
*51 pp., app., 19½ cms.*

The report of the committee set up to consider the McMahon–
Hussein correspondence in relation to Palestine which was presented to the Arab and United Kingdom Conference on Palestine.
In addition to the report there are appendices consisting of the
Arab interpretation of the correspondence regarding Palestine,
the British response and observations by the Lord Chancellor on
the legal aspects of the matter. Also reproduced are the terms of
Hogarth's message to Hussein in January, 1918; the declaration
to the Seven in June, 1918; Allenby's assurance to Emir Faisal
in October, 1918; the Anglo-French declaration of November
1918.
   The case made by the Arab delegation was that the Palestine
area was part of the area designated as part of an independent
Arab state. The United Kingdom contention was that on a proper
construction of the correspondence Palestine was excluded from
this understanding but that the language in which it had been
expressed was not so specific or unmistakable as was thought at
that time. The committee concluded, however, that Britain was
not free to dispose of Palestine without regard to the wishes and
interests of the inhabitants and that the British Government had,
as a result of the correspondence, incurred responsibilities
towards the inhabitants.

HUREWITZ, J. C.
**Diplomacy in the Near and Middle East:** A documentary
record: 1914–1956. Vol. II.
*London: Van Nostrand Co. 1956.*
*xviii, 427 pp., index, 23½ cms.*

The main annotation to this work will be found under Section 1c,
however, the following is of relevance to this section.
   The Mandate for Palestine, 24 July 1922 (p. 106).

\*INGRAMS, DOREEN
**Palestine papers, 1917–1922:** Seeds of conflict.
*London: John Murray. 1972.*
*xii, 198 pp., illus., map, notes, index, 22 cms.*

The situation in Palestine following the Peace Conference was
one of uncertainty as the British military administration had no
mandate other than the right of conquerors and immigration of
the Jews and the purchase of land were both restricted. Unrest
amongst the Arab population was building, however, partially

caused by the fear that the Jews would be buying large tracts of land and controlling the economy of the country. Indeed the Chief Administrator reported in August 1919 that although in sympathy with the idea for a Jewish National Home this was so 'as long as it is not carried out at the expense of the rightful inhabitants and owners of the land. There is no doubt whatever that the feeling of the great mass of the population is very antagonistic to the scheme . . .'

The San Remo Conference confirmed the British mandate for Palestine and Transjordan with the proviso that 'the mandate for Palestine is to have as its guiding objects the establishment of the Jewish National Home, the rights of the present inhabitants, of course, being adequately safeguarded . . .' Arab reaction was one of outright opposition and this section reproduces messages of opposition from various Arab sources. One such message from Bedouin Chiefs is partially quoted from as follows:

1. Palestine is dear to us therefore we can never accept that the newcomers should rob it from our hands.
2. Palestine is sacred to us, consequently we can never forget the dangers surrounding it.
3. The Zionist danger which threatens Palestine at present shall soon menace us and the Arab nation at large.
4. The national demonstrations which the people all over the country had made and the strong continual protests that were submitted to you . . . proved that the nation refuses the Zionist Emigration . . . and we say that the nation is prepared to protect this sacred charge, the charge of our fathers and forefathers with all its power.

*Jewish Agency for Palestine
**Documents relating to the McMahon Letters.**
*London: Jewish Agency for Palestine. 1939.*
*20 pp., map, 19½ cms.*

This publication lists documents relating to the McMahon letters in an attempt to prove that during the crucial period 1917–21 no claims were raised by the Arabs to Palestine on the basis of this correspondence and indeed in various ways the Arabs explicitly agreed to Palestine being treated differently from Arab territories.
Contents:

i Documents relating to the McMahon letters.
ii British Government pronouncements.
iii Statements by British negotiators.

# ARAB-JEWISH RELATIONS

AL-MIYAHID, SHARIF
**Arab Nationalism:** A historical analysis.
*Pakistan Horizon (Karachi), 1963, pp. 37-46.*

The problem of the Balfour declaration was the root of the Palestine problem as it increased the volume of Jewish immigration. Coupled with the increased Jewish population was the problem of the land which was being bought from Arab peasants and absentee Arab landowners resulting in increased resentment between the two peoples. The result of the Palestine problem was to teach the Arabs the bitter lesson that of making them 'conscious of their own weakness, inherent or otherwise, their disunity, their lack of singleness of purpose.' On the other hand, it made them intensely nationalist – and Arab.

*ARAB OFFICE OF JERUSALEM
**The Problem of Palestine:** Memorandum presented to the Anglo-American Committee of Enquiry.
*London: Arab Office. 1946.*
*8 pp.*

Although this pamphlet was presented in relation to the committee sitting to deal with the problem of Palestine and the termination of the mandate the historical introduction is of relevance.

This deals with the opposition of the Arabs to the Jewish immigration which was based on an historical connection which was effectively ended centuries before. Secondly the Arab case argues that the Allies had recognised the rights of the majority to make its own decisions by the various undertakings and statements made during World War I. Thirdly the Arabs argue that in terms of geography Palestine is part of Syria, 'its indigenous inhabitants belong to the Syrian branch of the Arab family of nations; all their culture and tradition link them to the other Arab peoples; and until 1917 Palestine formed part of the Ottoman Empire which included also several of the other Arab countries'.

Finally the Zionist presence and the support from the Western Powers has alienated Palestine from the other Arab countries being 'subjected to a regime, administrative, legal, fiscal and educational, different from that of the sister-countries'.

The remainder of the pamphlet deals with developments outside of the scope of this study.

ERSKINE, MRS. STEWART
**Palestine of the Arabs.**
*London: Harrap. 1935.*
*256 pp., illus., app., index, 21 cms.*

The mandate for Palestine was not resolved until 1923 and in the interim period the area was under British Military Administration and this period saw an increase in resentment shown by the Arabs, especially with regard to the increasing influence of the Jews. 'What made it harder to bear was the knowledge that the Jews, through their Agency, were in touch with the Palestine Government as well as with Downing Street and the League of Nations, while the Arabs, the rightful inhabitants of the country, had no means of direct communication with the Mandatory or the League.'

The military administration was followed by a Civil Administration in 1920 with Sir Herbert Samuel as High Commissioner, but the pattern of unrest continued in the light of the increased Jewish immigration into the country. Riots broke out in February of 1920 and again in April though these were far more serious lasting several days. 'The Arabs were the stronger fighters, and were armed by their desire to expel these invaders from their country; their greater casualties were occasioned after the soldiery and police went to the rescue of the Jews.'

The result of this unrest and the continuing influx of Jewish refugees caused further unrest between the Arabs and Jews and the Administration which meant that the granting of the Mandate was to receive unfavourable reaction from both communities.

*GILBERT, MARTIN
**The Arab-Israel conflict:** Its history in maps.
*London: Weidenfeld & Nicolson. 1974.*
*101 pp., maps, 25 cms.*

Part two is entitled 'The Jewish National Home' and the following maps are of interest:

10. Britain and the Jewish National Home, 1917–1923.
11. The Zionist plan for Palestine, February 1919.
12. Arab-Jewish conflict in 1920.
13. Arab-Jewish conflict in 1921.
14. Jewish settlement in the Valley of Jezreeh, 1921–5.

\*KIMCHE, JON
**Palestine or Israel:** The untold story of why we failed,
1917–1923: 1967–1973.
*London: Secker & Warburg. 1973.*
*xx, 360 pp., bibl., app., index, 29 cms.*

In this study the section of relevance is that dealing with the
period 1917–23. The work begins dealing with the British
approach to the Palestine question against the backcloth of the
European political situation with the powers bargaining amongst
themselves as to their relative territorial desires after the war and
with these desires changing as the fortunes of war changed.
Initially the Arab Bureau under Clayton pursued the furtherance
of the Arab cause in ignorance of what was developing with regard
to Palestine. However, the Zionist cause was being pursued in
political circles in Europe and this situation was further complicated by negotiations with France aimed at reconciling the
aims of the two nations in the Middle East coupled with Britain's
insistence on safeguarding the Suez Canal and the routes to India.

The second chapter deals with the Zionist view and is not within
the scope of this study. Suffice it to say that the chapter deals with
the roles of Weizmann and Lord Sieff in furthering the Zionist case.

Chapter Three is important to this study as it deals with the
Arab reaction to the handling of the Palestine Question. Following the failure of the Young Turks to grant Arab autonomy contact was made between the Arabs and Zionists to see if a common
front against Turkey was possible. However, these negotiations
had the contrary result as the Arabs felt that the Jewish delegates
were acting as Turkish agents and they considered that a Turkish-
Jewish front against the Arabs was a possibility. British support
for the Arabs was accepted mainly because of the fear of the
French with their emphasis on the Christian connection.

It is stressed in this section that the Palestinian role in the
Syrian National Movement was extremely important though they
soon emancipated themselves from the influence and control of
Damascus. Also the influence of Amin el-Husaini, the Mufti of
Jerusalem, is also stressed in shaping the policies of Palestinian
nationalism which formed the basis of future Arab policies on
Palestine. Despite negotiations between Weizmann and Faisal
events took another course with anti-Jewish riots in Jerusalem in
April 1920 which Amin el-Husaini saw as the beginning of the
struggle for independence with success hinging on the Arab
cause being led by the Palestinians and by driving a wedge
between Britain and the Zionists.

LUNTZ, YOSEF
**Diplomatic contacts between the Zionist movement and the Arab National Movement at the close of the First World War.**
*Hamizrah Hedadash (Jerusalem). 1962, pp. 212–229.*

Initially Jewish immigration was seen as beneficial in terms of economics and culture though in 1904 Negib Azoury predicted that the two movements were destined to become bitter rivals. Contact was made between the two sides prior to the war but these negotiations lapsed with the outbreak of war. Following the occupation of Palestine in 1917 by Britain contacts were renewed with the Jews strengthened by the Balfour Declaration and the Arabs by the success of the Arab Revolt.

The summary (main article in Hebrew) then continues to consider the various discussions between the two sides with the Zionists hoping that Feisal would prove to be a moderating influence. However, the move failed as it became clear to Feisal that Britain had abandoned Syria to France and Palestine to the Jews and as his support now rested with extremist elements any form of compromise was impossible.

*PERLMANN, M.
**Chapters of Arab-Jewish Diplomacy, 1918–1922.**
*Jewish Social Studies. Vol. VI, No. 2, April 1944, pp. 123–154.*

A lengthy article dealing with the problem of Arab-Jewish relations during the period in question. The first part, however, deals with the period prior to 1918 during which the problem of the Arab population of Palestine was not recognised and not really considered. Although some negotiations with the Arabs did take place with the knowledge of the Turkish authorities '. . . only a few Zionist leaders were alive to the difficulties which Arab resistance would place in their path'.

Following the Balfour Declaration events took a more serious turn as Arab opposition to Jewish immigration became widespread and Jewish diplomacy aimed at allaying Arab fears which were finally recognised as a serious obstacle. Although some measure of success was achieved between Weizmann and Feisal elsewhere anti-Jewish feeling grew. Problems arose at the Peace Conference because of America's approach to Palestine which favoured an eventual Jewish state, French opposition to a Sherifian regime in Palestine and growing extremism amongst Feisal's supporters.

Negotiations continued after the Cairo Conference in March

1921 but all efforts proved to be abortive with too many factors standing in the way of success. The Jews attempted to negotiate on the basis of the kinship of the two nations, the benefits to the whole area of Jewish settlement in Palestine, the non-imperialistic nature of Jewish aspirations and the safeguarding of the Palestinian Arabs. However, no adequate propaganda was carried out among the Arabs, the Jews were unprepared for Arab opposition and the British were non-cooperative.

PORATH, Y.
**The Emergence of the Palestinian-Arab National Movement, 1918–1929.**
*London: Cass. 1974.*
*IX, 406 pp., notes, app., bibl., index.*
*(Chapter One and Two, pp. 1–122.)*

These chapters deal with the situation in Palestine from the end of World War I to the assumption of the Mandate by Britain. The first chapter deals with the Arab rejection of Zionism and the crystallisation of Palestinian-Arab ideology and this is discussed in the light of the causes and effects of the anti-Zionist awakening at the end of World War I. This leads to the development of the Palestinian-Arab ideology and its reality in terms of Arab opposition.

The second chapter deals with the concept of the change from 'Southern Syria' to Palestine as an area with its own national identity following the territory being placed under a British Military administration with Jerusalem as the administrative centre of the country. 'There is no doubt that the meaning of the term "Palestine" was largely reinforced by this, for although it is true that the term was in general use among the population before the war, the division of the country into three separate districts certainly did not strengthen this concept.'

\*SCHECHTMAN, JOSEPH B.
**The Mufti and the Fuehrer:** The rise and fall of Haj Amin el-Husseine.
*London: Thomas Yoseleff. 1965.*
*336 pp., frontis., illus., notes, index, 21 cms.*

A biography, by a Zionist, of Haj Amin el-Husaine who was one of the driving forces behind the Arab nationalist movement between the two world wars. In his introduction the author states that the biography is an attempt to provide a fair portrait of '. . . the central person constantly exercising dynamic, powerful influence, occupying the fore of the troubled and often tragic Palestine scene'.

The centre of el-Husaini's political outlook was the idea of Arab nationalism and fierce opposition to the Zionist case for a Jewish national home in Palestine. He was believed to be responsible for the anti-Jewish riots of 1920 in Jerusalem and he fled to escape imprisonment but he was allowed to return in 1921 and was appointed to the post of Mufti of Jerusalem with British support. This move did not moderate his views and again in 1937 he was involved in provoking anti-Jewish riots and in agitating against the British mandate which once again led to his fleeing Palestine.

His political activity then became centred in Baghdad where he was the leading force behind the Axis coup of 1941 in Iraq. Following the collapse of the revolt he escaped to Tehran and from there made his way to Berlin where he joined the Fascist group organising propaganda broadcasts and espionage and the recruiting of Muslim units for Germany. Despite these activities he escaped trial following the war and continued to wage war against Jewish nationalism and British imperialism though his influence became less evident following the defeat of the Arabs in 1948.

The author considers that the Mufti's political philosophy was composed of three basic factors—that of Pan-Arabism, Pan-Islamism and the independence of Palestine. It was the latter factor which was dominant as the Mufti was a Palestinian Arab first with the other factors serving only to promote this aim. Such was his personal identification with an Arab Palestine and the pursuit of this idea that these '... constituted both the strength and weakness of the role Haj Amin played in the Middle East'.

\*TIBAWI, A. L.
**T. E. Lawrence, Faisal and Weizmann:** The 1919 attempt to secure an Arab Balfour Declaration.
*Royal Central Asian Journal. Vol. LVI, Part II, June 1969, pp. 156–163.*

An examination of Lawrence's involvement in the attempts to secure Arab recognition of the Zionist programme for Palestine. The crux of Lawrence's involvement is seen as his being Balfour's choice to attend the Peace Conference and to act as interpreter between Faisal and Weizmann which it is considered he manipulated to suit his own Zionist sympathies. Evidence for this assumption is a quotation from a note by Faisal attached to an agreement, in English, drafted by Weizmann to solve the problem of Arab opposition to the Balfour Declaration. The note by Faisal was in Arabic and contained the phrase 'Arab independence' as defined by his memorandum to the Foreign Office on 4 January 1919 as a condition of agreeing to this document. However, the translation given to Weizmann by Lawrence omitted the phrase and it was this translation that was used by the Zionists as proof of the Arab agreement. This attempt was nullified by Faisal's statement to the *Jewish Chronicle* on 3 October 1919 which in response to a question regarding the Arab attitude to the Balfour Declaration stated:

> 'To be sure they do . . . Palestine, Mesopotamia and Syria are inseparable and although we cannot legislate for the future, still we Arabs cannot yield Palestine as part of our kingdom. Indeed we would fight to the last ditch against Palestine being other than part of the kingdom and for the supremacy of the Arabs in the land.'

It can be seen therefore that the Zionist attempt to secure Arab support had failed and 'Vain, too, were the effects of such men as Sykes and Lawrence to intimidate and coax the Arabs into acquiescing in the Zionist policy of the British Government'.

## BIOGRAPHICAL WORKS

\*Ashbee, C. R.
**A Palestine Notebook, 1918–1923.**
*London: Heinemann. 1923.*
*xiii, 278 pp., frontis., 23½ cms.*

The author was Civil Adviser to the City of Jerusalem during the period in question and this book is an account of the administration and the people of Palestine during these years. The developments in Palestine he sees as having fallen into an inevitable sequence. 'There was, first, the confusion and fearful hazard of war, then the period of intense optimism that followed victory; next, a time of suspended creation ending in explosion and the coming of the civil administration, with all its new hopes and dreams. Next a spell of hard, conscientious, constructive work, a happy time, modified for many of us by the gradual realization that the base of our new building was unsure, and that we did not know our materials.'

STORRS, RONALD
**Orientations.**
*London: Nicholson and Watson. 1937.*
*xviii, 557 pp., illus., maps, index, 21 cms.*

See Sections 1b, 1c and 2b for annotations of the above work.

# (d) THE CAIRO CONFERENCE OF MARCH 1921

## GENERAL WORKS

\*ANTONIUS, GEORGE
**The Arab Awakening:** The story of the Arab nationalist movement.
*London: Hamish Hamilton. 1938.*
*xii, 13–471 pp., maps, app., index, 22 cms.*

The Cairo Conference was held to try and re-establish peace in the area and the Iraqi revolt was instrumental in causing the British government to change its policy and tactics in order to reduce its commitments. The result was for Iraq the 'election' of Faisal to the throne and for Abdullah the Emirship of Transjordan though the latter case was in effect a legalisation of a *fait accompli*. The claim by Lawrence that the Cairo Conference 'made straight all the tangle, finding solutions fulfilling (I think) our promises in letter and spirit' is disputed and this is evidenced by 'the measures of coercion which were subsequently resorted to in vain by France in Syria and by Great Britain in Palestine to force the mandates through upon an unwilling population'.

GASTER, Z.
**Lawrence and King Hussein:** the 1921 negotiations.
*National Review. 15 October 1918, pp. 512–515.*

This article discusses the attempts made by Lawrence in 1921 to negotiate a treaty with King Hussein but he was met with suspicion and mistrust because, although the treaty would free the Hedjaz it ignored Hussein's aspirations to a wider Arab empire. The treaty was unsigned and the reasons given by Hussein were as follows:

'It is impossible for him [Lawrence] to serve anything but

British interests. All these brilliant promises are not good enough for us. If they were sincere in the pledges they gave me prior to the Revolt, let them merely and simply fulfil them today . . . But to sign a treaty accepting much less than they originally promised me – I would rather surrender my soul than do it.'

\*GREAT BRITAIN: COLONIAL OFFICE
**Report on the Middle East Conference, Cairo and Jerusalem, March 12 to 30th 1921,** with appendix.
*London: H.M.S.O. n.d. (Secret).*
*210 pp., 30 cms.*

The official account of the Cairo Conference giving the background to the Conference, a report on the discussions and its recommendations.

\*KHAN, RASHEEDUDDIN
**Mandate and monarchy in Iraq:** A study in the origin of the British Mandate and the creation of the Hashemite Monarchy in Iraq: 1919–1921.
*Islamic Culture. Vol. XLIII, No. 3, July 1969, pp. 207–213 and No. 4, October 1969, pp. 255–276.*

Before discussing the Cairo Conference and its implications the article begins by discussing Faisal as a prospective king and the way in which he was regarded by the participants in the affairs of Iraq. 'His potential role as a hyphen between the demands of the nationalists and the interests of the imperialists, which throughout his active career as an Arab leader and as Arab king, he sought to reconcile with varying degrees of success, was his major qualification as the most suitable candidate for the throne of Iraq under the shadow of vigilant but indirect British dominance in the region.'

The article continues by discussing the Cairo Conference and the decision to support the candidature of Faisal for the throne of Iraq. Churchill, prompted by Lawrence, wanted to face the Iraqis with a *fait accompli* but Cox argued for the calling of a Congress to decide the form of rule and if monarchical to select the ruler. A carefully drawn up timetable for the ushering in of Faisal in Iraq was approved by the Conference '. . . so that Amir Faisal should appear on the horizons of Baghdad not as a British protégé but as a chosen and desired leader of the Iraqi people'.

Although the position of Faisal was satisfactorily agreed at the Conference the opinion in Iraq had swung against the Sherifians mainly at the instigation of Talib al-Naqib who was anxious to further his own cause though in the guise of campaigning for the Naqib of Baghdad. As Minister of the Interior it was feared that Talib could seriously prejudice the outcome and so Talib was arrested and deported to Ceylon using as a pretext certain indiscretions made at a dinner party on 13 April 1920 in the presence of a large influential gathering.

The latter part of the article deals with Faisal's arrival in Iraq and the reception arranged for him and the arrangements for the referendum which approved Faisal as king by 96% of the vote although the validity of the referendum is brought into question. 'It is surprising why such a fake show was needed formally to recognise Faisal as King. Had the election been strictly fair and representative the strong probability was that Faisal would have won. The sham tamasha organised by the High Commissioner was taken, and with justification, as yet another proof of British designs on Iraq and a clear exposure of Faisal as a person susceptible to British pressure and influence.' This situation was not helped by the Anglo-Iraqi treaty which was merely a change of name for the mandatory document and which caused political attitudes to become unfriendly towards Faisal and hostile to Britain. 'Faisal gave all the appearance of beginning his reign as a beneficiary of British diplomacy rather than the leader of the Arab Revolt, the spokesman of the Arab cause, the hero-son of an Arab King.'

*KLIEMAN, AARON S.
**Foundations of British policy in the Arab World.**
*The Cairo Conference of 1921.*
*London: Johns Hopkins Press. 1970.*
*xiv, 322 pp., illus., maps, bibl., index, 23½ cms.*

The Cairo Conference marked an important attempt on the part of the British Government to revise its policy with regard to the Middle East and to restore some direction to this policy. The work begins by examining Britain's policy with regard to the Ottoman Empire prior to World War I, that of bolstering 'the sick man of Europe' which was reversed when Turkey allied itself with Germany. This section also deals with the various commitments entered into by Britain on the one hand to the Arabs through the Hussein–McMahon correspondence and to the French through the Sykes–Picot agreement.

The author then considers the problems of the Peace Conference which was faced with the problems of reconciling the claims of the Arabs with those of the Great Powers, claims which were further complicated by the divergence of outlook between Britain and France. The differences between Britain and France arose mainly over the question of Syria which had an Arab Government under Feisal and which the French expected to be given control over under the peace settlement. The situation was not helped by British domestic policies which was forcing an early withdrawal of troops which dictated the need for an early settlement to the Middle East problems.

Despite these obvious problems the approach to the Peace Conference was one of optimism and the author discusses the failure of the conference to achieve a just peace. The Arabs found themselves as supplicants rather than being treated as partners in the victory and this led to a deterioration in relations between the Great Powers and the Arabs and between Britain and France. The result of all the deliberations was that the Arabs were forced to accept French control over Syria whilst Britain was interested only in a policy of disengagement whilst securing her interests in Arabia, Mesopotamia and Palestine. The French also moved from a policy which was willing to control Syria with Arab assistance to one of control regardless of Arab feelings or participation.

This imposed settlement led to a brief interlude of uneasy peace between the end of the war and the outbreak of violence in 1920. It is this year which is next considered by the author dealing firstly with the San Remo Conference which gave the French the mandate over Syria and Britain the mandate over Iraq and Palestine. The French intransigence over the problem of Syria caused bitter unrest amongst the Arabs and the certainty that the extreme sections of Feisal's supporters would take matters into their own hands. The result was an uprising against the French which was ruthlessly crushed by the French army and this was followed by a rising in Mesopotamia which was fanned by the Syrians and put down by the British.

The Cairo Conference began on 12 March 1921 firstly to consider the situation in the Middle East with the immediate objective being the reduction of military commitments. The question of Mesopotamia was considered first with the prime question being whether there should be an Arab ruler and if so whether it should be a member of the Sherifian family. If the first two were thought advisable the next task was to select a member of the family and it was decided that the chosen person should offer himself for election to the throne of Mesopotamia. The choice fell upon Feisal and it was agreed to offer him the throne and that the choice should be given popular appeal by means of an election.

The second problem to be considered was that of Palestine in company with Transjordan and it was decided, in Churchill's words: 'It had seemed best to support the Sherifian cause; in fact no other alternative presented itself.' This resulted in Abdullah being offered the governorship of Transjordan to ensure British control over the area and to prevent Abdullah interfering in Syria. Regarding Palestine it was decided that a defence force was necessary to maintain order, that the Arab population should be protected but Jewish immigration would not be halted.

The author then goes on to analyse the situation in Iraq, Palestine and Transjordan in the light of the Cairo Conference. The policy as evolved was a success in that it did achieve its primary objective of effecting economies but the author considers that it compromised British honour because: 'In the eyes of the Arabs Britain's reputation declined thereafter as she became the focus for nationalist resentment in each of the countries of the Fertile Crescent.'

The author concludes that the Cairo Conference was probably too ambitious in trying to graft monarchies and in projecting the Sherifians into the Arab World only to find that they were, in the end, largely unacceptable. However, 'As a forum for evaluating both the problems and prospects of the Arab World, the Cairo Conference of 1921 was therefore unprecedented in the long history of British relations with that region. And in its recognition of the importance of the Middle East for any global power and for world politics it has not been equalled since, not by Great Britain nor by the United States.'

LENCZOWSKI, GEORGE
**The Middle East in world affairs.**
*New York: Cornell University Press. 2nd ed. 1956.*
*xix, 576 pp., maps, bibl., index, 24 cms.*

The Cairo Conference of 1921 was an attempt to tidy up the Middle East following the Peace Settlement which had not solved the problems as unrest was prevalent. The essential features of the conference were that Faisal was given the throne of Iraq and Abdullah the Emirship of Transjordan which was removed from the terms of the Balfour Declaration regarding Jewish settlement. Hussein became an embittered and lonely ruler of the Hedjaz refusing to enter into a treaty with Britain or indeed to sign a peace treaty at all.

\*MONROE, ELIZABETH
**Britain's moment in the Middle East, 1914–1956.**
*London: Chatto & Windus. 1963.*
*254 pp., maps, notes, bibl., index, 22 cms.*

The situation in the Middle East following the decisions of the
San Remo Conference was one of considerable unrest with the
Arabs revolting in Iraq and in Syria and with growing unrest
evident in Palestine. To this must be added a worsening situation
in British domestic politics leading to a demand for less involvement in the Middle East both militarily and financially.

The outcome of this was the Cairo Conference which was
convened by Churchill once the administration of the mandate
had been transferred to the Colonial Office. The conference had
also been the result of pressure from officials in the Middle East
who had foreseen that the situation was getting out of control but
up till then had been unable to obtain government action.

The conference resulted in Faisal being given the throne of
Iraq subject to a referendum and Abdullah the Emirship of
Transjordan with responsibility for policing Iraq passing from
the army to the Air Force. The solutions were a compromise
'between the Middle Eastern wish for independence, and the
British wish to retain partial control. The British recipe was to
give moderate local leaders something to show for their
moderation.'

MONROE, ELIZABETH
**The Round Table and the Middle Eastern Peace Settle-
ment, 1917–1922.**
*Round Table. Vol. 60, November 1970, pp. 479–490.*

Lawrence's involvement in the aftermath of the peace settlement
began in September 1920 with a series of articles in the *Round
Table* expounding the concept of 'allies not subjects' in the
British mandates. At the same time, however, he was devising
with Trenchard an economy scheme for the air control of the
mandatory area instead of expensive military garrisons.

This activity by Lawrence was followed by his acceptance of a
post as adviser to Winston Churchill at the Colonial Office. At the
Cairo Conference in March 1921 Churchill and Lawrence were
instrumental in inducing Faisal to accept the throne of Iraq and
installing Abdullah as Emir of Transjordan having also secured
an agreement as to the non-involvement of the nationalists in the
affairs of Palestine.

POWELL, E. ALEXANDER
**The Struggle for power in Moslem Asia.**
*London: John Long Ltd. 1925.*
*320 pp., maps, index, 22½ cms.*

Following Churchill's appointment as Secretary of State for the
Colonies a new section was set up, that of the Middle Eastern
Department with T. E. Lawrence and Gertrude Bell as Arab
advisers. In March 1921 a conference was held at Cairo to try and
settle the outstanding Middle East problems including that of
Iraq which was proving to be a problem in domestic politics.

It was decided at the conference despite Cox's initial opposition
that Faisal should be given the throne of Iraq and arrangements
were made for any opposition to be stifled. Indeed Seyyid Talib,
Minister of the Interior, was arrested by the army and sent to
Ceylon for voicing opposition to the plan. The promised referendum was held and Faisal duly proclaimed the popular choice of
the people though 'the Sheikhs and the notables were perfectly
aware, therefore, that the cards were stacked against them. They
knew that if they voted against Faisal they would stand an excellent chance of meeting the same fate which had overtaken Talib,
and even if they escaped immediate exile, Feisal, once he came
into power, would see to it that their political careers, if not their
lives came to an abrupt end.'

This was followed in October of 1922 by a treaty of friendship
which could be regarded as a first step towards independence
though Britain continued to exercise a large measure of control.

STEWART, DESMOND
**The Middle East:** Temple of Janus.
*London: Hamish Hamilton. 1972.*
*viii, 414 pp., bibl., index, 24 cms.*

In Chapters Two and Three of the section entitled 'The Anglo-
Arab Twenties' the Cairo Conference is considered. The aim of
the conference was to deal with the future of the British Middle
East and in particular Iraq, Palestine and the area from the
Euphrates to the Jordan. As his adviser Churchill had recalled
T. E. Lawrence a move considered to have been an error of
judgement. 'Churchill was an innocent where complex characters
were involved. He had grabbed this young celebrity for his
adviser on Arab affairs. He did not know that Lawrence was an
inaccurate guide; he could not intuit that in 1921 Lawrence was
clasped by a psychological octopus . . .'

The author then deals with the solution as resolved for Iraq which was to provide the country with a ruler and an Arab administration which would be directed by British advisers. Faisal was put forward as candidate for the throne and was elected with 96% of the vote, a result which had been assured by the work of Sir Percy Cox and Gertrude Bell, with the tribal leaders recognising the realities of the situation as Faisal was the British choice which required endorsement by the people.

In dealing with the desert area of Jordan the position was further complicated by the arrival at Amman of Abdullah with the declared intention of leading his forces against the French in Syria to restore Faisal to the throne. Although such a move would have been doomed to failure it would have caused further trouble with the French and Transjordan was needed as a link between Palestine and Iraq. It was decided, therefore, to offer Abdullah the Emirship of Transjordan together with a subsidy which effectively stifled any designs that Abdullah might have on Syria and he also undertook to refrain from interference in the affairs of Palestine.

## BIOGRAPHICAL WORKS

ALDINGTON, RICHARD
**Lawrence of Arabia:** A biographical enquiry.
*London: Collins. 1955.*
*448 pp., illus., maps, bibl., index, 21 cms.*

See entry under 'The Arab Revolt and the War in the Middle East' for annotation.

ERSKINE, MRS. STEWART
**King Faisal of Iraq.**
*London: Hutchinson & Co. 1933.*
*288 pp., illus., app., index, 23½ cms.*

At the Cairo Conference it was decided to support the candidature of Faisal for the throne of Iraq and this move was supported by Sir Percy Cox and Gertrude Bell who worked to ensure that the result of the referendum to be held would be favourable. The result was a 96% vote in favour of Faisal's candidature though the Kurds refused to vote as they still sought autonomy for their own region.

*GRAVES, ROBERT
**Lawrence and the Arabs.**
*London: Cape. 1927.*
*454 pp., frontis., illus., app., index, 20½ cms.*
*(Chapter 29.)*

In considering the Cairo Conference Graves quotes from a letter he received from Lawrence in response to certain questions raised by Graves regarding the Cairo Conference in which Lawrence states that he was against complete withdrawal from the Middle East. 'Mr. Churchill was determined to find ways and means of avoiding so complete a reversal of the traditional British attitude. I was at one with him in this attitude.'

The account by Graves deals only briefly with the question of Palestine and the appointment of Abdullah with main emphasis being given to the solution in Iraq with Faisal being 'Elected' as king. He quotes again from a letter from Lawrence which considers the results of the Conference in which Lawrence wrote:

'I take to myself credit for some of Mr. Churchill's pacification of the Middle East, for while he was carrying it out he had the help of such knowledge and energy as I possess . . . When it was in working order, in March 1922, I felt that I had gained every point I wanted. The Arabs had their chance and it was up to them, if they were good enough, to make their own mistakes and profit by them. My object with the Arabs was always to make them stand on their own feet.'

HART, B. H. LIDDELL
**T. E. Lawrence in Arabia and after.**
*London: Cape. 1934.*
*490 pp., frontis., illus., maps, index, 22 cms.*
*(Part Four, Chapter III.)*

The question of the Cairo Conference is dealt with only briefly and whilst outlining the main points the work is really tailored to a consideration as to how the conference affected the part played by Lawrence and his commitment to the Arabs.

KNIGHTLEY, PHILIP AND SIMPSON, COLIN
**The Secret lives of Lawrence of Arabia.**
*London: Nelson. 1969.*
*x, 293 pp., plates, illus., bibl., index, 23 cms.*

Prior to the Cairo Conference Lawrence had been campaigning in the press for a settlement to the problems of Mesopotamia with British control to be transferred from the Army to the Air Force and a greater say for the Arabs in the government. Churchill persuaded Lawrence to join the Colonial Office as an adviser on Arab affairs with the aim of producing a solution to the Middle East question.

The Cairo Conference was held in March 1921 and the main

solutions were to be the 'election' of Faisal to the throne of Iraq and Abdullah was made Emir of Transjordan on the understanding that he put an end to anti-French and anti-Zionist activities. The important decisions were taken in London before the Conference had been held and Churchill was already committed to the Jewish National Home. It was Lawrence's opinion that the settlement was a good one and he was to write in 'Seven Pillars': 'So we were quit of the wartime Eastern adventure, with clean hands.' Lawrence also spent a period unsuccessfully trying to persuade Hussein to sign a treaty with Britain and a period reorganising the local administration in Transjordan.

*MONROE, ELIZABETH
**Philby of Arabia.**
*London: Faber. 1973.*
*332 pp., illus., maps, notes, bibl., index, 22½ cms.*
*(Chapter V.)*

In March 1921 Cox, Gertrude Bell and one or two pro-Hashemite Iraqis attended the Cairo Conference at which it was decided that Faisal should be offered the throne of Iraq after election by the people. On their return to Iraq the British delegates kept quiet about the decision and continued to draft electoral laws for the free selection of the future form of government by the people.

The rumour of Faisal being offered as a favoured candidate soon reached Baghdad and Philby found Talib difficult to handle as he began to curry favour with the extremist elements, censoring pro-Faisal newspapers and plotting with repatriates from Syria. Talib, had, however, overplayed his hand and on Cox's orders he was arrested by the British army and sent to Ceylon to forestall any trouble thus leaving Philby as acting Minister of the Interior.

Faisal's arrival and reception in Iraq was organised by Philby and he saw that the reception in the south was cool although Cox ensured a welcome for Faisal at Baghdad. Philby was ill with malaria and so was not present when Faisal complained of his treatment and Philby's lack of enthusiasm. On 11 July 1921 the Council of Ministers decided to end uncertainty and to proclaim Faisal as king which meant that Philby had to leave Iraq.

MORRIS, JAMES
**The Hashemite Kings.**
*London: Faber and Faber. 1959.*
*231 pp., illus., bibl., index, 22 cms.*

The unrest in the Middle East and the desire of the British government to reduce its military and financial involvement in the area led to the Cairo Conference at which Churchill attempted to settle the problems of unrest, especially in Iraq, and the reduction of British military presence in the area.

It was agreed that Faisal should be given the throne of Iraq subject to a referendum and that Abdullah should be made Emir of Transjordan, though the latter decision was forced upon the Colonial Office by circumstances. 'Abdullah had made himself master of Transjordan, with a government in Amman and an enthusiastic public support. The Syrian adventure was in abeyance: Abdullah had carved himself a new estate.' Faced with this situation the Cairo Conference moved to Jerusalem and set about legalising the position. 'Abdullah agreed that he would not attack the French in Syria, and that he would support Feisal's claim to the crown of Iraq; later, unlike his father, he also recognised the Palestine Mandate.'

MOUSA, SULEIMAN
**T. E. Lawrence:** An Arab view.
*London: O.U.P. 1966.*
*x, 301 pp., bibl., index, 22 cms.*
*(Chapter VIII.)*

The Cairo Conference was held in March 1921 but the important decisions had already been reached in London as it had already been agreed that Faisal should be made King of Iraq, the mandate annulled and a treaty would be signed to replace it.

The position of Transjordan had not been decided and the Emirship of Abdullah was a result of the crisis caused by the expulsion of Faisal by the French as Abdullah was bent on invading Syria to restore Arab rule. British attempts to resolve the situation resulted in Abdullah gaining Transjordan in return for an agreement not to invade Syria or to cause unrest in Palestine over the Balfour Declaration.

STORRS, RONALD
**Orientations.**
*London: Nicholson and Watson. 1937.*
*xviii, 557 pp., illus., maps, index, 21 cms.*

See Sections 1b, 1c, and 2b for annotations of the above work.

# Section 3

# The Fertile Crescent under the Mandate System

This section deals with Iraq, Syria including the Lebanon and Palestine from the assigning of the mandate by the San Remo Conference and dealing in each case with the period immediately following the assumption of authority by the mandatory powers. The date at which the study ends is dictated by events rather than by an arbitrary date.

## (a) Iraq

The situation in Iraq is marked by three differing aspects, the first being the initial occupation of the country following the defeat of the Turkish army and the assigning of the mandate to Britain. Secondly there is the uprising of 1920 with the subsequent desire of the British Government to reduce its involvement which resulted in the 'election' of Faisal to the throne of Iraq following the decisions taken at the Cairo Conference. Lastly there is the setting up of an administration under the terms of the mandate with Feisal at its head and the problem of the minority communities.

General works on Iraq covering the period include 'An introduction to the past and present of the Kingdom of Iraq' by a Committee of Officials which ends in 1946 with the main area being the period after World War I, and Fisher's *The Middle East: A History*. Of greater significance are *The Making of modern Iraq: A product of world forces* by Foster; *Iraq: A study in political development* by P. W. Ireland and Stephen Longrigg's *Iraq, 1900–1950*. The period prior to the civil unrest is dealt with in articles by C. J. Edmonds entitled 'Gertrude Bell in the Near and Middle East' and 'The Arab World Today' by D. G. Hogarth. Significant treatment of this aspect is provided by Harry N. Howard's *The partition of Turkey: A diplomatic history, 1913–1923*; *The Arab world: past, present and future* by Izzedin and Arnold Wilson's *Loyalties: Mesopotamia*, Vol. II.

The uprising in 1920 was partly the product of internal unrest and partly the result of the agitation of dissident Iraqi officers serving with Faisal's army in Syria. In addition to the general works already cited the uprising is dealt with by Abid A. Al-Marayti in his *Diplomatic history of modern Iraq*; Rasheeduddin Khan's *Mandate and monarchy in Iraq* . . . and the letter from T. E. Lawrence to *The Times* entitled 'Arab rights: Our policy in Mesopotamia'. The view of the British administration is reflected by Volume II of *The Letters of Gertrude Bell*; Lieutenant-General Haldane's article 'The Arab rising in Mesopotamia, 1920'; Sacher's *The Emergence of the Middle East, 1914–1924* and most significantly by the India Office publication of 1920 a 'Review of the Civil Administration of Mesopotamia'. The solution to the problem was provided by the Cairo Conference (see Section 2d) and works on this subject are interrelated to this section. Articles of relevance to the 'election' of Faisal to the throne are Churchill's 'Mesopotamia and the new government'; Rasheeduddin Khan's work already cited and E. W. P. Newman's 'The Middle East Mandates'. Other works of interest are Elie Kedourie's section in *England and the Middle East* . . .; J. de V. Loder's *The truth about Mesopotamia, Palestine and Syria* and Mrs. Erskine's biography *King Faisal of Iraq*.

The period immediately following Faisal's enthronement is dealt with by Lord Birwood in his biography of Nuri As-Said, Mrs. Erskine's biography of Faisal and Eli Kedourie's *The Kingdom of Iraq: A retrospect*. Articles of interest are Sir Percy Cox's 'Iraq'; Rasheeduddin Khan's work already cited and Slater's 'Iraq' which is a useful survey of the period. The question of the minorities is dealt with in an article entitled 'Kurdish Nationalism' and in his book *Kurds, Turks and Arabs: Politics, travel and research in North Eastern Iraq, 1919–25* with the Assyrian minority being considered by Heazell in 'The woes of a distressed nation, being an account of the Assyrian people from 1914 to 1934'. All of these are in addition to the works mentioned in the introductory paragraph.

## (b) Syria including Lebanon

The situation in Syria following the war falls into two distinct sections the first being the period between the fall of Damascus and the French Mandate, during which the French occupied the Lebanon, whilst Faisal was the head of a provisional Arab government in Damascus whilst the Great Powers debated the future of the area. The second part concerns the period from the assigning of the mandate to France, which resulted in the defeat of the Syrian nationalists and the exile of Faisal, to the early years of the mandate.

General works on the Middle East deal with Syria and Lebanon because of the importance of these events both at the time and to later events in the area. In this context the works by Fisher *The Middle East: A History*; the Naval Intelligence restricted publication on Syria and Lebanon and Lenczowski's *The Middle East in World Affairs* are of value whilst the general works on Syria and Lebanon by Hitti and Haddad are of significance.

The question of Syria prior to the French assumption of the mandate is extensively covered in both books and periodical articles as this was a significant development in the history of the Arab nationalist movement. An essential work on this section is the work by Antonious on *The Arab Awakening* as are Zeine's *The struggle for Arab Independence: Western Diplomacy and the rise and fall of Faisal's Kingdom in Syria* and Tibawi's article 'Syria from the Peace Conference to the fall of Damascus'. Also of significance is the section on Syria from 1918–1920 in *England and the Middle East; The destruction of the Ottoman Empire, 1914–1921* by Elie Kedourie.

The San Remo Conference assigned the mandate for Syria to France and this meant an immediate conflict between the French and the Syrian nationalists. The text of 'The Mandate for Syria and Lebanon' is to be found in *The emergence of the modern Middle East: Selected readings* edited by Landau and this should be contrasted with the 'Resolution of the General Syrian Congress at Damascus' which is reproduced in Hurewitz, J. C. *Diplomacy in the Near and Middle East* and also in Landau. Two works are indispensable to this section, the first being Elizabeth MacCallum's *The Nationalist Crusade in Syria* and Stephen Longrigg's *Syria and Lebanon under French Mandate* both of which cover the early period of the mandate in great depth. Also of relevance are Powell's *The struggle for power in Moslem Asia* and the articles 'The roots of Arab Nationalism' by Fatemi and 'Syria under the French Mandate' by Hourani.

In addition the general works cited in the opening paragraphs should also be used and it is stressed that this period cannot be examined in isolation from the earlier sections covering the Sykes–Picot agreement, France's traditional interest in the Levant and the problems of the Peace Conference.

## (c) Palestine and Transjordan

The vexed question of Palestine, 'The twice promised land', which bedevils the Middle East and world affairs today, though now as the State of Israel, was linked with Transjordan as part of the British Mandate following the San Remo Conference. In this study the concern is mainly with the Arab case for Palestine but some Jewish works have been included where they also present the Arab side of the argument, and some works by British administrators to try and illustrate the problems of trying to steer a middle course between the two peoples. Objective works are not easy to find as the question of Palestine is an emotional one which seems to many writers to have no shades of grey with each people convinced of the justice of their case.

The Arab case is represented by several entries dealing specifically with the problem and also in many of the general books on the Middle East covering this period. However, four representative works should be mentioned here as being of importance with the most significant being Boustany's *The Palestine mandate invalid and impracticable* together with *Palestine through the fog of propaganda* by Abcarius. Also of value are the works by Atiyah and Hadawi entitled *The Palestine Question* and *Bitter Harvest: Palestine, 1914–1967*. Two works which argue the Zionist case but which consider the Arab viewpoint as well are Broido's *Jews, Arabs and the Middle East* and the thesis by Hattis entitled 'The Bi-national idea in Palestine during mandatory times'.

Several works have appeared presenting the British view of the period but these are not all relevant to this study though Barbour's *Nisi Dominus*; Bentwich's *Mandate memories, 1914–48* and *Orientations* by Sir Ronald Storrs have been included as being representative of the views of the British administrators. Also of significance is the so-called Churchill Memorandum of 1922 presenting official British policy regarding Palestine which is to be found in Hurewitz.

Although objective works are difficult to find three are worthy of mention with the most essential being Jon Kimche's *Palestine or Israel. The untold story of why we failed* . . .; the work by Sachar covering the area during this period *The emergence of the Middle East, 1914–1924* and Koestler's *Promise and fulfilment: Palestine, 1917–1949* which has 'no heroes or villains only confused people all with implicit faith in their cause'.

The problem of Palestine is complicated by various arguments, documents and official statements and there are four useful publications which collect these together; Dodd and Sadler's *Israel and the Arab World*; Walter Laquer's *Israeli/Arab reader*; Khalidi's *From haven to conquest* and Doreen Ingrams' *Palestine papers, 1917–1922: The seeds of conflict*. Indispensable as a visual guide to the Palestine problem is the excellent work by Michael Gilbert *The Arab-Israeli conflict: Its history in maps*.

Transjordan was not a major problem during this period, being under a loose British administration and passed to Arab control under Abdullah by the Cairo Conference of 1921 and excluded from the terms of the Balfour Declaration. General works on the Middle East are of relevance here especially Fisher's *The Middle East: A History* and the Naval Intelligence section publication *Palestine and Transjordan*. A necessary study for the early years of the Emirship of Transjordan is the autobiography of Abdullah edited by Philip Graves and also Elizabeth Monroe's *Philby of Arabia*.

This is an important section because of the complexity of the Palestine problem and its interaction with the problem of the Peace Settlement and the future of the Middle East as a whole. The situation in the Middle East today is still beset by the problem of Palestine with the Arab case based on their historical claims to the country and the pledges made through the McMahon-Hussein correspondence.

# (a) IRAQ

## GENERAL WORKS

*al-Marayti, Abid A.
**A Diplomatic history of modern Iraq.**
*New York: Speller. 1961.*
*xvi, 222 pp., app., bibl., index, 22 cms.*

This work is mainly concerned with the diplomatic history of Iraq following the gaining of independence but the opening chapters deal with the question of the mandate. Also the value of the work is enhanced by the fact that the author is an Iraqi and the work is in English.

In dealing with the establishment of the mandate the author sets the background to the peace conference by outlining the MacMahon–Hussein correspondence and the conflict between these pledges and the Sykes–Picot agreement. The class A mandate granted to Britain over Iraq was considered to be a compromise between these two differing agreements and as a result the term became a discredited title in Iraq with its associations with colonialism.

The author continues by dealing with the Iraqi opposition to the mandate from, amongst others, those members of the Arab army who fought with Allenby. This leads to a consideration of the Revolt of 1920 with its cost in terms of human life and money which led to a realisation on Britain's part that it was 'unable to resist the overwhelming desire of the people of Irak for the formation of a national Government under an Arab ruler'.

The work has numerous footnotes and several appendices providing information about early Iraqi politicians, posts held under the British administration and biographical details of Iraqi diplomats. The bibliography is extensive and includes official and non-official items.

*Antonius, George
**The Arab Awakening:** The story of the Arab nationalist movement.
*London: Hamish Hamilton. 1938.*
*xii, 13–471 pp., maps, app., index, 22 cms.*
*(Chapter XVI.)*

Iraq following the San Remo Conference was also in a state of unrest and this was not helped by the activities of Iraqi officers serving with Faisal in Damascus. The result was a revolt lasting from July to October 1920 causing the loss of lives on both sides and at one stage the Arabs controlled most of the country with the exception of Baghdad, Basra and Mosul. The situation was resolved by the return of Sir Percy Cox who put down the revolt and proceeded to implement the preparation of an organic law by a representative Iraqi body.

A provisional Arab government was formed with British advisers and Sir Percy Cox as High Commissioner. This was followed in 1921 by the 'election' of Faisal to the throne of Iraq and further progress towards Arab control though the British advisers retained considerable power especially in the tribal areas. However, Antonius feels that there was a credit side to Britain's presence in Iraq. 'Just as hard things may legitimately be said of the British government's piratical attempts to grab Iraq after the war, so it can without exaggeration be said that the modern state of Iraq owes its existence to the efforts and the devotion of its British officials.'

BEN-HORIN, ELIAHU
**The Middle East:** Crossroads of history.
*New York: W. W. Norton & Co. 1943.*
*248 pp., map, index, 21½ cms.*

COKE, RICHARD
**The Arab's place in the sun.**
*London: Butterworth. 1929.*
*318 pp., illus., maps, index, 22 cms.*

*(A COMMITTEE OF OFFICIALS)
**An introduction to the past and present of the Kingdom of Iraq.**
*Baltimore. 1946.*
*x, 118 pp., illus., map, bibl., 25½ cms.*

This work aims at tracing the history of Iraq from earliest times until 1946 with the main areas of concentration being the period following the outbreak of World War I and the state of Iraq at the time of publication. The work deals with the Arab participation in the war against the Turks which was motivated by the promises of wholesale Arab emancipation in the event of the campaign succeeding.

In considering the operation of the mandate by Britain the authors make no secret of the fact that the Iraqi nationalists did not admit to the necessity of any form of mandatory period and that as a result the years of the mandate were unsettled ones. On the other hand they conclude that from a practical point of view the policy had succeeded mainly because of the astuteness of King Faisal I and the willingness of British officials to conduct Iraq towards nationhood which was achieved in 1932. The period following 1932 to the outbreak of World War II is dealt with briefly as being a period of improvement in Iraq which could be judged by improvements in the economy, education and social conditions. The involvement of Iraq in the war is outlined though the authors admit that some doubt was felt at the time due to the situation in other Arab states such as Syria and the political situation in Palestine.

The remainder of the work deals with the peoples that make up Iraq and a résumé of the progress made by Iraq following her rise to statehood. It also sees a need for Arab unity as disruption in the past was adjudged to be the main reason for its disintegration.

The work has an excellent bibliography but is not indexed.

FISHER, SYDNEY NETTLETON
**The Middle East:** A history.
*London: Routledge & Kegan Paul. 2nd ed. 1971.*
*xxx, 749 pp., maps, bibl., index, 22 cms.*

See Section 1a for annotation.
The chapter of relevance to this section is as follows:
Part IV. The Contemporary Middle East.
Chapter 31. The Fertile Crescent under the Mandate system.

FOSTER, H. A.
**The making of Modern Iraq:** A product of world forces.
*London: Williams and Norgate. 1936.*
*ix, 319 pp., illus., bibl., index, 23 cms.*

The mandate was not favourably received in Iraq and indeed both Sir Percy Cox and Gertrude Bell recognised this aversion as Cox said that 'the mere terms mandatory and mandate were anathema to them from the first . . .' and Gertrude Bell wrote that 'the word mandate isn't popular and a freely negotiated treaty would be infinitely better liked, besides giving us a much freer hand'.

Unrest among the tribes gradually mounted with attacks along the roads from Baghdad and Mosul together with attacks on British garrisons which were put down by punitive expeditions. However, the worst was yet to come and in the August of 1920 further troops had to be sent to the country followed by the return of Sir Percy Cox as Civil Commissioner in place of Colonel Arnold Wilson. 'In the competitive workput between the old ideas and new, the former won in crushing the Iraqi revolt, rather than yielding to the demand for withdrawal, but the latter won in a chastening of British imperialists and in a liberalization of Anglo-Iraqi policy.'

GREAT BRITAIN: ADMIRALTY, NAVAL INTELLIGENCE DIVISION
**Iraq and the Persian Gulf,** B.R. 524 (Restricted).
*London: Admiralty. 1944.*
*xviii, 682 pp., illus., stats., maps, app., index, 21½ cms.*
*(Geographical Handbook Series.)*

One of a series of handbooks written by the Geographical section of the Naval Intelligence Division of the Admiralty designed to supply material for discussion of naval, military and political problems.

A great deal of the material is outside of the scope of this study by nature of topic or date and the Persian Gulf section is outside by nature of geography. The historical section, the section dealing with the administration and that dealing with the peoples are of interest.

HOWARD, HARRY N.
**The Partition of Turkey:** A diplomatic history, 1913–1923.
*New York: Howard Fertig. 1966.*
*486 pp., maps, notes, index, 23½ cms.*

In addition to the problems of the peace settlement which are considered elsewhere this work also deals with the incorporation of Mosul into Iraq and the administration of the mandates. This is an extremely useful work backed by copious notes and references.

*IRELAND, PHILIP WILLARD
**Iraq:** A study in political development.
*London: Cape. 1937.*
*510 pp., illus., maps, app., bibl., index.*

An exhaustive study of the development of Iraq from its position as a vilayet in the Ottoman Empire to one of independence following the administration of the mandate. The work begins with a study of the growth of British interest in the Middle East brought about by a desire to protect the land route to India with the British presence being fostered by trade and diplomacy. This interest was finally completed by the British army during World War I when Mesopotamia was gradually occupied by the army closely followed by a military administration run by political officers attached to the India Office.

The work continues by discussing the British wartime administration and the immediate post-war problems prior to the granting of the mandate. Ireland also deals in detail with the question of Arab nationalism prior to the outbreak of the war and in particular the difference between it and the more developed Syrian nationalism. He deals with the early attempts to achieve some form of recognition from Turkey of the right to an Arab voice in the administration and especially the work of Saiyid Talib. At the time of the war the nationalist movement was in four main groups, the first consisting of Saiyid Talib and the Basra nationalists, the second favoured a link with Syria, the third were in correspondence with Egypt and the fourth formed a Baghdad party.

After the war these groups combined to present a united front to obtain independence and this had been assisted by British pronouncements regarding the future of the area. The resultant mandate caused considerable unrest despite the efficient administration by the political officers and although some of the unrest was the result of agitation from Syria Ireland feels that the unrest in Mesopotamia would have burst into open rebellion because of the various internal forces at work. Ireland then deals with the insurrection and the search for a ruler which led to the 'election' of Feisal to the throne of Iraq. The work concludes with a study of the progress towards eventual independence and the possible outcome of the termination of the mandate on the French position in Syria and the Lebanon.

The work has an extremely detailed bibliography covering official documents from the various government departments both in Baghdad and Arabia and general works dealing with Iraq. The appendices reproduce various documents relating to the Middle East and Iraq including General Maude's proclamation to the Iraq people in 1917, the Balfour Declaration and extracts from the speeches of King Feisal.

IZZEDDIN, NEJLA
**The Arab world:** Past, present and future.
*Chicago: Henry Regnery Co. 1953.*
*xvi, 412 pp., illus., index, 24 cms.*

The British position in Iraq is the subject of detailed consideration. The comments of Sir Arnold Wilson are cited as evidence that Britain was not in sympathy with the nationalist movement when, as Civil Commissioner, he stated that the mandatory system was not the solution as: 'The average Arab, as opposed to the handful of amateur politicians of Baghdad, sees the future as one of fair dealing and material and moral progress under the aegis of Great Britain.' The problems of the nationalist movement are considered in relation to the British administration and to the Syrian nationalist movement which was an influence in the repressed movement in Iraq.

LENCZOWSKI, GEORGE
**The Middle East in world affairs.**
*New York: Cornell University Press. 2nd ed. 1956.*
*xix, 576 pp., maps, bibl., index, 24 cms.*

Chapter Seven deals with Iraq after the Peace Settlement and the granting of the mandate through the gradual progress towards independence. The internal situation was one in which control rested with the British advisers though under the guidance of Sir Percy Cox, who returned after the uprising of 1920, more power was transferred to the Iraqis although the advisers were still retained. In fact the British district advisers succeeded in perpetuating British control irrespective of formal Anglo-Iraqi treaties especially in the tribal areas. The remainder of this section is outside of the scope of this study by virtue of date dealing with the progress towards independence, World War II and the problem of the Kurdish minority.

LONGRIGG, STEPHEN HEMSLEY
**Iraq, 1900–1950:** A political, social and economic history.
*London: O.U.P. 1953.*
*x, 436 pp., app., bibl., map, index, 22 cms.*

An extremely detailed history of Iraq and dealing extensively with the situation following the mandate decision at the San Remo Conference, the Revolt in 1920 and the Cairo Conference which resulted in the throne of Iraq being given to Faisal. Consideration is then given to the administrative set-up with British advisers and Arab ministers, the replacement of the mandate by a treaty and gradual progress towards independence.

LYELL, THOMAS
**The Ins and Outs of Mesopotamia.**
*London: A. M. Philpot Ltd. 1923.*
*237 pp., 21½ cms.*

It is the second part of this work entitled 'Political Situation and the Future' which is of relevance to this study dealing with the period following the war. The author was a member of the British administration and the study is very much from this viewpoint. The attitude can be gathered from the following extract:

'That the Arabs of Mesopotamia "don't want us" is nothing new. They have never wanted anyone or any form of government which could restrain their inherited instinct for lawlessness and violent crime. They are now crying out to a sentimental Europe, pleading for the right to express the soul-consciousness of the "Arab Nation", bolstered up by English sentimentalists who ought to know better.'

MANSFIELD, PETER, ED.
**The Middle East:** A political and economic survey.
*London : O.U.P. 4th ed. 1973.*
*xi, 591 pp., map, app., index, 22½ cms.*

See Section 1b for annotation.

*SACHAR, HOWARD M.
**The Emergence of the Middle East, 1914–1924.**
*London : Allen Lane, The Penguin Press. 1969.*
*xiii, 518 pp., xxix, maps, notes, bibl., index, 24 cms.*

The question of the mandate for Mesopotamia is considered in the section entitled 'The Second Arab Revolt'. Iraq at first was relatively peaceful as the populace seemed to accept a British presence and the nationalist movement had not developed as rapidly as in Syria. This was, however, upset by the Revolt in 1920 and the outside influences of the Syrian nationalists together with the belief of the British government that the country was not worth the expenditure and that moves should be made towards independence to relieve the burden on the exchequer.

The work has extensive notes and a detailed bibliography arranged by topic together with an exhaustive index.

SINDERSON, SIR HARRY C.
**Ten thousand and one nights:** Memoirs of Iraq's Sherifian Dynasty.
*London : Hodder and Stoughton. 1973.*
*287 pp., illus., app., index, 22 cms.*

The autobiography of the physician to the Sherifian family of Iraq which, although not a detailed political study of Iraq, is useful as a first-hand narrative of events relevant to this study. The author began service in Iraq in 1918 as part of the occupation administration during the period from the end of hostilities to the granting of the mandate and the 'election to the throne of

Faisal'. Subsequent to Faisal becoming King of Iraq the author became physician to the royal household.

SLATER, S. H.
**Iraq.**
*Nineteenth Century. April 1926, pp. 479-494.*

This article is a comprehensive review of the administration of the British mandate in Iraq and the installation of Feisal as a constitutional monarch. It was considered by some writers that the military administration in Iraq had been a failure and this was illustrated by the Revolt which took place in 1920 but the writer feels that were it not for outside intervention the Revolt would never have taken place and even more so when one considers that many of the nationalist demands were in the process of being implemented.

The article continues with a discussion of the Cairo Conference and the proposals put forward regarding Iraq which were motivated by a need for economy in costs being borne by Britain. The most important proposal was that of the setting up of a constitutional monarchy with Feisal as the first king but at the expressed wish of the population. The election was administered by Sir Percy Cox who was an expert at this sort of exercise and, together with the political officers, arrangements were made for the election which resulted in a 96% vote in favour of Feisal. Consideration is then given to the administrative and executive machinery set up to govern the country with Feisal at its head.

The author concludes by dealing with the setting up of the new state and the economic problems which it faced. In particular the article deals with the problem of the repayment of that part of the Turkish Public Department allotted to Iraq by the Allies, although this had to some extent been alleviated by the satisfactory arrangements with Britain over the development costs incurred in various projects. The writer feels that the problems of Iraq was going to be a British one for some time as the Feisal government was by no means secure with the balance of power having shifted and the Sherifian regime no longer as respected as it had been.

WILLIAMS, KENNETH
**The Significance of Mosul.**
*Nineteenth Century. March 1926, pp. 349-355.*

A consideration of the implications of the League of Nations' decision to include Mosul as part of Iraq with the case having been argued on the basis of being necessary for the fulfilment of

Arab pledges, an Arab renaissance, and the question of oil. These reasons were really subsidiary to the real question which was the aim of maintaining a series of buffer states between the Mediterranean and India and it is in this context that the Mosul decision was important.

In its wider context Mosul can be seen as necessary to the integrity of Iraq as a sovereign state and to its completeness as an economic unit. The author feels that this decision could be 'regarded either as the end of the preliminary chapter of British work in the Middle East, or as the beginning of a new one that shall last – who knows how long?'

## SPECIFIC WORKS

CHURCHILL, WINSTON SPENCER
**Mesopotamia and the New Government.**
*The Empire Review. Vol. XXXVIII, No. 270, July 1923, pp. 691–698.*

An examination of British policy with regard to Mesopotamia which was a continuation of the policy outlined by the Cairo Conference of 1921. This changed the three-fold administration of the country whereby the India Office had administered the country, the War Office provided the army of occupation and the Foreign Office general over-lordship all of which was expensive in terms of manpower and finance. It was also alarming in terms of administration as it was aimed at building 'up a kind of little India with an elaborate and frightfully expensive administration, utterly unsuited to the people or conditions of Mesopotamia and violently contrary to their wishes'.

Churchill felt that this new policy could succeed and that eventually Mesopotamia would cease to be a burden on Britain's resources and instead become a credit with valuable openings for trade. The one condition for this success was a lasting peace with Turkey as any conflict in this area exposed Britain's military and economic deficiencies. A sound peace 'will secure to the newly created state of Iraq and to the Arab race as a whole the opportunity of reviving, if they are worthy of them, the old culture, glories and prosperity of the Arab World'.

COX, PERCY
**Iraq.**
*United Empire. March 1929, pp. 132–144.*

Despite the expressed intent of the British and French governments to establish national governments and administrations Iraq was made the mandatory territory controlled by Britain. The announcement of this move was unfavourably received in Baghdad and although it was announced that an Arab government would be established unrest was prevalent and a revolt broke out in June 1920.

Cox was recalled to Iraq to become High Commissioner with the prime task being the establishment of a National Government. This was achieved with the cooperation of the Naqib of Baghdad who became President of the Council of State which was representative of all classes and sects of the community. Its initial tasks were the repatriation of Iraqi officers from Syria and the Hedjaz, the re-organisation of a civilian administration under Iraqi officials and the preparation of an electoral law.

HOGARTH, D. G.
**The Arab World Today.**
*Foreign Affairs (New York). April 1926, pp. 406–414.*

The first part of this article is considered in the section dealing with Syria and the Lebanon.

The position in Iraq is seen to be different from Syria because the initial attempt to overthrow Western control had failed and because the British were not really regarded 'as the Syrian regards the French, as masters come to stay. He half believes that . . . there is something in the actual British profession of being in Iraq simply to guide and protect an infant state constructed out of destruction.'

In conclusion Hogarth considers that the Arab world is no more united than it was before the war for although a common policy can sometimes be discerned there is little sign of the common effort that prevailed under the Caliphs.

*GREAT BRITAIN: INDIA OFFICE
**Review of the Civil Administration of Mesopotamia.**
*(Cmd. 1061.)*
*London: H.M.S.O. 1920.*
*748 pp., index, 33 cms.*

A paper prepared by Gertrude Bell under the direction of Sir A. T. Wilson on the civil administration during the period of military occupation from the outbreak of war to the acceptance of the mandate by Britain in 1920.

The paper considers the organisation of the administration, the gradual defeat of the Turks in Mesopotamia, and the increasing administrative problems which the increase in area of occupation caused. It also considers Britain's relationship with the Arab tribes that came under British control and in particular the Kurds.

The report ends with a consideration of the nationalist movement in Iraq, its complex nature and the outside influences which were brought to bear on it. The first of these was that brought by the extremist elements in Syria who caused ferment among the dissident tribesmen in the Dair al Zar region. The second of these influences was represented by the Iraqis who had served the Turkish administration, fled on its defeat and returned after the signing of the peace treaty with Turkey.

Further difficulties were caused by the religious problems and the fact that the tribesmen in the remoter areas were opposed to any form of government at all whether French, British or Arab. The report then deals with the various uprisings that took place and the inadequacy of the military presence to deal with them until the advent of an aerial presence. The unrest was a direct result of the hereditary animosities from which Turkey had profited and the example of the unrest in Syria created by Mesopotamia in Faisal's army and the French presence. The anarchy which followed the uprising resulted in the alienation of some of the nationalist movement's support especially in the urban areas whose notables had suffered considerably from the pillaging of crops by the tribesmen who took advantage of the lack of military control outside of Baghdad. It was during this period of looting that Colonel Leachman was murdered as were many other administrative officers and their staffs.

HALDANE, LIEUTENANT-GENERAL SIR AYLMER
**The Arab rising in Mesopotamia, 1920.**
*Royal United Services Institute Journal. Vol. LXVIII, February 1923, pp. 63–79.*

This article describes the Arab rising in Mesopotamia and the attendant difficulties in dealing with it from the military aspect. The author deals with the campaign especially with regard to the difficulties of engaging an enemy that used 'hit and run' tactics and the problems of the terrain. The operations were also carried out in a climate of political pressure from the British Government which wished to disengage from any conflict which held up the demobilisation of the army.

HOGARTH, D. G.
**Present discontents in the Near and Middle East.**
*Quarterly Review. Vol. 234, No. 465, October 1920, pp. 411–423.*

This article deals with the discontent in Mesopotamia following the granting of the mandate and the problem of reconciling the promises made to the Arabs with the Sykes–Picot agreement and international politics. The problems were partly created by the difficulty of evolving a unified policy for the area when different government departments were involved. Hogarth saw the Revolt in Mesopotamia as being the direct result of the policy of the India Office which did not seek to enlist the support of the Arabs but to impose on the area the same form of administration as that used in the Indian Empire.

HUREWITZ, J. C.
**Diplomacy in the Near and Middle East.** A documentary record, 1914–1956. Vol. II.
*London: Van Nostrand Co. 1956.*
*xviii, 427 pp., index, 23½ cms.*

The main annotation to this work will be found under Section 1c, however, the following is of relevance to this section.

Treaty of Alliance: Great Britain and Iraq. 10 October 1922 (p. 111).

*KEDOURIE, ELIE
**England and the Middle East:** The destruction of the Ottoman Empire, 1914–1921.
*London: Bowes and Bowes. 1956.*
*xiii, 9–236 pp., app., bibl., index, 21½ cms.*

Mesopotamia 1918–1921.

The British administration in Iraq following the end of the war was complicated by dissent from dissident Iraqi officers serving with Faisal's army in Damascus who wanted Iraq to be an independent state and not under British control. The situation was not helped by the administration of Sir Arnold Wilson who was not able to cope with the crisis and events moved towards organised civil unrest.

The Revolt broke out in March 1920 lasting until October when Sir Percy Cox was brought back as High Commissioner in an attempt to quell the unrest. The new policy adopted was the pursuance of a middle course aimed at safeguarding British interests in Mesopotamia whilst reducing the financial and military commitment and satisfying what the British administration considered to be national aspirations.

217

KEDOURIE, ELIE
**The Kingdom of Iraq:** A retrospect.
*In: Kedourie, Elie*
*The Chatham House Version and other Middle Eastern Studies.*
*pp. 236–285.*

An examination of the Kingdom of Iraq only parts of which are of relevance to this study. It considers the British administration in Iraq following the war and the enthronement of Faisal as King of Iraq which was engineered as a result of the Cairo Conference. Kedourie also deals with the internal problems of Iraq with the opposition of the Baghdad Shi'ites to Faisal whom they regarded as a foreigner and a usurper. As a result Faisal is seen as retaining control only with the military support of Britain and by intrigue with the various anti-British factions active in the country.

KHAN, RASHEEDUDDIN
**Mandate and monarchy in Iraq:** A study in the origin of the British Mandate and the creation of the Hashemite monarchy in Iraq, 1919–1921.
*Islamic Culture. Vol. XLIII, No. 3, July 1969, pp. 189–213.*

The mandate system was a result of the passing of the age of outright annexation and the failure of the Arab case for unity and independence at the Peace Conference in 1919. 'It was a curious situation: the Arabs were powerless to assert independence but the French and British were equally inhibited in their plans of incorporating outright the ex-enemy territories within the framework of their colonialism. The incipient Arab national movement presided over by the politically unskilful and fickle leadership of the Sherifians was obviously not cohesive and strong enough to establish unity and proclaim independence on its own initiative.'

The period between the armistice and the taking up of the mandate was one of increasing unrest with 'tribal restiveness, urban agitation, militant thrusts from Dayr az-Zur backed by the firm and consistent demands of the Iraqi officers in Faisal's Arab Army'. The result was the return of Sir Percy Cox as High Commissioner with the brief of setting up an Arab administration. A committee was set up by Colonel Wilson to examine the problem prior to Cox's return though the majority of its proposals were adopted by Cox and can be summarised as follows.

1. The acceptance of the mandate.
2. A provisional constitution for an interim period.
3. The definition of the rights of the mandatory power in this provisional constitution enumerating its 'reserved rights'.

4. The nomination of an Arab Emir to head the government.
5. The establishment of a Council of State to act as the Chief Executive Authority with a majority of British members in the ratio of six to five.
6. The President of the Council to be an Arab.
7. The High Commissioner to have the power of veto.
8. The British Secretary of the Department to be the Chief Executive with the Arab members as advisers.
9. Arab members of the Council need not be elected from the Legislative.
10. The Legislative Assembly to be appointed by elected local bodies with representation from Jewish and Christian minorities.

These proposals were implemented by Cox who took over as High Commissioner following the unrest and violence of 1920 and the Provisional Government was organised on these lines. It still met with opposition from the 'Sh'i community who, although in a majority, were almost completely excluded from the government and administration as they would have had to have taken out Mesopotamian citizenship before they could take up any official position. Also they maintained that the Arab government should have been elected by the people and not a provisional one under British patronage. Although some moves were made towards the problem of electoral law the question was postponed until after Faisal's accession.

LAWRENCE, THOMAS EDWARD
**Arab rights:** Our policy in Mesopotamia.
*The Times (London)*. 23 July 1920, p. 15.

A letter to *The Times*, whilst Lawrence was at All Souls, discussing the Arab Revolt in Mesopotamia in response to the debate on the situation in the House of Commons and articles in the press expressing surprise at the Arab reaction to the British administration.

According to Lawrence the main cause of unrest was the continuance of the military administration in which the Arabs had no say and the presence of a large army of occupation. The solution advocated by Lawrence was to allow the Arabs a greater say in the government and to permit them to form volunteer units to help preserve law and order thus enabling reductions to be made in the size of the garrison. 'I believe the Arabs in these conditions would be as loyal as anyone in the Empire, and they would not cost us a cent . . . Of course, there is oil in Mesopotamia, but we are no nearer that while the Middle East remains at war, and I think if it is so necessary for us, it could be the subject of a bargain. The Arabs are willing to shed their blood for freedom; how much more their oil.'

LODER, J. DE V.
**The Truth about Mesopotamia, Palestine and Syria.**
*London: Allen & Unwin. 1923.*
*221 pp., maps, index, 19 cms.*

The author considers the relations between the Arab nationalists and the British administration in Mesopotamia leading to the various uprisings against the mandate. In discussing the unrest the author also considers the outside influences at work especially the agitation of the Mesopotamian members of Feisal's army from Syria.

MARLOWE, JOHN
**Arab Nationalism and British Imperialism:** A study in power politics.
*London: The Cresset Press. 1961.*
*viii, 236 pp., bibl., index, 22 cms.*

The second chapter of this work deals with the granting of the mandate in Iraq to Britain and the conflict between this and the aspirations of the Arabs. The subsequent problems in Iraq are seen as a result of the imperialistic policies of Britain which were bound to conflict with the rising tide of Arab nationalism.

MONROE, ELIZABETH
**Britain's moment in the Middle East, 1914–56.**
*London: Chatto & Windus. 1963.*
*254 pp., maps, notes, bibl., index, 22 cms.*

The third section of this work is entitled 'The years of good management, 1922–45' though only the earlier parts are of relevance to this study. In Iraq following Faisal's accession British control was not looked on too unfavourably as 'a new state needed a protector; King Faisal, inoculated by experience in Syria, probably saw no alternative to working with a great power'.

The situation in Iraq under the guidance of Sir Percy Cox saw the dropping of the term mandate and its substitution by a treaty which although maintaining the status quo did at least nullify local resentment over the use of the word mandate. Although progress was slow the early years did see some progress towards Arab control though Britain through its advisers maintained the final authority.

NEWMAN, E. W. POLSON
**Middle East Mandates.**
*The Contemporary Review, pp. 705-711.*

In the main this article is concerned with the British position in
Iraq and Palestine which is examined in the light of the Balfour
Declaration and Britain's imperial policy. The position in Iraq is
seen as the result of a need for a series of buffer states between
the Mediterranean and India and as a necessary dependency to
safeguard the position in Palestine. The question of Britain's
promises to the Arabs are considered to have been met by the
installation of Faisal as King of Iraq though it was also evident
that the mandate in Iraq 'was far from being entirely based on a
desire for the emancipation of the peoples so long oppressed by
the Turks'.

ORMSBY GORE, W.
**Great Britain, Mesopotamia and the Arabs.**
*The Nineteenth Century. August 1920, pp. 225-238.*

The article begins by outlining the terms of the mandate for
Iraq and by giving details of the population, agricultural prospects
for the area and the exploitation of the oil deposits. Also considered are the financial problems with regard to the subsidies
needed for the area, the prospects for the civil administration, the
continuing need for a military presence and these questions
related to the demand for economies being expressed in parliament and the British press.

The latter part of the article deals with the outlook of the Arabs
who saw the war as a reopening of their opportunities which at
this time were focused on Damascus. The problems of Mesopotamia are seen as the problems of the Arab World in general and
'what is now required is the wider vision, the keener foresight,
and above all, faith in the peoples and in our own capacity to
help them'.

*POWELL, E. ALEXANDER
**The Struggle for power in Moslem Asia.**
*London: John Long Ltd. 1925.*
*320 pp., maps, index, 22½ cms.*

The British presence in Iraq is seen to rest solely on conquest as
before 1914 she had no real interest in the area and although it
was recognised as an independent state this was qualified by
placing it under a mandate which was assigned to Britain. This
presence was in itself a deception as the people were promised

221

independence but the pledge was not kept. 'On the contrary, the people of Mesopotamia have been forced to accept as their king an alien, belonging to another creed, whom they neither knew nor trusted; and a form of government which they did not want, and which is maintained only by British bayonets.'

The result of the continuing occupation was a revolt in 1920 which was to prove costly in terms of British lives and property with peace being restored only by force of arms. Sir Percy Cox returned to Iraq as High Commissioner 'pledged to support the policy of self-determination for the people of Mesopotamia, as enunciated in the Anglo-French Declaration, thus securing for himself the confidence and co-operation of the most influential opinion in the country . . .' This was followed by the 'election' of Faisal to the throne of Iraq in 1921 following the Cairo Conference though he refused 'to perform as a well-trained puppet should; Arab confidence in British sincerity and good faith has been completely shattered; and that "honour" of which British statesmen are for ever prating has been indelibly stained'.

ROGERS, A. L.
**Arab nationalism in Iraq and Palestine.**
*Asiatic Review. July 1928, pp. 397–402.*

The article is an appreciation of Arab opinion in Iraq and Palestine where British interests were most immediately affected. It examines the structure of the Arab society in the desert areas where the rule of the Sheikh was by popular consent of the tribe, and the peoples of the urban areas many of whom were only concerned that the country should be stable to ensure prosperity. It concludes that the governments or mandatory powers in Arabia could count on strong support where their prestige was high and their strength evident but any weakness would place their position in jeopardy. It was, he maintains, not only British policy in the Arabia peninsula which would affect her position in the area, but the general imperial and foreign policy, as the restoration and maintenance of British prestige was essential if the growing nationalist movement was to be held in check and allowed to develop at a pace compatible with the mandate.

WHITE, WILBUR W.
**The Process of change in the Ottoman Empire.**
*Chicago: University of Chicago Press. 1937.*
*ix, 315 pp., map, bibl., index, 23½ cms.*

Immediately prior to the granting of the mandate the Iraqis in Damascus proclaimed Abdullah as Emir of Iraq in the wake of the installation of Faisal as King of Syria, but the move was dashed by Britain being granted the mandate in April 1920. Opposition to the mandate ran high with the extremists demanding that Britain should leave Iraq. In an attempt to placate some of this feeling it was suggested that a council of notables be set up to advise the government and for the number of Iraqi advisers in the government to be increased.

However, the unrest continued to spread resulting in rioting and attacks on British garrisons which were put down only after the arrival of reinforcements. Sir Percy Cox returned as Civil Commissioner to try to settle the problem and it was he who arranged the referendum following the Cairo Conference which 'elected' Faisal to the throne of Iraq and the replacement of the mandate by a treaty. Although peace had been restored pressure was to continue for independence which was to follow Iraq's admission to the League of Nations.

**The Working of the Iraq Parliament.**
*The Round Table. Vol. XVII, December 1926, pp. 18–36.*

This article considers the setting up of parliamentary government in Iraq although the move was viewed with some misgivings by the political officers used to working with the military administration of the occupation army. It deals with the parliamentary machinery which was set up and the electoral system which was complicated by the lack of identifiable political parties.

It concludes that the Iraq parliament is not as representative as the British parliament as there is no body of public opinion as such to be represented but that it was more democratic than anything the country had previously known. These changes also meant that the differences between the Iraqis and Britain's representatives were made more public but the changes were in keeping with Britain's responsibilities under the terms of the mandate.

## THE MINORITIES IN IRAQ

EDMONDS, C. J.
**Kurdish Nationalism.**
*Journal Contemporary History. Vol. 6, No. 1, 1971, pp. 87–107.*

A great deal of this article is outside of the scope of this study but the earlier part is of interest in setting the pattern of future dissention in Iraq following independence. The first part of the article examines the historical roots of Kurdish nationalism which developed in its modern form from the second half of the nineteenth century in parallel with other movements within the Ottoman Empire. Following the defeat of the Ottoman Empire the Treaty of Sevres provided for an independent Kurdistan, but this treaty was never ratified owing to the rise of Ataturk and was replaced by the Treaty of Lausanne in 1923 which made no mention of Kurdistan. The result was the split-up of Ottoman Kurdistan between Turkey, Iraq and Syria and the seeds of future trouble were sown.

*EDMONDS, C. J.
**Kurds, Turks and Arabs:** Politics, travel and research in north-eastern Iraq, 1919–25.
*London: O.U.P. 1957.*
*xiii, 457 pp., plates, maps, bibl., app., index, 22 cms.*

The author was a political officer in the Mosul district at the time of the dispute between Britain and Turkey and a member of the British delegation to the Commission of the League of Nations set up to investigate the dispute and to recommend a solution. This work deals with the history of the dispute during the years in question and the eventual decision to include the Mosul district into the mandatory area of Iraq. This work is also interesting for its description of life in Iraq and in particular the problem of the Kurdish peoples not only in the internal affairs of Iraq but as a factor in the secular border dispute with Iran.

Also considered is the role of the Royal Air Force in Iraq in its role as an internal peace-keeping force in addition to its role as part of Iraq's external defence. This view is interesting in the light of Lawrence's views on the possible role of the Air Force in the post World War I world and the vision of Trenchard in this respect.

HEAZELL, F. N.
**The Woes of a distressed nation, being an account of the Assyrian people from 1914 to 1934.**
*London: The Faith Press. 1934.*
*iv, 24 pp., frontis., 19 cms.*

A very brief work setting out the case for some assistance for the Assyrians who had supported Britain against the Turks during World War I. It describes the treatment of the Assyrians by the Turks after the Russian troops had withdrawn from Urmi because of Turkish attacks in the Caucasus. It details the post-war problems created by the denial of the Assyrians' ancient home by the League of Nations in its settlement of the Iraq–Turkey frontier.

The author deals with the treatment meted out to the Assyrians by the Moslems in the area in which they had settled and their subsequent flight to Syria. The return of the Assyrians from Iraq was not successful as conflict broke out between the returning peoples and the Iraqi forces resulting in several deaths. Even those villages of the Assyrians who had remained loyal to Iraq were not immune from these strained relationships and were subject to looting and murder.

The writer considered that Britain had a responsibility to the Assyrians not only for their assistance during the war but under the terms of the mandate, a responsibility which had been too easily relinquished and with too much optimism for the future.

## BIOGRAPHICAL WORKS

\*BELL, GERTRUDE
**The Letters of Gertrude Bell,** selected and edited by Lady Bell. Vol. II.
*London: Benn. 1927.*
*vii, 405–791 pp., illus., map, index, 23 cms.*

The middle part of this volume is extremely interesting as it deals with the unrest in Iraq and the Cairo Conference. In considering the question of unrest she wrote, in a letter dated 18 December 1920, that it was necessary for the government to be backed by force whether British or Arab. 'The bedrock on which this argument rests is that no administration can exist without force behind it. I think you have seen enough of the country to know that it's correct . . . In setting up an Arab state we are acting in the interests of the urban and village population which expects and rightly expects that it will ultimately leaven the mass.'

BIRWOOD, LORD
**Nuri As-Said:** A study in Arab leadership.
*London: Cassell. 1959.*
*xi, 306 pp., frontis., illus., maps, glossary, bibl., index, 22 cms.*

After leaving Syria with Faisal in 1920 Nuri As-Said returned to Iraq in 1921 to become Minister of Defence. He took an active part in the campaign to secure Faisal's election to the throne of Iraq and following Faisal's enthronement he continued as Minister of Defence. In this capacity Nuri organised the Iraqi army and set up the administration necessary to support it.

At this stage the biography moves on to deal with Nuri As-Said's periods as Prime Minister of Iraq and for a few months prior to his death on 14 July 1958 as Prime Minister of the Federation of Jordan and Iraq.

EDMONDS, C. J.
**Gertrude Bell in the Near and Middle East.**
*Royal Central Asian Journal. Vol. LVI, Part III, October 1969, pp. 229–244.*

During the period following the armistice and prior to the granting of the mandate Gertrude Bell found herself at variance with Arnold Wilson over matters of policy and 'by the end of the summer (i.e. 1920), if not earlier, influenced perhaps by the contacts she had had in London, Paris and Damascus the previous year, she had come round to favouring the immediate establishment of a purely Arab administration under one of the sons of the Sharif of Mecca'.

In the October of 1920 Sir Percy Cox returned to Iraq as High Commissioner charged with a definite policy of setting up an Arab administration and Gertrude Bell worked closely in these moves. She was also present at the Cairo Conference which supported Faisal's candidature for the throne of Iraq and this added to her enthusiasm for the task. 'More than ever she came to regard herself as the vital spark in the body politic, and throughout her letters we find such passages as : "My business is now to set up an Arab State"; or "I can't go on leave this summer, we are in the middle of a Cabinet crisis"; or "It is we two [Cornwallis being the other] who ultimately guide Faisal and with him the destinies of the Arab world, if I'm not mistaken".'

The remainder of the article is outside the scope of this study as it deals with the period following the Anglo-Iraqi treaty following which she became more and more involved in her archaeological work.

ERSKINE, MRS. STEWART
**King Faisal of Iraq.**
*London : Hutchinson & Co. 1933.*
*288 pp., illus., app., index, 23½ cms.*

Despite Faisal's gaining the throne of Iraq agitation against the mandate continued one of the problems being to maintain the delicate balance when 'there were differences of opinion between the British advisers who had been building up the foundations of the Kingdom with care and a knowledge based on experience of Eastern as well as Western forms of government, and those of the extremists who naturally wanted to throw off supervision and to govern the country themselves. To these the very word "Mandate" was anathema; they took it in the sense of a command instead of a trusteeship, which was its true significance.'

The biography then continues to deal with the transition of Iraq from a mandated country to one with a treaty with Britain with gradual progression towards independence and admittance to the League of Nations. The book ends in 1933 and was at the printers when Faisal died in September and an epilogue has been added as a final tribute to the country's ruler for twelve years.

\*Monroe, Elizabeth
**Philby of Arabia.**
*London: Faber. 1973.*
*332 pp., illus., maps, notes, bibl., index, 22½ cms.*

Following the decision not to replace Philby as British representative at Ridayh he remained in England until the crisis broke in Iraq during the summer of 1920, immediately after the deposing of Faisal by the French and Mustafa Kemal's nationalist renaissance in Anatolia. The situation was most serious with British officers being murdered and Arnold Wilson having given up hope of reconciling the extremists advised London to restore order and govern or withdraw.

The response of the British government was to send Sir Percy Cox to calm the situation, and as one of his team Cox selected Philby. On their arrival in August 1920 the rebellion was on the wane but the country was still in a turmoil with British officers ruling with British advisers. The first task facing Cox, Gertrude Bell and Philby was to reverse the trend and to secure administration by Arabs under British advisers after the forming of an Arab council of ministers. This was a difficult task but a solution was found with the Naqib of Baghdad agreeing to preside over the council. Under this arrangement Sayyid Talib became Minister of the Interior with Philby as his adviser, and Philby was of the opinion that once Talib had learned the art of good administration he could well be a worthy successor to the Naqib, as he had an outstanding intellect and was of good character. Events in the shape of the Cairo Conference were to prove Philby wrong.

\*Morris, James
**The Hashemite Kings.**
*London: Faber and Faber. 1959.*
*231 pp., illus., bibl., index, 22 cms.*

Faisal was confirmed as King of Iraq by a referendum and he was enthroned on 23 August 1921. The kingdom was, however, a curiosity as it was, by British decree, a constitutional monarchy with no constitution, a mandated territory which had not been ratified, a country in treaty relationship with Britain, but without a treaty. 'The Arabs demanded its complete independence. The Anglo-Indians wanted it to be a buffer state, an Arab Bhutan. The British coveted its unexploited deposits of oil. The Turks claimed part of its northern territories.'

The control of the government was securely in the hands of the British advisers and although many of them were sympathetic to the Arab cause in practice Iraq remained a British dependency. Faisal hoped that the promised treaty would see the end of the mandate but when the treaty was presented for signature in 1922 it confirmed Britain as the power behind the throne responsible for all foreign relations and retaining general control. The result was widespread unrest and demonstrations and it took harsh measures by Sir Percy Cox before order was restored.

The remainder of the section deals with the history of Iraq to independence with each Anglo-Iraq treaty giving the Arabs more authority and reflecting the decline of the British Empire and the rise of Iraqi nationalist.

WILSON, ARNOLD T.
**Loyalties:** Mesopotamia, Vol. II, 1917–1920.
*xix, 420 pp., plates, maps, bibl., index, 24½ cms.*

This second volume of Wilson's memoirs deals with the armistice and the subsequent military administration. In this volume he deals with the problems of trying to administer a country peopled by so many divergent groups. In particular concern is expressed about the mandate with reservations about the limited period proposed before the granting of independence. 'In Iraq as elsewhere a kingdom to be stable must in the ultimate resort be based on the character of rulers, the strength of social bonds and the assent of the subjects. The path on which we have set the feet of the peoples of Iraq is steep and stony; the journey has been made more difficult by the pace at which their leaders have traversed the first stages.'

# (b) SYRIA AND LEBANON

## GENERAL WORKS ON THE MIDDLE EAST

\*ANTONIUS, GEORGE
**The Arab Awakening:** The story of the movement.
*London: Hamish Hamilton. 1938.*
*xii, 13–471 pp., maps, app., index, 22 cms.*

The unrest in Syria whilst the Peace Conference was sitting became worse following the San Remo Conference and was aggravated by the French ultimatum the terms of which were unacceptable to the nationalists. Indeed Antonius maintains that the motives were ulterior and that 'it is clear beyond all doubt that the French had made up their minds in any case to extend their military occupation to the rest of Syria, and that the ultimatum was no more than a tactical move to that end'. Although Faisal finally accepted the ultimatum the French advanced on Damascus and occupied the city after a brief struggle with Faisal deposed and exiled.

The French administration of the mandate was not to the benefit of the population or within the spirit of the mandate. 'Its record is largely one of wasteful conflict: and it is no exaggeration to say that, in the period from 1920 to 1926, that is to say in the years between San Remo and the conclusion of the Franco-Syrian Treaty, the harm done in the name of the mandate to French and Arab interests was far greater than its incidental benefits.'

ATIYAH, EDWARD
**An Arab tells his story:** A study in loyalties.
*London: John Murray. 1946.*
*226 pp.*

This work is the autobiography of a Christian Arab who spent his boyhood in Beirut prior to World War I and who grew up with an awareness of the differences between Muslim and Christian society which led to his seeking an identity within Western culture. After an education in England he returned to the East as an inner conflict between his Western ideals and his Eastern upbringing and he deals at great length with his belief in Britain and his incapability to accept all aspects of Arab nationalism.

229

The latter part of his book deals with the position of the Arabs during World War II and ends with a warning that no genuine friendship between East and West could exist unless the West accepted the intransigence of the Arab desire for independence and unity and did not hinder this realisation.

BEN-HORIN, ELIAHU
**The Middle East:** Crossroads of history.
*New York: W. W. Norton & Co. 1943.*
*248 pp., map, index, 21½ cms.*

BUTLER, ROHAN AND BURY, J. P. T., EDS.
**Documents on British Foreign Policy, 1919–1939.**
*First Series. Vol. XIII, The Near and Middle East, January 1920–March 1921.*
*London: H.M.S.O. 1963.*
*lxxxiii, 747 pp., 24½ cms.*

See the section on the Peace Settlement for annotation.

COKE, RICHARD
**The Arab's place in the sun.**
*London: Butterworth. 1929.*
*318 pp., illus., maps, index, 22 cms.*

FISHER, SYDNEY NETTLETON
**The Middle East:** A history.
*London: Routledge & Kegan Paul. 2nd ed. 1971.*
*xxx, 749 pp., maps, bibl., index, 22 cms.*

See Section 1a for annotation.

The chapter of relevance to this section is as follows:
Part IV. The Contemporary Middle East.
Chapter 31. The Fertile Crescent under the Mandate System.

GREAT BRITAIN: ADMIRALTY, NAVAL INTELLIGENCE DIVISION
**Syria:** B.R. 513 (Restricted).
*London: Admiralty. 1943.*
*xv, 485 pp., illus., stats., maps, app., index, 21½ cms.*
*(Geographical Handbook Series.)*

One of a series of handbooks written by the Geographical Section of Naval Intelligence Division of the Admiralty designed to supply material for discussion of naval, military and political problems.

A great deal of the material is outside of the scope of this study by nature of topic or date but the historical section, the section dealing with the administration and that dealing with the people are of interest.

HOURANI, ALBERT, ED.
**Middle Eastern Affairs, Number Two.**
*London: Chatto & Windus. 1961.*
*(St. Antony's Papers, No. 11.)*
*167 pp.*

In this section only one article is of relevance to this study: Marmorstein, Emile.
*A note on Damascus, Homs, Homa and Aleppo, pp. 161–165.*

See entry under author for annotation.

IZZEDDIN, NEJLA
**The Arab world:** Past, present and future.
*Chicago: Henry Regnery Co. 1953.*
*xvi, 412 pp., illus., index, 24 cms.*

In considering the question of the Arab reaction to the administration of the mandates the position of Syria and the Lebanon is dealt with in some detail and the bitterness of the Arab to the whole Syrian question is evident here. The extent of the French control in Syria as permitted by the Sykes–Picot agreement and the Mandate is regarded as a painful betrayal which '. . . must be told – for it reveals the cause at the root of much of the restlessness and confusion which have afflicted and continue to afflict not only Syria but the rest of the Arab world as well'.

*LENCZOWSKI, GEORGE
**The Middle East in world affairs.**
*New York: Cornell University Press. 2nd ed. 1956.*
*xix, 576 pp., maps, bibl., index, 24 cms.*

In considering Syria and the Lebanon Chapter VIII begins by setting the background to the problems following World War I by dealing briefly with the history of France's association with the Levant. This leads to a consideration of the events following the granting of the mandate which resulted in the French assuming the control by force and Faisal being expelled from Damascus.

The French then proceeded to rule by encouraging the minority communities in the country and by failing to fulfil the terms of the mandate regarding the progress towards independence. This caused considerable unrest in the country which was politically conscious and relations deteriorated to such an extent that the threat of an uprising was ever present. The revolt took place in 1926 but this and the events that followed are beyond the scope of this study.

MANSFIELD, PETER, ED.
**The Middle East:** A political and economic survey.
*London: O.U.P. 4th ed. 1973.*
*xi, 591 pp., map, app., index, 22½ cms.*

See Section 1b for annotation.

MORRISON, S. A.
**Arab nationalism and Islam.**
*Middle East Journal. Vol. 2, No. 2, April 1948, pp. 147–159.*

Following the peace settlement the nationalist movement split with the Lebanese nationalists favouring independence from the Muslim nationalists of Syria and this caused the non-Muslim minorities to look to the Christian governments for protection. This resulted in hostility between the two factions as the Arabs considered that they had been betrayed by these Western powers.

The article then goes on to consider these developments in the light of post World War II events and the creation of Israel.

*POWELL, E. ALEXANDER
**The Struggle for power in Moslem Asia.**
*London: John Long Ltd. 1925.*
*320 pp., maps, index, 22½ cms.*

At the time of the San Remo Conference Faisal was crowned as King of Syria, a move which the French suspected as being a ploy of Britain though with the full support of the Syrians. Faisal, however, over-estimated his position and strength and chose to defy the French with the result being the defeat of his army and his flight to Palestine. The French did little to try and recoup their position because they imposed a fine of ten million francs on the people of Damascus for supporting Faisal thus further antagonising the population.

Instead of pursuing a policy of reconciliation the French pursued a policy of rule by force with demonstrations of military strength, harsh court martial verdicts and petty restrictions. Further mistakes were made with the choice of French officials, many of whom had seen service in the North African colonies and tried to use the same techniques on the cultured Syrians. The Syrians were actively opposed to a French presence with the following being voiced as the main reasons for opposition:

1. The French by substitution of their customs and language virtually forced the Syrians to preserve *their* language, culture and national identity.
2. The French losses in the war had prevented her restoring France let alone give adequate financial assistance to Syria.
3. The French intended to exploit Syria for the profit of Frenchmen rather than the benefit of Syrians.
4. The French acted as conquerors rather than temporary guardians.

PRIESTLEY, HERBERT INGRAM
**France Overseas:** A study of modern imperialism.
*London: Frank Cass. 1966.*
*ix, 463 pp., maps, statistics, bibl., index, 23½ cms.*

A study of French imperialism in general but of interest to this study is the section dealing with Syria. It considers the historical involvement of France in the area and then continues to consider the position following World War I. As this is a brief study it cannot deal with the complexities of the situation but it does provide a useful synopsis.

ROBERTS, STEPHEN H.
**The History of French Colonial Policy, 1870–1925.**
*London: King & Co. 1929 (rep. Cass 1963).*
*xvi, 741 pp., bibl., index, 23 cms.*

A study of French colonial policy during the period in question and as such a great deal of the work is outside of the scope of this study. Chapter XV is relevant to this study as it deals with Syria, though some of the earlier chapters dealing with general colonial policy are of interest for useful background information.

The section on Syria considers briefly the period of colonisation following the French occupation after World War I until 1925 and considering the political developments and the relationship between the Arabs and the French. It also deals with French policies in Syria and especially the effect of the political and social insecurity on the economy of the country. It concludes that the French policy in Syria was a failure due to the alienation of the natives both in the rural and urban areas. The result was the nationalist revolt in 1925 which resulted in heavy initial defeat for France followed by a military re-occupation and a resultant weakened position not only in Syria but in her other Mediterranean colonies.

WOODWARD, E. L. AND BUTLER, ROHAN, EDS.
**Documents on British Foreign Policy, 1919–1939.**
*First Series. Vol. IV, 1919.*
*London : H.M.S.O.*
*xciii, 1,278 pp., maps, 25 cms.*

See entry under Section 2a on the Peace Conference for annotation.

# SYRIA AND LEBANON – GENERAL WORKS

\*HADDAD, GEORGE
**Fifty years of modern Syria and Lebanon.**
*Beirut : Dar-al-Hayat. 1950.*
*xvi, 264 pp., illus., maps, bibl., index, 23 cms.*

A readable account of the history of Syria and the Lebanon beginning with a brief geographical and historical introduction, leading to the rise of the nationalist movements. The author considers in detail the rise of the nationalist movement in relation to the Turkish administration before and during World War I. The work then considers the struggle to obtain independence following the defeat of Turkey beginning with the reign of Faisal from 1918–20 and the subsequent period of French occupation under the mandate until 1936, concluding with the gradual progression towards independence in 1946.

The work ends with a consideration of the government and economic life of the two countries dealing with the form of government, the political parties and the economic progress of the area. Also considered are the social and cultural changes that have taken place not only in the structure of society but in terms of the emergence of a national identity in social and cultural life.

HITTI, PHILIP K.
**History of Syria including Lebanon and Palestine.**
*London : Macmillan. 2nd ed. 1957.*
*xxv, 750 pp., illus., maps, index, 22 cms.*

An extremely detailed history of which only the last chapters are relevant to this study. The latter part of the work deals with Syria as a Turkish province, the rise of Arab nationalism in the latter half of the nineteenth century and the involved process of attaining independence.

HITTI, PHILIP K.
**A short history of Lebanon.**
*London: Macmillan. 1965.*
*xi, 249 pp., maps, index, 20 cms.*

HOURANI, ALBERT
**Syria and Lebanon:** A political essay.
*O.U.P. (for Royal Institute of International Affairs). 1946.*
*x, 402 pp., maps, app., bibl., index, 22 cms.*

This extremely detailed work deals with the political history of Syria and the Lebanon from World War I until the time of writing though the question of foreign interests in the area is only dealt with until World War II. The work is divided into four main sections covering a brief history of Syria and World War I and the peace settlement; the impact of Westernisation and the growth of nationalism; the French mandate and the Franco-Syrian treaties and the early part of World War II; the final section deals with Mr. Hourani's conclusions followed by a postscript updating the work to 1945.

The spread of Western ideas is dealt with in great detail as these are considered by the author as having been the cause of fundamental change in the political life of the area as in other parts of the Arab world. This development brought with it two inseparable problems, that of fusing the two civilisations together and of establishing a relationship based on equality and mutual respect. Nationalism is considered in the light of this Westernisation as is the Arab's political response to these problems in an attempt to defend the Arab community from possible disruption. At the time of writing the author considered the movement to be 'unformed' with the choice of moving away from the West, borrowing only its strengths to resist encroachment, or to reconstruct Arab society by assimilating the best elements of Western society.

The work concludes by examining the position at the time of the Allied occupation during World War II and by considering the problems which needed to be solved regarding the independence of the area and future relations with France and Great Britain.

The appendices reproduce the texts of various documents ranging from the Mandate for Syria and Lebanon to the various proclamations from the French on constitutional developments in Syria and the population figures for them are by province.

*KEDOURIE, ELIE
**England and the Middle East:** The destruction of the Ottoman Empire, 1914–1921.
*London: Bowes and Bowes. 1956.*
*xiii, 9–236 pp., app., bibl., index, 21½ cms.*

Syria, 1918–1920.

This chapter deals with the limbo period between the fall of Damascus and the French occupation of Syria by force in 1920. After his visit to Paris Faisal hoped that the proposed International Commission in Syria would decide the fate of the country and this was also felt by Allenby and his political officers though subsequent events proved this hope to be ill founded.

Clemenceau, however, decided on the full implementation of the Sykes–Picot agreement and Faisal was forced to return to Paris to negotiate again. This caused problems amongst his own supporters who felt that the French should be resisted by force as should the Zionist interest in Palestine. The Syrians opposed the French by setting up their own Syrian Congress and declaring Faisal as king though this was futile in the face of the granting of the mandate to France by the San Remo Conference and the subsequent invasion of Syria by the French army. Faisal was forced to flee to Palestine where he was received by Sir Herbert Samuel and *The Times* devoted two articles to the events and pronounced Faisal a modern Saladin.

KHADDURI, MAJID
**Constitutional development in Syria:** With emphasis on the Constitution of 1950.
*Middle East Journal. Vol. 5, No. 2, Spring 1951, pp. 137–161.*

A discussion of the various constitutional developments in Syria which, the writer feels, should not be regarded as a sign of inherent instability but as a transitory stage in its development. Syria had not been free long enough from French domination to adjust fully to national and international circumstances.

The article begins by considering the rule of Emir Faisal and the Syrian Congress held between 3 June 1919 and 19 July 1920 to consider all matters of national and foreign policy and a constitution. The resultant constitution of 148 articles was blocked because of the San Remo Conference which gave France the mandate for Syria resulting in the deposing of Faisal. It was from this point that the Syrian situation began to deteriorate even further with further revolts against the French and a policy of non-cooperation in all matters from the nationalists.

PETRAN, TABITHA
**Syria.**
*London : Benn. 1972.*
*284 pp., plates, maps, index, 22 cms.*
*(Nations of the Modern World Series.)*

A detailed history of Syria dealing briefly with its early history
and continuing in detail from the middle of the nineteenth century
to the present day though only the first third of this work is of
relevance to this study. The author deals with the position of the
Arab nationalists during World War I, the participation of the
Arabs in the Revolt and the short life of the Arab Government
after the capture of Damascus.

The problem of the mandate is also dealt with in some detail
with the Syrians' struggle to obtain independence in the face of
French resistance and although the revolt of 1925–1927 was put
down the French control was undermined. Despite this full independence was not achieved until 1946, due to various delaying
tactics on the part of the French administration in Syria and the
various French governments. Consideration is also given to the
problems of Palestine both in the general context of Arab affairs
and on the effect that the 1948 defeat had on internal Syrian
affairs with its independence still in a precarious position.

STEIN, LEONARD
**Syria.**
*London : Benn. 1926.*
*vii, 9–94 pp., bibl., index, 19 cms.*

A very brief study of the position in Syria from the granting of the
French mandate until 1924 aimed at the general reader. The work
deals with the terms of the mandate, the structure of the French
administration and its relationship with the Arab population.
The author deals with the 1920 Revolt and the problems of finding
a peaceful solution and although the point is made that any mandatory power would have problems it is stressed that the French
position was complicated by its traditional role as protector of the
Christian minority.

TIBAWI, A. L.
**A modern history of Syria including Lebanon and
Palestine.**
*London : Macmillan. 1969.*
*441 pp., plates, maps, notes, bibl., index, 23 cms.*

YAMAK, LABIB ZUWIYYA
**The Syrian Social Nationalist Party:** An ideological analysis.
*Massachusetts: Harvard University Press. 1966.*
*vi, 177 pp., bibl., notes, 20½ cms.*

The majority of this work is not directly related to this study as
the Syrian Social Nationalist Party did not come into being as a
force until 1932. The earlier part of the work is of interest, however, dealing with the making of the Lebanon State from 1840,
covering its historical background, the structure of Lebanese
society in religious and social terms.

The work has a full bibliography covering works in Arabic,
French and English and a section of detailed notes.

\*ZEINE, ZEINE N.
**The Struggle for Arab Independence:** Western Diplomacy
and the rise and fall of Faisal's Kingdom in Syria.
*Beirut: Khayat's. 2nd ed. 1966.*
*xii, 297 pp., plates, app., bibl., index, 22 cms.*

A valuable study dealing with the rise of Arab nationalism in
Syria and the Lebanon from the Arab Revolt to 1920. It con-
siders the Sykes–Picot agreement and its effects upon the Arab
Revolt together with the Peace Conference in 1919 and the resul-
tant settlement. Detailed consideration is given to the Franco-
British rivalry at the Peace Conference and the conflict between
Lloyd George and Clemenceau over the Syrian question.

The work continues by discussing Faisal's rule in Syria, the
granting of the mandate and the resultant fall of Faisal's government. The reasons for the downfall are considered in the light of
the promises made to the Arabs at the time of the Arab Revolt
and the French interests in Syria. The writer feels that the
promises have to be considered against the backcloth of war, the
differences in interpretation between the promises made and the
process of implementation within the framework of the mandate

The work has copious notes, a good bibliography and is well
indexed.

ZIADEH, NICOLA A.
**Syria and Lebanon.**
*London: Benn. 1957.*
*312 pp., maps, bibl., index, 22 cms.*

A general work aimed at analysing the contemporary scene in
Syria and Lebanon and as such it cannot be detailed. The section
of relevance to this study is that dealing with the granting of the

mandate to France and its early administration, though the section dealing with the land and its people is also of interest for its background information.

# ADMINISTRATION OF THE MANDATE

Duff, Douglas V.
**The Mandate in Syria and Palestine.**
*Quarterly Review. January 1933, pp. 71–83.*

The article begins by sketching in the background to the French interest in Syria with its origins in the Crusades. The granting of the mandate resulted in France having to forcibly remove Faisal from Damascus and the quelling of the Syrian rising with a heavy hand though at some cost. 'Dissatisfaction with the Mandatory is rife in the country, and only the presence of large, armed forces ensures peace.'

Earle, Edward Mead
**Syria – Acid test of the Mandates System.**
*The Nation (New York), January 1926, pp. 28–29.*

The article was prompted by the revolt of the Syrians against the French and the bombardment of Damascus and it examines the reasons for the revolt which stem from the granting of the mandate by the League of Nations. The French were unpopular from the start as was evidenced by the King–Crane Commission and the Syrian General Congress of 1919. Also the French treated Syria as a colony rather than a mandated territory. 'In short, a situation faced France which required unusual tact, sympathy and punctilious regard for native susceptibilities; she was obliged to meet it unprepared from every point of view – psychological, financial, administrative.'

The remainder of the article deals with the subsequent relations under the mandate and the events leading up to the revolt in 1926.

Fatemi, Nasrollah S.
**The Roots of Arab nationalism.**
*Orbis (Philadelphia). 1959, pp. 437–456.*

Despite the King–Crane report on Syria the mandate was given to France though the people had expressed the wish that if foreign assistance had to be received it should come from the United States or Britain. The first action of the French after expelling Faisal from Damascus was to inaugurate their rule by dissolving the unity of the country by creating six states. 'This artificial division was clearly intended to accentuate religious and local differences and to encourage a religious outlook at the expense of the national unity of the country.' The result was that Damascus was the centre of revolts, uprisings and demonstrations against imperialism.

GHEERBRANDT, J. L.
**Syria and the Lebanon.**
*Asiatic Review. July 1927, pp. 393–400.*

A brief article surveying the position of Syria in relation to the mandate. It outlines the area covered by the mandate and the responsibilities of the mandatory power. The article also gives a brief summary of the economic position of Syria and the future prospects for the country.

HOGARTH, D. G.
**The Arab World Today.**
*Foreign Affairs (New York). April 1926, pp. 406–414.*

This article considers the Arab World in 1926 which is defined by Hogarth as being the Asiatic block of Arab societies and territories. Hogarth considers Syria and the Lebanon in relation to the mandate and the effects of twenty years of Syria Arabism on the mandate. One of the major problems was the fact that France was not welcome because of its unfavourable war record and because its assimilative colonial policy was considered to be the prime count against the granting of the mandate.

HOGARTH, D. G.
**Present discontents in the Near and Middle East.**
*Quarterly Review. Vol. 234, No. 465, October 1920, pp. 411–423.*

The situation in Syria is judged to have been inevitable because the Hedjaz revolt had reached its borders and because prior to the war the nationalist thinking in Syria had reached an advanced state. Thus the British army was placed in the position of freeing Syria whilst the government was pledged to introduce a national home for the Jews in Palestine and to support the French mandate in Syria. Although the British Government maintained that promises to the Arabs were made subject to French interests '. . . we have put forward an ideal of Arab unity only to render its realisation impossible, in this generation at least, and, having betrayed the Arab sentiment of independence, we had not secured to the Syrians anything they counted as material gain'. Hogarth felt that only two courses were open to Britain, either the subjection of the Arabs by force or the fulfilment of pledges of independence, with either course requiring a unity of policy.

HOURANI, G. F.
**Syria under the French Mandate.**
*Contemporary Review. Vol. CXLVIII, 1935, pp. 591–598.*

The most striking political feature of the French mandate is seen as one of division based on religion, social cross-divisions and geographical divisions imposed by the French in their administration of the mandate. The French attitude following her seizure of the mandate by force was one of divide and rule with French administrators coming from areas of French Africa which were less advanced politically than Syria. The author admits that some unrest was '. . . not surprising. Syrians are awkward people to govern: but the Lebanese were willing to be friendly at first, and the French should have done better in Lebanon.'

The remainder of the article is not within the scope of this study as it deals with the problems of the National Assembly, the moves towards self rule and the corruptibility of the French administration.

JOARDER, SAFUIDDIN
**Syria under the French Mandate:** An overview.
*Journal Asiatic Society of Pakistan. Vol. XIV, No. 1, pp. 91–104.*

The French mandatory rule in Syria began with three distinct disadvantages. First informed Syrians were aware of French colonial rule in North Africa which created a bad impression. Secondly the French were regarded as the traditional protectors of the Maronite Christians and there was constant friction between this minority group and the Sunni Muslims. Lastly the French occupation could not be justified as a spoil of war as the area had been occupied by the British armies with the French playing a relatively insignificant role.

It was from this unstable base that the French began their mandatory rule and proceeded to worsen the situation by pursuing a policy of 'Balkanising' the country creating, dissolving and recreating states in quick succession. The aim seemed to be to rule by division, setting off one faction against another and exploiting traditional differences.

The overall administrative machinery also caused bad feelings as it was highly centralised and in the hands of French functionaries headed by the High Commissioner whose power was overwhelming. Control was then exercised through a hierarchy of officials which ensured that the Government could implement no decision without French approval.

The expulsion of Faisal had left the nationalists in a state of confusion and without a national leader. The factions lacked cohesion but did not break up and the continuing economic problems gave it the impetus it needed leading to unrest and revolution though the latter events are beyond the scope of this study.

LODER, J. DE V.
**The truth about Mesopotamia, Palestine and Syria.**
*London: Allen & Unwin. 1923.*
*221 pp., maps, index, 19 cms.*

This work deals at some length with the relationship between the Arab nationalists and the French in the Lebanon and Syria. The author also deals with the downfall of Feisal and his expulsion from Syria by the French and the problem of the extremist elements within the Arab ranks.

The appendices reproduce some of the relevant agreements including the Sykes–Picot agreement.

*LONGRIGG, STEPHEN HEMSLEY
**Syria and Lebanon under French Mandate.**
*London: O.U.P. 1958.*
*xii, 404 pp., maps, bibl., index, 21½ cms.*

A significant work which considers the political history of Syria and the Lebanon from before World War I to 1946. It deals with the period of Turkish rule, World War I, the mandate and its consequences, World War II and the decline of the mandate.

The work considers Syria as a Turkish province, its peoples and their religions, the methods by which the province was ruled and the economic structure of the country. It then deals with the Arab Revolt and the promises that were made to the Arabs regarding Syria and the conflict between these and the Sykes–Picot agreement which influenced the eventual settlement. The mandate is considered in some detail especially that part related to French relations with Feisal and the gradual transfer of power from the mandatory country. It was the tenor of French rule and the lack of progress towards independence which led to the revolt of 1925. The work then considers the re-assertion of French control and the further promises made to the Syrians which were never ratified by the French government which led to further frustration of nationalist feeling.

The work concludes with an appreciation of the position in Syria at the end of World War II and the effects of the French defeats in Europe on her influence in Syria resulting in the eventual breakdown of the mandate and the gradual transfer of power to the Syrians. It discusses the problems accompanying the transfer of power and the relationship between the Syrians and Lebanese and the French embittered by previous events.

The book is enhanced by an exhaustive index and an extremely detailed bibliography.

MacCallum, Elisabeth P.
**The Nationalist crusade in Syria.**
*New York: The Foreign Policy Association. 1928.*
*299 pp., app., bibl., index, 18½ cms.*

In any consideration of the nationalist movement in Syria this is an indispensable work providing a detailed study of the Syrian Mandate and in particular the French interpretation of the mandate system which aimed at preserving a French presence in the Levant. The problem was accentuated by the belief of the French that the Syrians were not ready for self government after generations of control by the Ottoman administration and by the Syrian belief that the French colonial policy was aimed at denying the Syrians a voice in their own form of government.

One of the main complaints voiced by the nationalists concerned the division of Syria into several administrative districts which, they charged, destroyed Syrian unity and was aimed at the creation of diversive religious and tribal factions within the country. A further cause of discontent was the lack of individual freedom as demonstrated by the control of the press, the courts and the activities of French intelligence officers. Whilst some allowance must be made for exaggeration the author is clear that the injustices against which the population complained in 1925 were something more than the fictitious grievances of troublemakers who resented all limitations placed upon their own activities.

The work then considers the declining economy of Syria and the failure of the agricultural policy which together with the political questions led to the rebellion of 1925. Although the rebellion was put down it took the French two years to restore order and this did nothing to enhance their prestige. The rebellion also resulted in a retarding of the natural development of opportunity for young Syrians and its commercial progress which led to an emigration that the country could ill afford. However, the author considers that on the credit side the rebellion helped to extend among the ordinary people an understanding of the principles and aims of nationalism, which resulted in an extension of a political awareness which showed itself in the far greater interest shown in the elections to the Constituent Assembly of 1928. It should not, however, be assumed that the nationalists presented a united front as there was the grave problem as to whether the movement should cooperate at all with the French administration to secure independence and also power rivalry within the movement.

The work concludes with an examination of the Permanent Mandates Commission in relation to Syria and its responsibilities towards the League of Nations. Both bodies were criticised at the time for a lack of action at the time of the rebellion especially when the reports of the Commission seemed to confirm some of the grievances of the nationalists.

The appendices reproduce the French mandate for Syria and the Lebanon, notes on the religious sects in Syria and the Ponsat declaration of 1927. The work has an excellent bibliography relating to Franco-Syrian relations although the majority of the works represent European and American viewpoints.

*MANDATE FOR SYRIA AND LEBANON, 24 JULY 1922
**Geneva: League of Nations.**
*In : Landen, Robert G., ed.*
*The Emergence of the Modern Middle East : Selected readings, pp. 205–210.*

A copy of the mandate for Syria and Lebanon under which France was to administer the territory under the general supervision of the League of Nations. Although the mandates were supposed to prepare the territories for eventual independence, France's administration was blemished by its repressive nature and the numerous uprisings which were put down with extreme severity. The French aim was to divide and rule and parliamentary life was marked by bitter recriminations and numerous suspensions of the legislature. Independence for the two countries was finally achieved during World War II.

NEWMAN, E. W. POLSON
**The Revolt in Syria.**
*Nineteenth Century. January 1926, pp. 33–41.*

A discussion of the French position in Syria at the time of the Revolt and in particular the problem of Jebel Druse where the Revolt had originated. The Druses had always been a sect apart in

Syria with their own country, religion and customs and even under the Ottoman administration they had enjoyed a certain measure of independence. The rebellion started by the Druses soon spread and the whole country was in a state of rebellion and it was only the lack of co-ordinated policy amongst the insurgents which prevented a complete French defeat.

The article examines the problems faced by the French in Syria which were threefold, military, administrative and religious and discusses possible solutions to these problems. In considering the military aspect the writer concludes that more reinforcements were needed and that a strategy somewhat akin to that used by Britain in the Boer War was called for, i.e. protection of large centres of population, ensuring safety of communication, followed by the restoration of authority in rural areas. It is the military situation which the author sees as the key to the whole situation as administrative reform and the religious problems could only be solved once peace had been restored.

RESOLUTION OF THE GENERAL SYRIAN CONGRESS AT DAMASCUS, 2 JULY 1919.
*In: Hurewitz, J. C.*
*Diplomacy in the Near and Middle East, pp. 62–65.*

This resolution resulted from the arrival of the King–Crane Commission in Damascus with the Arab nationalists taking the opportunity to express their dislike of the idea of a French mandate over Syria and the establishment of a Jewish state in Palestine. In particular the resolution stressed that there should be no separation of Palestine or Lebanon from Syria thus resulting in a Greater Syria concept.

*Also in: Landen, Robert G., ed.*
*The Emergence of the Modern Middle East: Selected readings, pp. 227–230.*

RONDOT, PIERRE
**Lebanese institutions and Arab nationalism.**
*Journal Contemporary History. Vol. 3, No. 3, 1968, pp. 37–51.*

A large amount of the article is outside of the scope of this study, however, the earlier part of the article dealing with the development of Arabism and Lebanese nationalism from 1861 to 1914 is of interest. It also deals with the formation of the Greater Lebanon in August 1920 and the relation between the new state of Lebanon and the Arab regime in Damascus.

RYAN, A.
**The Syrian rebellion.**
*Contemporary Review. February 1926, pp. 186–195.*

A consideration of the rebellion in Syria at the time of the uprising which concerns itself with the reasons for French unpopularity in Syria, the course of the rebellion and the problems to be faced in concluding a settlement.

*TIBAWI, A. L.
**Syria from the Peace Conference to the fall of Damascus.**
*The Islamic Quarterly. Vol. XI, Nos. 3 & 4, July/December 1967, pp. 77–122.*

An extremely important article dealing with the complex situation in Syria and Palestine from the negotiations prior to the peace conference to the occupation of Damascus by French troops in 1920. The article is, in effect, a complete re-assessment of the whole question from the Arab viewpoint based on the release of Foreign Office material not available to earlier writers. The problems of the area were complicated because of the three conflicting interests namely those of the Arabs, the Zionists and the French with the complexities of international politics causing shifts in policy to achieve compromise.

Initially the author deals with the vexed question of Palestine retracing the initial promises to the Arabs, the conflict between these and the Sykes–Picot agreement and in the tide of Zionism in Palestine. In addition all of these were influenced by the determinations of the American, French and British Governments both at the peace conference and behind the scenes. In this particular area Tibawi casts doubts on the part played by Lawrence accusing him of bias in the translation of Feisal's speeches and altering telegrams and letters relating to the negotiations.

It is considered by Tibawi that by the peace conference Britain was already committed to a policy of securing the mandate for Palestine and, therefore, by default ensuring French control over Syria. This agreement reached between the two powers meant that at the peace conference the Arab case was lost before it was presented. The British domestic situation also caused problems in the Middle East with the need to withdraw troops for economic reasons adding to the crisis. This left a vacuum which was destined to be filled by the French after the granting of the mandates at the San Remo Conference, though the mandate over Syria had to be assumed by force. Further fragmentation of the area was to result from the Cairo Conference in 1921 which resulted in the creation of Transjordan and though this was to come under the control of Emir Abdullah it was mainly an attempt to prevent Arab action against the French rule in Syria and a price for non-interference in Palestine.

WHITE, WILBUR W.
**The Process of change in the Ottoman Empire.**
*Chicago: University of Chicago Press. 1937.*
*ix, 315 pp., map, bibl., index, 23½ cms.*

The mandate was given to France but had to be taken by force with the French entering Damascus and forcing Faisal to flee to Palestine and 'setting up this new type of control of "backward" peoples by the same old method – military power'. The French pattern of administration was to break the country up into units forming the autonomous states of Great Lebanon, Damascus and Aleppo, the territory of the Alouites and the emirate of the Hairan.

The mandate which had been assumed by force had to be retained by force in the face of continuing opposition from the Syrian nationalists both within the country and from the exiles in Transjordan.

# (c) PALESTINE AND TRANSJORDAN

## *GENERAL WORKS*

\*BARBOUR, NEVILL
**Nisi Dominus.** A survey of the Palestine controversy.
*London: Harrap. 1946.*
*248 pp., maps, app., index, 20 cms.*

A survey of the Palestine problem which aims to present both sides of the dispute and stressing that the solution is the strict interpretation of the Balfour Declaration with Palestine being a Jewish National Home without prejudice to the position of the Arab population.

The work begins by considering the position of the Jews in history through the Roman Empire to the growth of Political Zionism. This leads to a Zionism related to Palestine and the resultant Balfour Declaration which provided for a Jewish National Home with the backing of the Great Powers. The author then deals with the position of the Arabs and their relations with the Jews in the early history of Palestine, the Arabs under Ottoman rule and the Arab Revolt. This section also deals with the McMahon–Hussein correspondence and the promises made to the Arabs to secure their support against the Turks.

The latter part of the work deals with the mandate system which dismembered the Arab world and the relations between the Arabs and Jews before the granting of the mandate to Britain. The relevant sections of the book conclude with a consideration of the administration's policies with regard to land, education and the Muslim community.

COKE, RICHARD
**The Arab's place in the sun.**
*London: Butterworth. 1929.*
*318 pp., illus., maps, index, 22 cms.*

DANN, URIEL
**The Beginning of the Arab Legion.**
*Middle Eastern Studies. Vol. 5, No. 3, October 1969, pp. 181–191.*

Although this subject is only of passing interest to this study it is included for the light that it throws upon the problems of the administration of Transjordan from July 1920 which was based on limited assistance to the native administration. 'There must be no question of setting up any British Administration in that area and all that may be done at present is to send a maximum of four or five political officers.' The article then proceeds to detail the development of the administration and the part played by the Reserve Force in maintaining order in Transjordan prior to it becoming the Arab Legion.

ERSKINE, MRS. STEWART
**Palestine of the Arabs.**
*London: Harrap. 1935.*
*256 pp., illus., app., index, 21 cms.*

The official granting of the mandate was for the Arabs the dashing of all their hopes as the terms of the mandate provided for the implementation of the Balfour Declaration. 'By these clauses the Jewish immigrants were given full rights not only to colonize but to undertake public works and to acquire Palestinian nationality; and all these benefits were given without consulting the inhabitants of the country. Had we said that we had conquered the country and were prepared to arrange its affairs according to our pleasure it would have been far better; the Arabs might have accepted the conditions . . .'

The remainder of this section deals with the breakdown of relations between the communities and opposition from both communities to the mandate and to the British administration.

FERGUSON, PAMELA
**The Palestine problem.**
*London : Martin Brian & O'Keeffe. 1973.*
*158 pp., bibl., index, 22 cms.*

As this work attempts to deal with the problem of Palestine from the beginning of the twentieth century to date, a large amount is outside the scope of this study. The earlier parts are of relevance, however, as the author considers the problems of the mandate as a legacy of the McMahon–Hussein correspondence and the Balfour Declaration.

Problems were also caused by increased Jewish immigration coupled with their pattern of settlement and the land problem. The early administration is considered with the problems faced by Britain in trying to administer to suit the wishes of the two communities in the context of the contradictory agreements relating to the area and the terms of the mandate.

FISHER, SYDNEY NETTLETON
**The Middle East:** A history.
*London : Routledge & Kegan Paul. 2nd ed. 1971.*
*xxx, 749 pp., maps, bibl., index, 22 cms.*

See Section 1a for annotation.
The chapter of relevance to this section is as follows:
Part IV. The Contemporary Middle East.
Chapter 32. Palestine and Transjordan.

GILBERT, MARTIN
**The Arab-Israeli conflict:** Its history in maps.
*London : Weidenfeld & Nicolson. 1974.*
*101 pp., maps, 25 cms.*

Part two is entitled 'The Jewish National Home' and the following maps are of interest:
    18. Arab fears of a Jewish Majority in Palestine, 1920–1939.
    19. Roads and riots in Palestine, 1920–1947.

GLUBB, JOHN BAGOT
**Peace in the Holy Land:** An historical analysis of the Palestine problem.
*London : Hodder & Stoughton. 1971.*
*384 pp., maps, bibl., index, 24 cms.*

An examination of the Palestine problem through the eyes of the former commander of the Arab Legion. The aim of this work is to examine the problem from earliest times in its historical setting and with the human problem '. . . rationally and without emotion, for it is the violent passions which this problem has aroused which made it so difficult to solve'.

The earlier part of this study is outside of this bibliography and the relevant portion begins with the section entitled 'The Coming of Zionism' which deals with the latter part of the nineteenth century and the increased Jewish immigration from Eastern Europe, not all of which was to Palestine, and ending with the Balfour Declaration. The work continues with a consideration of the mandate and the gradual movement towards anarchy with acts of violence being perpetrated by both sides. In considering the immediate post-mandate war between Israel and Jordan Glubb deals with the various claims and counter claims regarding the responsibility for starting the war and the conduct of the war thereafter. The work ends with a brief consideration of the six-day-war and a proposal for the settlement of the problem.

GREAT BRITAIN: ADMIRALTY, NAVAL INTELLIGENCE DIVISION
**Palestine and Transjordan:** B.R. 514.
*London: Admiralty. 1943.*
*xv, 621 pp., illus., stats., maps, app., index, 21½ cms.*
*(Geographical Handbook Series.)*

One of a series of handbooks written by the Geographical section of the Naval Intelligence Division of the Admiralty designed to supply material for discussion of naval, military and political problems.

A great deal of the material is outside the scope of this study by nature of topic or date but the historical section, the section dealing with the administration and that dealing with the peoples are of interest.

HUREWITZ, J. C.
**Recent books on the problem of Palestine.**
*Middle East Journal. Vol. III, January 1949, pp. 86–91.*

This review article begins by detailing the problems facing the student of the Palestine problem including the mass of material, some of which is not generally available, the language problem and the wideness of the subject matter which must include the domestic policies of Britain and America. The article then continues by examining the most important material on the subject, beginning with the Palestine Royal Commission Report (Cmmd.

Paper 5479) which the author feels is indispensable for an understanding of the background and which he praises for its fair and frank assessment.

The review also indicates the problem of the partisan nature of the majority of the literary contributions which are characterised by preoccupations with theories, 'Arabs as well as Zionists, could, and did, muster powerful moral arguments. But instead of presenting both sides objectively, the partisans see the issue as black and white without intermediate shades.' The article then deals with the subject from both the Zionist and Arab viewpoints assessing the strengths and weaknesses of the various titles. The final part of this review article considers the literature from the Great Power aspect and stresses the need for a balanced work on Britain's position with regard to the mandate.

IZZEDDIN, NEJLA
**The Arab world:** Past, present and future.
*Chicago: Henry Regnery Co. 1953.*
*xvi, 412 pp., illus., index, 24 cms.*

The section on Palestine puts forward the Arab case against the establishment of a Jewish state in the light of the historical evidence. The author also argues that Britain had no right to issue the Balfour Declaration as it conflicted with the promises made to the Arabs through the McMahon–Hussein correspondence. It concludes that Palestine cannot exist as a separate entity as it is artificial and unjust and will cause unrest until it is once more integrated into the Arab world to which it belongs.

*KIRKBRIDE, ALEC SEATH
**A Crackle of thorns:** Experiences in the Middle East.
*London: John Murray. 1956.*
*viii, 201 pp., illus., map, index, $21\frac{1}{2}$ cms.*

In 1920 Kirkbride was one of the political officers based in Transjordan charged with the setting up of an administration to run the area which was 'intended to serve as a reserve of land for use in the resettlement of Arabs once the National Home for the Jews in Palestine, which they were pledged to support, became an accomplished fact. There was no intention at that stage of forming the territory east of the Jordan into an independent Arab state.'

In this section Kirkbride discusses the administration of the area prior to the Cairo Conference and he deals with the arrival of Abdullah from the Hedjaz on his way to Syria following the expulsion of Faisal.

Abdullah was made Emir of Transjordan following the Cairo Conference in return for promises not to interfere in the domestic affairs of Syria and the Jewish presence in Palestine and Kirkbride remained as the representative of the British Government.

\*KOESTLER, ARTHUR
**Promise and fulfilment:** Palestine, 1917–1949.
*London: Macmillan. 1949.*
*xv, 335 pp., map, 22 cms.*

The author presents a picture of Palestine in which there are no heroes or villains, only confused people all with implicit faith in their cause. The Balfour Declaration is seen by Mr. Koestler as 'one of the most improbable political documents of all time, [by which] one nation solemnly promised to a second nation the country of a third'.

This book is a useful contribution to the literature of a complex problem which attempts to examine the problem from both sides and concluding that the Arabs and Jews were 'both right in their own terms of reference and in their own universe of discourse' and British attempts at finding a solution failed not because of territorial and economic aspirations but because of mental blocks and 'psychological imponderables' which Mr. Koestler feels are the only possible explanations for the fluctuations in British policies.

LAQUEUR, WALTER
**A History of Zionism.**
*London: Weidenfeld & Nicolson. 1972.*
*xvi, 640 pp., illus., bibl., index, 24 cms.*

An extremely detailed survey of the Zionist movement from the beginning of the nineteenth century to the birth of the State of Israel in 1948. As such the majority of the work is outside of the scope of this study but it does cover the clash with the Arab nationalist movement.

Laqueur makes the point that initially the Zionist movement was unaware of the Arab nationalist movement and indeed it has been argued by their critics that the Zionists regarded Palestine as an empty country created specially for their national home. The danger of conflict gained real substance with the Arab attacks on the Jews in 1921 and the friction gathered momentum over the years, though Laqueur does make the point that friction was evident even under the Turks, though this could be regarded as part of the lawlessness of the outlying provinces of the empire.

The work continues to deal with the position during the war when political activity ceased on both sides as they were subjected to restrictions imposed by the Turkish authorities. It deals with the immediate post-war relations between the two communities in the light of the Balfour Declaration and Britain's promises to the Arabs. The author traces the tortuous history of the mandate with the increasing Jewish immigration and their resultant economic strength in Palestine which was a further cause of friction. In the 1930s the last real chance of Jewish-Arab rapprochement was dashed by the massive increase in Jewish immigration caused by the persecution of the Jews by Hitler. This led to the conviction that the Jews had no home but Palestine and that the Arabs would have to be absorbed into the surrounding country and the German persecution led to the psychological fear that whilst in a minority the Jew would always be persecuted. The Zionists also believed that the Arabs finding themselves economically better would accept minority status in a Jewish state and it was only increasing Arab resistance which led to the problem of incompatability being faced.

The work also deals in detail with the last years of the mandate and the Jewish struggle against the British to secure independence. It considers the increasing tension between Arab and Jew and the violent clashes which flared up from time to time culminating in civil war with the British maintaining only a semblance of control. It also deals with the struggle to create a Jewish state in the face of complex political situations with the decision being taken in the United Nations to partition the country to provide areas for each community. The work considers finally the first Arab-Jewish war and the resultant creation of the State of Israel in 1948.

The work has a full bibliography and is well indexed.

MARLOWE, JOHN
**Arab Nationalism and British Imperialism:** A study in power politics.
*London: The Cresset Press. 1961.*
*viii, 236 pp., bibl., index, 22 cms.*

In considering the Palestine problem the author examines the confrontation which was bound to result between the Balfour Declaration and the aspirations of the Arabs. The British part in the history of Palestine during this period comes in for some criticism with regard to the treatment of the Arab population and the genuine desire of the Arabs for independence.

PARKES, JAMES
**Palestine.**
*London: O.U.P. 1940.*
*32 pp., maps, 17½ cms.*
*(Oxford Pamphlets on World Affairs, No. 31.)*

A résumé of the problem of Palestine setting out the reasons for Britain's involvement in the area following World War I, the conflicting promises made to the Arabs and Jews and the relationship between the two communities and their relationships with Britain. The pamphlet also discusses the political history of the mandate from its inception to date and the problems still presented by Palestine.

\*ROYAL INSTITUTE OF INTERNATIONAL AFFAIRS
**Great Britain and Palestine, 1915–1936.**
*London: Royal Institute of International Affairs. 1937.*
*111 pp., tables, notes, app., 22 cms.*
*(Information Department Papers, No. 20.)*

The period just prior to the granting of the mandate saw Palestine under British Military Administration followed by a Civil Administration in 1920 though disturbances were evident among the Arabs mainly as a result of the unrest in Syria and the Arab fear of being swamped by Jewish settlement. The civil administration which assumed control in July 1920 began to implement the Balfour Declaration with the first immigration ordinance. Alarm spread amongst the Arab population partly because the Arab effendi class felt it would lose its feudal position if the Jewish immigration changed the social structure of Palestine and further, though limited, rioting ensued.

In an attempt to make the position clear to both parties and to reassure the Arabs the Colonial Office issued a statement of British policy on 3 June 1922 commonly known as the Churchill memorandum which stressed that:

1. Britain did not contemplate the creation of a wholly Jewish Palestine or any adverse effects upon the Arab population.
2. That the terms of the Balfour Declaration did not mean anything other than a National Home for the Jews.
3. The status of the Jews was to be one of right rather than sufferance.
4. Immigration to be controlled and at an economically viable level.

254

The appendices reproduce the Mandate for Palestine and the text of the Churchill Memorandum.

SACHAR, HOWARD M.
**The Emergence of the Middle East, 1914–1924.**
*London: Allen Lane, The Penguin Press. 1969.*
*xiii, 518 pp., xxix, maps, notes, bibl., index, 24 cms.*
*(Chapter XIII.)*

The consideration of the problem of Palestine begins by examining the negotiations between Faisal and the Zionists in 1918 which seemed to reach some measure of agreement though it was difficult for Faisal to negotiate in the face of his own people and apparent harmony soon turned into discord.

Gradually an authentic Palestinian nationalism began to evolve among the younger Arabs in the cities and the gradual deterioration in relationships was not helped by Abdullah's actions in Transjordan, though they resulted in his being made Emir by Britain as an inducement to cease opposing the Jews in Palestine. Relations between Jews and Arabs continued to worsen, however, and during the period that this work ends the area was being totally administered by the British.

The work has extensive notes and a detailed bibliography arranged by topic together with an exhaustive index.

STEWART, DESMOND
**The Middle East:** Temple of Janus.
*London: Hamish Hamilton. 1972.*
*viii, 414 pp., bibl., index, 24 cms.*

Despite Arab opposition the mandate for Palestine was given to Britain on the understanding that the Balfour Declaration would be implemented. The problem of this condition and the question of the Arabs haunted the administrators for although some favoured one side or the other the majority tended to be impartial.

The Arab reaction was to argue for their natural right to the country and to democratic institutions though Britain realised that if these institutions were permitted the Arabs would use them to prevent further Jewish immigration. Although there had been little trouble between the Jews and the Arabs in the past the Arabs were suspicious of the post-war immigrants from Europe. The Arabs viewed with alarm the steady increase of a minority, feeling that if the Jews ever became a majority they would either evict the Arabs by force or reduce them to an insignificant minority.

\*Toukon, Baha Uddin
**A Short History of Transjordan.**
*London: Luzac & Co. 1945.*
*49 pp., frontis., 21½ cms.*

A useful survey of the history of Transjordan from earliest times before it had a separate identity as a sovereign state until 1944. As such only the latter part of this work is of relevance to this study beginning with the section entitled 'Transjordan in Modern Times'.

The work deals with the early days of Turkish rule in the area leading to the unrest which began to manifest itself at the beginning of the twentieth century with revolts at Shabeh in 1905 and Karak in 1910, both of which were suppressed. The author then considers the Arab Revolt which began in June 1916 after extensive negotiations between Hussein and the British Government. The work considers the events leading to the establishment of Transjordan after the collapse of Feisal's rule in Syria and the creation of an Arab administration headed by Abdullah to rule an area which had previously formed the Syrian province of Dera'a to Ma'an.

The work concludes by examining the various uprisings that took place in Transjordan, the Wahhabi invasions of 1922 and 1924 which were defeated by the Arab Legion and the Royal Air Force, and the part played by the Arab Legion in World War II.

Although very brief this is a useful survey of the history of Transjordan by a Transjordanian.

## ARAB-JEWISH RELATIONS

Abcarius, M. F.
**Palestine through the fog of propaganda.**
*London: Hutchinson & Co. 1946.*
*240 pp., app., 22½ cms.*

This work puts forward the Arab case for an Arab nation in Palestine based on the historical concept of the problem and in the light of the promises made to the Arabs in the Hussein–McMahon correspondence. It also deals in detail with the military administration in Palestine and the arrival of the Zionist Commission which Abcarius feels adopted a provocative attitude from the outset and which wielded considerable power. He then moves to a consideration of the civil administration and the mandate with the gradual increase of Jewish influence at all levels of public and commercial life, and what Abcarius described as double standards in relation to wages paid to Arab and Jew for the same job.

Abcarius continues by examining various aspects of the Palestine problem such as land tenure and agriculture, the claims that the Arabs benefited from Jewish capital, and the economic position of the Jews in relation to their Arab neighbours. The problem is seen as none other than that caused by the creation of a Jewish National Home which conflicts with the true principles of democracy. 'The Arabs feel with the Jews in their plight; but it is not their sympathy that the Jews require: they demand the Arab's land and are ready to extend to them their sympathy.'

\*ATIYAH, EDWARD
**The Palestine Question.**
*London: Diplomatic Press & Publishing Co. 1948.*
*16 pp., 20½ cms.*

This pamphlet examines the question of Palestine from the Arab point of view beginning with an examination of the situation prior to the outbreak of World War I and especially with regard to the relationship between the Arabs and Jews and the relative positions of the two peoples. In addition this section examines the Balfour Declaration and concludes that it did not provide for a Jewish State only a National Home which meant a self-contained community without sovereign status, an interpretation which is supported by the Command Papers of 1922, 1930, and 1939.

Atiyah continues by examining the Balfour Declaration and the mandate both of which he considers to be invalid as they made promises which had been made without the knowledge of the Palestinians and against their wishes. He also raises the question of the correspondence between Hussein and McMahon, raising once again the question of whether Palestine was included in the area designated as an independent Arab state. This leads to a consideration of the Zionist movement at large which was instrumental in pursuing the establishment of a Jewish state which Atiyah considers was a conspiracy against the rights of the Arabs.

The pamphlet concludes with a study of events outside of the scope of this study dealing with the increased immigration in the thirties and the subsequent relinquishment of the mandate to the United Nations.

*BOUSTANY, W. F.
**The Palestine Mandate invalid and impracticable:** A contribution of arguments and documents towards the solution of the Palestine problem.
*Beirut : American Press. 1936.*
*iv, 168 pp., app., bibl., 25 cms.*

The author was a member of the Third Palestine Arab Delegation to London to present a case to the Royal Commission on Palestine and the mandate and this material aims at investigating the problem. The work is divided into ten parts representing the Jewish, Arab and British aspect of the problem with the first nine parts having been formally presented to the British Government and the tenth added for publication.

The first five parts deal with the whole question of the mandate beginning by arguing that the mandate was invalid from the start as Palestine was not excluded from the area of support for Arab independence in the discussions between Britain and Hussein. The mandate is then compared to those in operation for Syria and Lebanon and Iraq in relation to the covenant to the League of Nations to which, the author claims, it did not conform.

The last five sections deal with the problems of the mandate from the administrative aspect, the complexity of the operation and the conflicting interests in Palestine. It concludes with a consideration of the policy of the Jewish National Home which is considered to be the main defect and of Britain's policy in the country.

The work is prefaced by an index of events from the early history of the Jews through to the Royal Commission of 1936, and an index of documents arranged by Jewish, Arab and British and Legal aspects. The appendices reproduce official documents related to the subject such as the terms of the mandate and the Treaty of Lausanne.

BROIDO, EPHRAIM
**Jews, Arabs and the Middle East.**
*London : Poale Zion. 1944.*
*47 pp., 18 cms.*

A brief analysis of the problem of Arab-Jewish relationships in Palestine seen against the Middle East situation as a whole. It concludes that the case of the Arabs as a separate nation in Palestine is an oversimplification of the case and that the Jewish case for a national home is a baffling one because of its unique and complex character.

Initially the author considers the involvement of both peoples in Palestine and he feels that the comment of the Royal Commission was probably correct when it defined the conflict as 'fundamentally a conflict of right with right'. The Arab claim was that Palestine was part of the area of independence discussed in the Hussein–MacMahon correspondence and was part of Syria with historical and linguistic links with the Arab world as a whole. The Jewish National Home, however, had its boundaries within the state of Palestine whereas the Palestinian Arabs had an interest in a wider area.

The author discusses the problem in its wider setting dealing with its impact on Middle East affairs in general and the effects of Jewish immigration on life in the country. He also deals with negotiations between Hussein and the Allies, the position of Palestine in these negotiations and the Feisal–Weizmann agreement. The author then considers the Zionist policy towards the Arabs and the possibilities for a future partnership. The work concludes with an essay on the rebuilding of a Jewish Commonwealth on socialist lines which the author sees as being ideal for the task of national reconstruction.

These essays first appeared in *The Left News* for November 1942 and December 1943.

\*DODD, C. H. AND SALES, MARY
**Israel and the Arab World.**
*London: Routledge & Kegan Paul. 1970.*
*xvi, 247 pp., bibl., index, 22 cms.*

A collection of official papers, maps, reports from journals and quotations from other works illustrating the Arab-Israeli conflict from World War I to 1968 and as so much of the material is beyond the limits of this study, the following sections are of relevance.

Part 1: Place and People.
A series of maps and graphs to illustrate territorial and population changes in the area.

Part II. The Basic Argument.
Extracts from a document by Weizmann 'The Jewish People and Palestine' and Zurayk's 'The Conflict between Principle and force in the Palestine problem' representing the Arab viewpoint.

Part III. The Written Undertaking.
Extracts from the McMahon–Hussein correspondence, the Sykes–Picot Agreement and the Balfour Declaration.

Part IV: The Peace Settlement.
Article 22 of the Covenant of the League of Nations and extracts from the mandate for Palestine.

\*Hadawi, Sami
**Bitter Harvest:** Palestine, 1914–1967.
*New York: The New World Press. 1967.*
*xx, 385 pp., maps, refs., index, 22½ cms.*

The Arab viewpoint of the Palestine problem written by a Christian Arab sometime Director for the Institute for Palestine Studies, member of the Palestine Government 1920–48 and thereafter various other posts in the Middle East and America. The bulk of this work is outside of the scope of this study but the first five chapters are of relevance to this period and even more so because the case is argued from the Arab viewpoint.

The work begins with the historical background to Palestine and its peoples and the relations between the Arabs and Jews throughout history. The author then considers the British wartime pledges of Arab independence centred mainly upon the McMahon–Hussein correspondence, the Sykes–Picot agreement and the Balfour Declaration. Following these aspects of the problem the author considers the reassurances given to the Arabs including the Hogarth message of 4 January 1918 and the British declaration to the Seven of 16 June 1918. This section concludes with a consideration of the role played by the Arabs in the war and the growing problem of Zionism.

The author then moves to the Jewish aspect of the problem, devoting two chapters to this side of the problem dealing with the links between Palestine and the Jews and the Zionist Movement. The fifth chapter deals with Palestine under the mandate from 1920 firstly with the system in general and then to the administration set up in Palestine to administer the mandate, the Arab opposition to the mandate and the British statement of policy in relation to Palestine. The remainder of the chapter gradually leads on from this period with which this study is concerned dealing with the deteriorating situation in Palestine, the growth of civil unrest between the two communities and the termination of the mandate.

Hattis, Susan Lee
**The Bi-national idea in Palestine during mandatory times.**
*Israel: Shilmona Pub. Co. 1970.*
*355 pp., bibl., index, 22½ cms.*

A thesis presented to the University of Geneva which considers the question of whether Palestine could have achieved the status of a bi-national state as one of the possibilities under the mandate. The attitudes towards bi-nationalism were clear from the beginning as the Arabs saw Palestine as remaining a predominantly Arab land with the Jews having minority rights whilst the Jews believed that their presence was internationally recognised and that the Arabs could be won over by economic benefits. In the early part of the nineteenth century '. . . the realisation that Arab interests in Palestine existed and were likely to clash with those of the Jews unless careful attention were given them was still far way off from a definite theory of how the problem should be tackled, never mind a theory on a bi-national state'.

The work considers the theory behind bi-nationalism as shown in the case of Switzerland and the U.S.S.R. and as one stage in the political thought of the Young Turks which was never put to the test. The concept is then considered in relation to the two communities though the main area of Arab sympathy for the idea was amongst the Christian Arabs of Syria as they were seeking to find their place as a minority in a Muslim world whilst the Christian Arabs in Palestine 'had a natural reason to unite with their Moslem brethren – Anti-Zionism. Any other position would have placed them in the eyes of the Moslem Arabs as traitors to the Arab cause.'

The work then considers the idea of bi-nationalism throughout the mandate with each chapter dealing with a period of years, with a concluding chapter which brings together the threads to see what had happened to the idea and whether, if circumstances had been different, the concept could have worked.

KATIBAH, H. L.
**The New spirit in Arab lands.**
*New York: Published by the Author. 1940.*
*320 pp., bibl., index, 23 cms.*

The question of Arab nationalism in relation to Zionism is dealt with in some detail though the majority is outside the scope of this study by virtue of period. The conclusion is that the Jews should have accepted a place in the Arab world as promised in the Balfour Declaration and not an independent Jewish state which, by its very presence, would invite perpetual hatred and opposition from the Arabs.

*KHALIDI, WALID, ED.
**From Haven to Conquest:** Readings in Zionism and the Palestine problem until 1948.

*Beirut: Institute for Palestine Studies. 1971.*
*lxxxiii, 914 pp., maps, app., index, 22½ cms.*

An anthology of readings dealing with the history of Zionism and Palestine from 1897 until the creation of the State of Israel in 1948. The work is divided into four main sections:

1. Background and early development of the Palestine problem.
2. 1919–39 and the establishment of the Zionist presence.
3. Zionist links with America.
4. The partition of Palestine and the creation of Israel.

Although the anthology as a whole is of interest to the study of the Palestine problem much of the material is concerned with the Zionist viewpoint and the involvement of the Great Powers and as such is not directly relevant to this study. The following articles are of direct relevance:

No. 19. Memorandum by Mr. Balfour respecting Syria, Palestine and Mesopotamia, pp. 201–11.
Deals with the problems of the conflicting interests in these three countries in the Middle East and especially the problem of conflicting interests in Syria between the French in Syria and the conflict raised between this and the Sykes–Picot agreement and the promises to the Arabs. It deals also with the problems of a Jewish state of Palestine and the integrity of Mesopotamia. It puts forward five proposals.
   1. Fundamental conception of Sykes–Picot to remain.
   2. Sykes–Picot special privileges in respect of red and blue areas to be abandoned.
   3. Economic monopolies to be abandoned.
   4. French zone of Syria to also include Alexandretta and its hinterland.
   5. British zone in Mesopotamia to include Mosul.
43. Reid, T. 'Reservations on the Plans for the Partition of Palestine, 1938'. (Reprint from *Gt. Britain, Palestine Partition Commission Report, 1938.*) pp. 409–32.
Deals with the various plans put forward regarding the partition of Palestine and the problems in trying to partition the country to give the areas to the dominant community. Maps of the various partition suggestions are reproduced.

51. Hocking, W. E. 'Arab nationalism and political Zionism', pp. 499–507.
(Reprinted from *The Moslem World*, xxxv, No. 3, 1945.)
An examination of the Jewish aspirations in Palestine and the problems of the Arabs and their political aspirations. It also deals with the position of the Arab society striving to find its new identity after four centuries of Turkish rule.

Also of relevance:

53. Roosevelt, K. *The U.S. and the Arab World*, pp. 515–25.
63. *Bi-nationalism not partition*, pp. 645–95.

\*KIMCHE, JON
**Palestine or Israel:** The untold story of why we failed, 1917–1923: 1967–1973.
*London: Secker & Warburg. 1973.*
*xx, 360 pp., bibl., app., index, 29 cms.*

The latter part of the section covering the period 1917–23 considers the period following the mandate which was approved at the San Remo Conference. In 1921 Amin el-Hussani became Mufti of Jerusalem and he immediately began to pursue his policy of driving a wedge between Britain and the Zionists. This was evidenced by the riots of May 1921 during which the Arabs supported the British administration whilst opposing the Jews. Success was gained by Herbert Samuel feeling the need to ban further Jewish immigration following the riots, but it had also set the scene for future discord as he had established the Arab refusal to accept Zionism. This policy also forced the Zionists to abandon the policy of accommodation and to pursue the aim of statehood and control over Palestine.

The appendix reproduces the Balfour Declaration and the work also has a note on sources, a detailed bibliography and index.

\*LAQUEUR, WALTER, ED.
**Israeli/Arab reader:** A documentary history of the Middle East conflict.
*London: Weidenfeld and Nicolson. 1969.*
*xi, 371 pp., map, bibl., 22 cms.*

The work reproduces documents relating to the Israeli-Arab conflict though only the first two sections are of relevance to this study dealing with the period leading up to the mandate and the period from 1920.

The first section covers the period from the beginning of the Jewish and Arab national movements to the British Mandate. The Zionist movement found its political expression in the latter part of the nineteenth century and the Arabs began to express the desire for self-determination which, following the Turkish defeat in 1918, gained considerable momentum.

*Documents Reproduced:*

The Manifesto of Bilu 1882, pp. 3–4.
An exhortation to the Jews to fulfil their desire for a Jewish National Home.

Negib Azouri: Program of the League of the Arab Fatherland, pp. 5.
An excerpt from 'Reveil de la Nation Arabe dans l'Asie Turque' which was the first open demand for the secession of the Arab World from the Ottoman Empire.

Theodor Herzl: The Jewish State. 1896, pp. 6–11.
The exposition of Herzl's philosophy for the restoration of the Jewish State.

The Sykes–Picot Agreement, pp. 12–15.
The draft agreement between Britain and France regarding the post-war division of interests in the Middle East.

The McMahon Letter 24 October 1915, pp. 15–17.
This letter deals with the undertakings given by McMahon regarding Arab independence following the revolt against the Turks.

The Balfour Declaration, 1917, pp. 17–18.

The Feisal-Weizmann Agreement & Feisal Frankfurter Letters 1919, pp. 18–22.

Recommendations of the King–Crane Commission, 1919, pp. 23–30.

Memorandum presented to the King–Crane Commission by the General Syrian Congress, 1919, pp. 31–33.

The British Mandate 1922, pp. 34–42.

Part II. Palestine, 1920–1947:

The Churchill White Paper, 1922, pp. 45–50.

The Arab Case for Palestine: Evidence submitted by the Arab Office, Jerusalem. 1946, pp. 94–104.

LODER, J. DE V.
**The Truth about Mesopotamia, Palestine and Syria.**
*London: Allen & Unwin. 1923.*
*221 pp., maps, index, 19 cms.*

In his consideration of the Palestine problem the author lends great weight to the Arab cause in relation to the Zionist movement. Indeed in his foreword to this work Lord Robert Cecil states that being a confirmed Zionist he could not subscribe to the author's views on the Palestine problem. Although it is true that the Arab case is treated in far greater detail than the Jewish case the approach is valuable if only to act as a counter to the mass of pro-Zionist material.

The work ends with a consideration of the system of mandates in general terms and the appendices reproduce the texts of some of the relevant documents.

PORATH, Y.
**The emergence of the Palestinian-Arab Nationalist Movement, 1918–1929.**
*London: Cass. 1974.*
*ix, 406 pp., notes, app., bibl., index.*
*(Chapters Three to Five, pp. 123–208.)*

These chapters deal with the situation in Palestine following the granting of the Mandate to Britain with conflict between the Arab and Jewish communities and each, in turn, with the British administration. Chapter Three is entitled 'Confrontation with the British Government' and deals with the various representations to Britain regarding the problems of Jewish immigration and increasing Jewish influence in Palestinian affairs and economic life. Also considered are the various British proposals to solve the problems of the two communities and the moves to produce a Legislative Council.

Chapter Four is devoted to the emergence as an Arab leader of al-Hajj Amin al-Husayni following his appointment as Mufti of Jerusalem. This was followed by the establishment of the Supreme Muslim Council and its role as a stronghold for Arab opposition to Zionist aspirations in Palestine. This leads in Chapter Five to a detailed consideration of the origins and development of Arab opposition in Palestine considering the basic reasons for this opposition and its political and organisational development.

The work has appendices dealing with the composition of the Arab Executive Committee from 1920–34, the composition of the Supreme Muslim Council and a Chronological Table of events.

A detailed bibliography is also given covering material in Archives, manuscript material, official publications, books, articles and journals.

QUANDT, WILLIAM B., JABBER, FUAD AND LESCH, ANN MOSELY
**The Politics of Palestinian Nationalism.**
*London: University of California Press. 1973.*
*xi, 234 pp., maps, bibl., index, 24 cms.*

The greater part of this work falls outside of this study but Part I which deals with the Palestine Arab Nationalist movement under the mandate is of interest. This section of the work by Ann Mosely Lesch is the result of research carried out for a doctoral dissertation on the 'Frustration of a Nationalist Movement: Palestine Arab Politics, 1917–1939'.

The section begins by considering the problems faced by Britain in relation to the Sykes–Picot agreement and the Balfour Declaration which was seen by the Arabs as incompatible with the undertaking expressed in the McMahon–Hussein correspondence. Arab aspirations were dashed by the peace settlement which gave Britain responsibility for Palestine, and by the mandate which was entrusted to Britain on the understanding that the Balfour Declaration was to be implemented. The growth of the nationalist movement in reaction to British control following the war and the expansion of the Jewish community is traced showing a gradual movement from moderate political reaction to outright civil disorder culminating in the general strike of 1936 and the uprisings of 1937–39.

ROGERS, A. L.
**Arab nationalism in Iraq and Palestine.**
*Asiatic Review. July 1928, pp. 397–402.*

As this work deals with the reaction to the mandates in general terms rather than specifically by area the annotation to the article is placed in the section dealing with the mandate in Iraq.

## ADMINISTRATION OF THE MANDATE

DUFF, DOUGLAS V.
**The Mandates in Syria and Palestine.**
*Quarterly Review. January 1933, pp. 71–83.*

In dealing with Palestine the article has no sympathy towards the Arabs as their hostility is seen as a misrepresentation of Britain's policy towards the establishment of the Jewish National Home.

'We have been held up to the illiterate, fanatical peasants as In-
fidels, tyrannical oppressors of Islam, who wish to expel the
Moslems from their lands and homes in order to supplant them
with the new Zionist settlers.'

It is also argued that the Palestinians as a nation have no
substance in fact either from the racial, geographical or historical
aspects as prior to the war they were part of the vilayet of Beirut
and there 'were no pro-Arab sympathies as were in parts of
Arabia and elsewhere in Syria, and the question of a Palestinian
nationality had never entered their heads'.

The remainder of the article is chronologically outside of the
scope of this study.

HYAMSON, ALBERT M.
**Palestine under the mandate.**
*London: Methuen. 1950.*
*ix, 210 pp., index, 20 cms.*

This work represents a Jewish view of Britain's role under the
mandate and is, in the main, concerned with the record of Britain
in fulfilling the terms of the mandate regarding the establishment
of a national home for the Jews. It also considers the position of
the Arabs in Palestine and in particular the areas of cooperation
and disagreements between the Jews and Arabs.

The author deals with the anti-Jewish riots which were motivated by the increased Jewish immigration and the increasing role
being played by the Jews in the affairs of the state. Also considered are the events leading up to the termination of the mandate and in particular the problems faced in trying to provide a
solution acceptable to both communities. Some consideration is
also given to the armed clashes between the Arabs and the Jews
as the mandate was running out, dealing not only with the major
clashes on a more formal basis but also with the terrorist acts that
were perpetrated by both sides.

The work concludes that although the mandate was a failure
and Britain's record imperfect, the mistakes were made in good
faith and in an attempt to fulfil the trust that had been undertaken. On the credit side the state had made enormous progress
in the economic, social and administrative fields, and in these
areas both sections of the community had benefited.

*INGRAMS, DOREEN
**Palestine papers, 1917–1922:** Seeds of conflict.
*London: John Murray. 1972.*
*xii, 198 pp., illus., map, notes, index, 22 cms.*

Although the mandate for Palestine was not confirmed by the League of Nations until July 1922 and did not officially come into being until September 1923 the country continued under British administration, only in 1920 the military gave way to a civil one under a High Commissioner. The appointment was given to Herbert Samuel, a move which Allenby viewed with concern as the Arab population would resent and mistrust the appointment of a Jew as the first Governor.

'Consternation, despondency, and exasperation express the feelings of the Moslem–Christian population, the Christians being, if possible, even more bitter than the Moslems.' The seeds of future conflict had indeed been sown and the Haifa delegation to Churchill during the Cairo Conference wrote: 'If England does not take up the cause of the Arabs other powers will. From India, Mesopotamia, the Hedjaz and Palestine the cry goes up to England now. If she does not listen then perhaps Russia will take up their call some day, or perhaps even Germany. For though today Russia's voice is not heard in the councils of the nations, yet the time must come when it will assert itself . . .'

In 1921 serious rioting broke out in Palestine between the Arabs and Jews at Jaffa during a Labour Day procession when about one hundred people were killed. The cause of the riots is summed up in a memorandum from Captain Brunton of General Staff Intelligence as follows:

1. The special privileges accorded to the Jews.
2. The influence of the Zionist Commission and the openly declared political aims of the Zionists.
3. The use of Hebrew as an official language.
4. The immigration of great numbers of low-class Jews.
5. The behaviour and immorality of the immigrants.
6. The fall in price of land, trade depression, and the prohibition of export of cereals affecting the peasantry.
7. Arrogance of Jews towards Moslems and Christians.
8. No representation in the Government of the country or control of expenditure being accorded to the Arabs . . .
9. Loss of confidence in the Palestine Administration and in the British Government.
10. The realisation of the injustice of self-government being given to nomadic savages in Transjordania and refused to Palestine.
11. Moslem and Christian religious feeling aroused by conduct and aims of the Jews.
12. The Government attitude towards Moslem and Christian

petitions, protests and complaints which are frequently not answered or disregarded while Jews appear to have at all times the ear of the administration.

13. The use of the Zionist flag . . .

In August 1921 an Arab delegation led by Kazem Pasha al Husseini, who had been removed from the post of Mayor of Jerusalem for supposed involvement in the 1920 riots, went to London to plead their case and they remained there until September 1922. It cannot be said that their mission was successful as the British Government persisted in the policy already laid down. The delegation was still in London when the first White Paper on Palestine was issued in June 1922 by Churchill, and this is sometimes known as the Churchill Memorandum. This was issued as a definitive public statement of policy for Palestine, summarising the correspondence between Churchill and the Delegation and stating conclusions reached after deliberations. This reiterated the promise that the Jewish National Home would not mean the imposition of Jewish nationality on the inhabitants as a whole but the Jews had to have guarantees that they were in the country by right and their numbers must be allowed to increase to make the National Home a viable undertaking.

The White Paper also stressed that Palestine had been excluded from the promises given to Sherif Hussein as McMahon's letter supporting Arab independence excluded the portions of Syria lying west of Damascus. 'This reservation has always been regarded by His Majesty's Government as covering the vilayet of Beirut and the independent Sanjak of Jerusalem. The whole of Palestine west of the Jordan was thus excluded . . . .' The paper also put forward proposals for self-government which the Arabs rejected as the balance of voting power on the proposed Legislative Council was given to the *ex-officio* members and the High Commissioner assuming that the Jews would always vote with the official members.

Future British official policy was based on the attitude assumed by Sir Herbert Samuel who wrote in December 1922 that 'if it appears there is a prospect of change, the opposition will be stimulated . . . If, on the other hand, a definite and unqualified statement is made that the policy expressed in the White Paper of last July . . . will be maintained, then there is some prospect that a rapprochement may be effected between the opposing parties . . .' A judgement which subsequent events were to prove wrong.

NEWMAN, E. W. POULSON
**Middle East Mandates.**
*The Contemporary Review, pp. 705–711.*

The position of Palestine with Britain as the mandatory power is seen as a result of the Balfour Declaration which had been essential to secure the support of world-wide Jewry for the Allied cause during the war. The operation of the mandate is seen as a failure as it was based on a belief that the Arabs and Jews could work together and this was a delusion. It is considered that the problem can only be solved by the Jews accepting that the concept of a National Home does not imply dominance and for the Arabs to accept a Jewish presence in a predominantly Arab country with special arrangements being made for the Holy Places.

PONK, VINCENT
**Great Britain and the Near East after World War I:**
H. St. John Philby as Chief Representative in Transjordan.
*Islam and the Modern Age. Vol. 4, No. 1, 1973, pp. 66–87.*

After the Peace Conference it was undecided as to whether Transjordan should be controlled by Britain or be allowed to evolve as an independent Arab state. Initially the area was controlled by an administration which was an offshoot of the Palestine administration. This situation remained until 1921 when the Cairo Conference, under pressure from Abdullah's intention to invade Syria, decided to grant him the Emirship of Transjordan for a period of six months under the supervision of the High Commissioner for Palestine.

At the end of the six months the situation was far from satisfactory as Abdullah was constantly at variance with the policy of the High Commissioner, especially over the spending of the subsidy. Lawrence, however, persuaded Churchill to reaffirm Abdullah's position and Philby was appointed to try and advise on the situation and to prevent friction with the Palestine administration. His first year was a considerable success and by the winter of 1922 talks were under way towards granting Transjordan independence and this was achieved on 25 May 1923 when the High Commissioner travelled to Amman and conferred formal recognition of Transjordan's independence.

The article continues the study of Philby's term of office though this is beyond the scope of this study.

POWELL, E. ALEXANDER
**The Struggle for power in Moslem Asia.**

*London: John Long Ltd. 1925.*
*320 pp., maps, index, 22½ cms.*

The treatment of the situation in Palestine is wholly sympathetic to the rights of the Muslim and Christian Arabs concluding that the concept of a Jewish National Home would only be achieved by force of arms. The author does, however, credit Britain when trying to find a middle way between the two communities, though a powerful Zionist lobby in the British Government ensured that the Jewish case was safeguarded.

Although the right of the Jews to a National Home is not denied 'that does not mean that 80,000 Jews have a right to impose their rule, no matter how just or tolerant that rule may be, on nearly ten times that number of Moslems and Christians'.

## *Statement of British policy (Churchill Memorandum) on Palestine 1 July 1922.
*In. Hurewitz, J. C.*
*Diplomacy in the Near and Middle East, pp. 103–106.*

This statement was given by Churchill as Colonial Secretary because of the conflicting pressures from the Arab nationalists and the Zionists, whilst Britain could only exercise a de-facto administration in Palestine whilst the final provisions of the mandate were being worked out.

It aimed at trying to pacify both communities by pointing out that the British interpretation of the Balfour Declaration did not mean the disappearance or subordination of the Arabs, their language or their culture. To the Jews it re-affirmed the declaration of the policy of a national home though this did not mean the establishment of a Jewish state but the right of the Jews to live in Palestine under international guarantees. The statement also rejects the claim that Palestine was designated to be included in an independent Arab state under the terms of the McMahon–Hussein correspondence but that Palestine should achieve self-government in gradual stages.

WILLIAMS, KENNETH
**Palestine: Strategic and political.**
*English Review. June 1927, pp. 707–13.*

An article which examines the need for a British presence in Palestine in relation to Egypt and the Suez Canal. It examines the political and economic situation and concludes on an optimistic note regarding the future as 'the very indeterminateness of her [Britain] policy in Palestine is something that, in its seeming eventlessness, should breed not despair but hope'. It fails, however, to appreciate that this lack of policy was bound to lead to conflict between the Jewish population and the aspirations of the Arabs who considered themselves let down by the failure of Britain to exclude Palestine from the area of Arab nationalist aspirations.

## BIOGRAPHICAL WORKS

ABDULLAH I, KING OF TRANSJORDAN
**Memoirs of King Abdullah of Transjordan** edited by Philip P. Graves.
*London: Cape. 1950.*
*278 pp., illus., refs., app., index, 20½ cms.*

Abdullah glosses over the question of the Peace Conference as he was appointed by Hussein to lead the Arab delegation whereas the Allies recognised Faisal as the leader of the delegation but not as ruler of Syria. As a result Abdullah resigned his position of responsibility for foreign affairs in the face of overwhelming difficulties from his father.

In 1921 Abdullah became Emir of Transjordan following the Cairo Conference and the area was removed from the National Home provisions of the Balfour Declaration.

The remainder of the memoirs are outside the scope of this study by nature of date as they deal with the history of Transjordan up to World War II.

*BENTWICH, NORMAN AND HELEN
**Mandate memories, 1918–1948.**
*London: Hogarth Press. 1965.*
*231 pp., index, 22½ cms.*

A valuable account of the Palestine mandate by a legal officer in the military administration of Palestine from 1918–20 and in the Mandatory Government from 1920–31, and subsequently a lecturer in the Hebrew University of Jerusalem. The work is an attempt to describe the forces and personalities in Palestine during the time in question based on diaries, letters and personal memories with the social side of the picture being provided by Helen Bentwich. Of particular interest is the chapter on 'The Arab Opposition' with its outline of the personalities, their various outlooks and the problem of trying to establish a bi-national state on mutual cooperation and understanding.

\*Monroe, Elizabeth
**Philby of Arabia.**
*London : Faber. 1973.*
*332 pp., illus., maps, notes, bibl., index, 22½ cms.*

After Faisal's 'election' to the throne of Iraq Philby became British Representative in Transjordan which had become, following Faisal's expulsion from Syria, left very much to its own devices with only the existence of a few British advisers including Alec Seath Kirkbride. The arrangement was upset in March 1921 when Abdullah arrived in Transjordan intent on attacking Syria and the French. Churchill immediately left Cairo for Jerusalem to meet Abdullah and offered him a temporary assignment as Emir, but within the mandated territory of Palestine and on a trial period of six months. This initial six months was full of problems as Abdullah squandered his allowances and the country was full of Syrian refugees bent on causing trouble for the French.

In this climate Lawrence arrived to settle the problem and he decided that it was possible to maintain a sound administration with Abdullah as its head, provided he was supplied with 'some good strong Englishman' who would promote Arab control, advise on setting up an administration and stop the financial drain on British allowances. It was a result of this judgement that Philby was sent to Transjordan, remaining there until 1924.

Storrs, Ronald
**Orientations.**
*London : Nicholson and Watson. 1937.*

See entries under Sections 1b, 1c, 2b and 2c for annotations to this work.

# General Bibliographies

DOFAN, URI, COMP.
**A Bibliography of articles on the Middle East, 1959–67.**
*Israel: Tel Aviv University. 1970. 24 cms.*
*(The Shiloah Center for Middle Eastern and African Studies Research Aid No. 2.)*

This work continues the series of bibliographies issued by the Hebrew University of Jerusalem and follows the pattern of the previous works listing some 2,902 items. Index is by author only using the entry number as the point of reference.

\*EARLE, EDWARD MEAD, ED.
**Problems of the Near East.**
*Washington: Carnegie Endowment of International Peace. 1924. 23 pp., 24 cms.*
*(International Relations Club Bibliography, Series No. 2.)*

A narrative bibliography confined largely to material available in American Libraries and covering the pre-World War I Ottoman Empire including Egypt, the Balkan countries and the Caucasian provinces of Russia, Persia and Arabia. The work is divided into the following sections:

1. General works of reference on the Near East.
2. Historical and economic Geography of the Near East.
3. Western Imperialism in the Near East.
4. The rise of nationalism in the Near East.
5. Religious problems of the Near East.
6. The Near East in the World War.
7. The Near East since the Armistice of 1918.
8. American interests in the Near East.
9. Periodical Literature.

The annotations are very brief giving author, title, date and an indication as to strength or bias. The periodical section does not list articles but guides the reader to those journals which are of relevance.

THE HEBREW UNIVERSITY, JERUSALEM: ECONOMIC RESEARCH INSTITUTE
**A Selected bibliography of articles dealing with the Middle East.**

In three volumes.

> Vol. I.   1939–50, published 1954, 1,442 entries.
> Vol. II.  1951–54, published 1955, 1,163 entries.
> Vol. III. 1955–58, published 1959,  841 entries.

Each volume covers a wide range of periodicals, but as the work is intended for Israeli readers the selected journals are those which are available in Israeli libraries. The entries are arranged by country with general sections covering the Middle East and Arabian Peninsula. Each section is divided by subject covering:

| | |
|---|---|
| (a) General works. | (g) Economics. |
| (b) Geography. | (h) Finance. |
| (c) Modern History (1798–1918). | (i) Arab League and Inter-Arab relations. |
| (d) Politics and Government. | |
| (e) Society. | (j) Regional organisations and agencies. |
| (f) Religion and culture. | |

Entries are not annotated but give author, title and journal references. The index is by author only with the point of reference being the consecutive entry number.

HOPWOOD, DEREK AND GRIMWOOD-JONES, DIANA, EDS.
**Middle East and Islam:** A bibliographical introduction.
*Switzerland: Inter Documentation Co. 1972.*
*viii, 368 pp., index, 20½ cms.*

The aim of this work is to provide an introduction to the subject and in many areas is highly selective to reduce the whole to manageable proportions. Each area of study has been contributed by a specialist in the area and the format and content reflect their tastes and interests. As a general rule works in non-European languages have been excluded except where no satisfactory European work exists or where Arabic material is essential.

The work is divided into the following sections.

1. Reference.
2. Islamic studies.
3. Subject bibliographies.
4. Regional bibliographies.
5. Arabic language and literature.

The format of each section reflects the approach of each contributor with some being lists with introductions, some annotated lists and others texts in which the items are included.

\*Khalidi, Walid and Jill
**Palestine and the Arab-Israeli Conflict:** an annotated
bibliography.
*Beirut: Institute for Palestine Studies. 1974.*
*XXI, 736 pp., index, 24½ cms.*

An extremely valuable and detailed bibliography covering the
Palestine problem though part of the material is irrelevant by
virtue of date. 'The purpose of this bibliography is to provide a
reasonably balanced core of primary and secondary sources on
the various aspects of the Palestine question; on which future
bibliographic work can build.' The organisation of the bibliography is by subject and covers printed material both published
and unpublished. This includes books, periodical articles,
periodicals and newspapers in their entirety but not individual
newspaper articles. Unpublished material is only included where
it is reasonably accessible to researches.

The arrangement of the subject organisation is as follows;
though this is an abbreviated version of the contents list.

    i General sources of the Palestine problem.
    ii Historical background.
    iii Development of the Palestine problem, 1880–1947.
    iv The Palestine War, The Establishment of Israel
       and the expulsion of the Palestinians, 1947–1949.
    v The Palestinian people, 1948–1967.
    vi The Palestine Question, The Arab States and Israel,
       1948–1967.
    vii The 1967 war.
    viii The Palestine Question, The Arab States and Israel,
       1967–1971.
    ix The Palestinian people, 1967–1971.

Each entry has been given a consecutive number and this is the
point of reference from the index.

Ljunggren, Florence and Hamidy, Mohammed
**Annotated guide to journals dealing with the Middle East
and North Africa.**
*Cairo: American University in Cairo Press. 1965.*
*viii, 108 pp., index, 21½ cms.*

The work aims at providing an annotated listing of journals
dealing with the Muslim countries of the Middle East and North
Africa. It excludes popular and women's magazines and news
weeklies as well as scientific and highly technical journals.

The work is alphabetical by title in two sections, one of non-Arabic journals and the other Arabic journals. Each section has its own subject index and the work has an authority list of libraries visited, guides and journals consulted and a sample of the questionnaire sent to publishers.

MACRO, ERIC
**Bibliography of the Arabian Peninsula.**
*Florida: University of Miami Press. 1958.*
*xiv, 80 pp., index, 26½ cms.*

A listing of some 2,000 items on the Arabian Peninsula covering all aspects of the area and, as a result, much of the material is outside of the scope of this study either by virtue of its context or by geography.

The entries are arranged alphabetically by author with anonymous works arranged alphabetically by title under the author heading 'anonymous'. The entries covered include books, periodicals and from official sources regardless of language. Each entry is given a consecutive number and this is the point of reference between the index and the text. The weakness of the work is that the index is an author index only and as the listing is alphabetical there is no subject guide and the reader is forced to examine the complete list to extract material of specific interest. Despite this the work is a useful listing though its political content is minimal.

PATAI, RAPHAEL, COMP.
**Jordan, Lebanon and Syria:** An annotated bibliography.
*New Haven: HRAF Press. 1957.*
*vii, 289 pp., 21½ cms.*

This bibliography is part of the Human Area Files project and is intended primarily to satisfy the student with an interest in the peoples and the cultures of the three countries. The emphasis is therefore on the social sciences and in the main anthropology, economics, sociology and human geography with political history and history taking second place. Some works listed are, however, of interest to a study of Arab nationalism although their location is not easy as one has to carefully examine all the entries in each section.

The work is arranged in four sections, the first dealing with the general items which contain information pertinent to two or more of the countries in question, or which contain information pertinent to the Arab world as a whole but containing material of value to a study of the three countries. The remaining sections are by country beginning with handbooks, guide books and maps, followed by the general listing which is in each case alphabetical by author with a running entry number. No further breakdown was considered practical because of the relevance of listed works to more than one subject.

PEARSON, J. D., COMP.
**Index Islamicus:** 1906–1955 plus supplements to date.
*London: Heffer. 1958.*
*(Supplements now published by Mansell.)*

A catalogue of articles on Islamic subjects in periodicals, fest-schriften, congresses and other collective works.

The work is arranged by subject, dealing first with general material and then subjects in general terms, such as Art, Religion, and Literature. Further sections are devoted to area studies which are further subdivided by subject and each entry is given a running number which forms the point of reference in the index. Entries are not annotated and give author, title, bibliographical details and cross references to other entries.

Recent supplements are now being produced annually and the index has been changed to refer to the main subject number and subdivision number rather than by entry number. Arrangement of entries within the subject breakdown is alphabetical by author.

*QUBAIN, FAHIM I., COMP.
**Inside the Arab Mind:** A bibliographical survey of literature in Arabic on Arab nationalism and unity with an annotated list of English Language books and articles.
*Arlington, Virginia: Middle East Research Associates. 1960. 100 pp., 23 cms.*

The bibliography is divided into two parts, the first consisting of ninety-six Arabic titles and the second one hundred and forty-five English language titles. In the Arab section the works cited are books and articles whilst the supplement is mainly comprised of articles. Each part is divided into six sections as follows:

1. Arab Nationalism (General).
2. Arab Nationalism and unity.
3. Arab Nationalism and Islam.
4. Arab Nationalism and Communism.
5. Arab Nationalism and separatism.
6. Arab Nationalism and Part Movements.
   (a) The Ba'th Party.
   (b) The Syria Social National Party.

(In the English Language section there is an additional section, that of Arab Nationalism and Nasserism.)

Part I is heavily annotated to provide the reader with a synopsis of the work which is listed in English and with the original Arabic title. The English Language supplement is less detailed in its annotations as the works can be read in the original and are easily obtainable.

Selection is by personal choice of the compiler with the aim being to list serious material on the subject with an ideological emphasis and excluding ephemeral material and material having only propaganda value. The material selected includes items that consider parallel movements to Arab nationalism, counter-currents and important intra-Arab party movements. The work has an author and subject index.

UNITED ARAB REPUBLIC: MINISTRY OF CULTURE AND NATIONAL GUIDANCE
**A Bibliography of works about Iraq.**
*Cairo : National Library Press. 1960.*
*60 pp., 24½ cms.*
*(In Arabic and English.)*

An alphabetical listing by author of works about Iraq in the Cairo National Library. The entries are brief catalogue entries consisting mainly of material in English and with a few items in French. The work has a title index.

UNITED ARAB REPUBLIC: MINISTRY OF CULTURE AND NATIONAL GUIDANCE
**A bibliography of works about Lebanon.**
*Cairo : National Library Press. 1960.*
*46 pp., 24 cms.*
*(In Arabic and English.)*

An alphabetical listing by author of works about the Lebanon in the Cairo National Library. The entries are brief catalogue entries consisting mainly of materials in English and French. The work has a title index.

UNITED ARAB REPUBLIC: MINISTRY OF CULTURE AND NATIONAL GUIDANCE
**A Bibliographical list of works about Palestine and Jordan.**
*Cairo : National Library Press : 2nd ed. 1964.*
*338 pp. of English text, 24 cms.*
*(In English and Arabic.)*

A listing of items dealing with Palestine and Jordan in the Cairo

National Library. The bulk of the Bibliography, comprising 948 entries, deals with Palestine with only 49 devoted to Jordan. The listing is by subject arranged within by author giving brief catalogue entries. The index covers authors, titles and subject and uses the entry number as the point of reference.

YAARI, A.
**A Post-war bibliography of near eastern mandates:** a preliminary survey of publications on the social sciences dealing with Iraq, Palestine and Transjordan and the Syrian States. From 11 November 1918 to 31 December 1929.
*Beirut: American University of Beirut. 1933.*
*xix, 227 pp., index, 24½ cms.*
*(Social Science Series, No. 1.)*

The bibliography is available in eight fascicles by language with entries in English and the language of the fascicle. The listing is alphabetical by author with a subject index referring to the running entry number. A great deal of the bibliography is outside of the scope of this study but some entries dealing with the relations between the Jews and the Arabs and the disturbances in Palestine are of relevance to this work.

*ZIADEH, NICOLA A.
**Recent Arab Literature on Arabism.**
*Middle East Journal. Vol. 6, No. 4, Autumn 1952, pp. 468–473.*

A review article which discusses recent Arabic literature by providing a summary of the development of Arab nationalism. The writer considers that the nationalist movement began to show itself during the last decades of the nineteenth century but did not come to maturity until World War I, having been brought to this state by the Ottoman administration of the Arab lands.

At the time of the Young Turks constitution in 1908 three trends had developed among the politically conscious:

1. A Muslim conviction that the Caliphate should be Arab.
2. A desire for reforms to give the Arabs sufficient autonomy to develop their own distinctive character.
3. An outright case for complete independence of the Arab lands and the formation of a united Arab state.

These hopes were dashed by the Turkification of the Ottoman Empire and of the Arabs and this policy more than anything brought impetus to the more extreme Arab nationalists.

First Arab Conference, 18–23 June 1913.

A landmark in the development of Arab nationalism as the conference was representative of all shades of opinion and came to the following conclusions:

1. Real and basic reforms were necessary for the Ottoman Empire and were needed immediately.
2. A guarantee of Arab political rights with an active part in the central administration.
3. Each Arab province should be given a wide scope of autonomy to ensure the fulfilment of its needs and the development of its resources.
4. Arabic to be recognised as an official language in the Ottoman Empire.

It is significant that the conference represented the Arab communities as both Muslims and Christians were present, and many of them were not willing to consider separatism from the Turks but reform within the framework of the Empire. Some progress was being made, albeit reluctantly, in this direction when World War I broke out. The advent of war led to Arab soldiers being posted outside the Arab lands and the declaration of martial law followed by the repressive policy of Djemal Pasha in Syria. These policies were in part responsible for the declaration of the Arab Revolt in 1916.

The article then proceeds to examine literature that has appeared in Arabic together with a brief assessment of the problems discussed such as what constitutes an Arab, what political boundaries the Arab states should have and the relationship between Arabism and Pan-Islamism.

# INDEX

The index is an alphabetical listing of authors and titles with the reference being to the relevant page numbers. In the case of items by different authors with the same title the author's name is given, in parenthesis, following the title entry. In some cases due to their length title entries have been abbreviated and omissions are indicated by . . . .

283